Faces on the Clock

Faces on the Clock

Larry Bauer-Scandin

First Edition

Copyright © 2010 Larry Bauer-Scandin

Cover art formatted by David Hoffman, Gloomwing Author Resources

Published by Eagle Entertainment USA
130 Teton Lane #2
Mankato, MN 56001

Website: www.eagleentertainmentusa.com

ISBN # 978-0-615-37516-8

Dedication

To Richard Hazuka, my cousin, for giving me the idea to re-write this entire book and to concentrate on the kids' stories. If I'd had more time with him, I might have saved myself the first fourteen years of writing and fighting with my computer.

To Corrine Scharnhorst, a very wise woman. About forty five years ago, this lady made a prediction about my future parenting skills that wasn't particularly complimentary. I want to admit now that she was probably right, and I'm proud to admit it.

To my family, my wife, Peg, my four oldest friends, Marty, Wayne, Mich, and Fr. "The Chief" Jim, all of "my kids," my friends and acquaintances who have honored me with their presence in my life.

And to my friend and advisor, Steve Ulmen, for being kind enough to believe that someone might actually be interested in reading this work.

Introduction

Originally, this autobiography was going to concentrate on my medical history. That history has been somewhat out of the ordinary, and it was thought that it might be encouraging for people experiencing similar medical problems.

The idea for the autobiography was that of a cousin who was a professor at a major university. It was mentioned that there might be a possibility of getting it published through the university, but at the time, I was about twelve years old, and the thought of reliving my medical experience (if only in my mind) was not something I would have enjoyed doing. So the idea lay dormant for a while, about 35 years or so. I know; it takes a little time for me to make decisions.

By the time I'd made the decision to write the autobiography, the reasons for doing so had changed and expanded. By that time, I had approached the end of my working career, and it seemed safe to assume that I could start, and maybe even complete, the work without having to worry about missing much at the end. That may, or may not, wind up being the case. In any event, for better or worse, here we go.

I'd like you to remember a few things while reading this autobiography. First, always remember the title, "Faces On The Clock." The title is meant to suggest that each of us has a finite amount of time on this earth, and what we do or don't do with that time is the measure of our success or failure, our happiness or unhappiness with that life.

Secondly, as you read, I would ask you to consider a Higher Power, a Supreme Being, a God, if you will, operating in your life. I hope it becomes as clear to you, as it is to me, that you couldn't have lived my life without believing in such a Being.

Thirdly, I'm convinced that people are put into our lives for a reason, perhaps to teach us something like optimism, patience, or faith, or even humor. And people create events. And people and events constitute one's life. So it's very important that we not allow people and events to pass us up unnoticed, like cars on a freeway.

If we do this, we'll have maximized the potential in our lives and will have learned how to squeeze our lives for everything they have to offer, just as every life has something to offer. In the end, one's life results in a sort of tapestry. The only question is how rich and bright and detailed it will be.

So I'm hoping that the stories I tell will entertain, make a point occasionally, encourage you to reflect on your lives, and above all, enhance your appreciation for the people and experiences, good and bad, pleasant and unpleasant, that you run into during the course of your lifetime.

The Family and Original Neighborhood

I was born in the city of Duluth, Minnesota. Duluth is a city situated on the north shore of Lake Superior. During my childhood, the population of Duluth was slightly over 100,000 people. I think the city's largest employer was United States Steel Corporation. As I recall, it employed some 5,000 people, including my father.

We were what would probably be referred to as a "working class" family. My family and our home blended in quite well with the others in the neighborhood.

We lived in a predominantly Italian neighborhood referred to as Central Hillside. We attended St. Peter's Catholic Church, referred to as the "Italian Church." And my Dad came from a very Italian family, made up of Marietta, the oldest child, my Dad, Yolanda, the youngest and their parents, Dominic and Mary.

Some advice for the reader, especially younger readers: Ask questions. Get to know your family and your heritage, or you may leave this world with some serious questions about your life and/or family unanswered. I can almost promise that, sometime during your lifetime, you'll wish you had the answer to some questions that you should have asked long ago.

A case in point: My paternal grandfather had a brother, Uncle Ralph, who lived about a block from my grandfather's house. I knew what he looked like, but I never met him, and I never saw my grandfather or anyone else in my family speak to him or of him. Every member of my Dad's family is dead, and I'll never know what happened between Grandpa and Uncle Ralph. Recently I heard a story, told by my brother, which suggested Uncle Ralph was, at some point, found to have "put the make" on Grandma. Yup, that would do it!

Dad's Family

Now to introduce Dad's family. First of all, there was Grandpa Dominic. What can I say about Grandpa Scandin? I can say that I always considered him to be a very lucky man, but he would never have said that. For example, I never heard of his ever having seen a doctor or dentist, and I don't ever remember his feeling like he had need of either. Also, he never missed a day of work during the entire period of the Great Depression. And he also had a wife who took very good care of him and the family, work that I'm sure was not appreciated as much as it should have been. He was a very lucky man, but his attitude seemed to preclude any possibility of his ever realizing it.

Grandpa lived to a ripe old age of 96 years. He had the constitution of a caveman. For as long as I knew him, his almost daily routine involved walking to downtown Duluth and then back up the hills to his home. In total, I would guess that this was a daily walk of three to four miles. Not bad for a 96-year-old.

To give you one more example of Grandpa's constitution, I once walked into the house to check on him, as my brother and I often did. As I recall, he was in the bathroom when I walked in the house. As I was scanning the house, the bathroom door opened, and standing before me was one bruised, cut up little man with two black eyes. When I asked him what happened, he took me out to the porch and showed me a broken hand railing. The hand railing was one story above a concrete slab that separated the house from the lower level of the garage. Over the next few days, we watched Grandpa turn into a walking scab, but he never would go to a doctor.

Then there was Grandma. I think she was the real strength in the family, and she had to be. I suspect that Grandpa was very hard to live with. Part of the problem, I think, was the Italian culture which, in my opinion, had a male gender bias. Italian women seemed to be into taking care of their men, and this certainly was the case in my Dad's family. I've said many times that my Dad had the world's worst luck. He was born the only male in an Italian family, and he was sandwiched between two girls.

My favorite memory of Grandma is walking into the house on Saturday mornings and seeing all the freshly made pasta hanging from clotheslines hung all around the kitchen and the smell of homemade spaghetti sauce, all of which was being prepared for the family dinner on Sunday, after Mass. We didn't always have homemade meals for Sunday dinner, but we almost always ate together.

Grandma died on June 23, 1956, after surviving another of several heart attacks. As I recall, she was getting herself ready to go home. She reached for a hairbrush, fell out of bed and broke a hip. She developed pneumonia or other complications, and passed away as a result. I think Grandma's was the first funeral I ever attended.

Aunt Marietta was a very rotund woman who was very proud of her boobs. Actually, they were gross and had to be very uncomfortable to carry around, but hey, she was happy.

My favorite memory of Aunt Marietta was my first day of kindergarten at St. Peter's Catholic School. Before I get into this, I should explain that we lived two blocks from my Dad's parents, and Aunt Marietta and her family lived a block and a half from them, and Aunt Yolanda lived with my grandparents. So you see, we were a VERY close family! Anyway, school was two and a half blocks from our house.

On the first day of kindergarten, I decided I didn't want to go to school, and for some reason, I decided I could take refuge at Aunt Marietta's house. The first thing I knew, my mother walked in the house and dragged my sorry butt, with me kicking and screaming, the block and a half to school. I don't ever remember skipping school again, at least until I got to the university.

Last, but certainly not least, is Aunt Yolanda. Aunt Yolanda was stricken with Multiple Sclerosis somewhere around 1960. The doctors told her that if she chose to fight, she might be able to delay the effects of the disease. My family asked me to talk to her and encourage her to fight and accept the therapy. They thought she might listen to me, given my medical problems during the previous few years, which I'll get into later. I did talk to her, and she agreed to try the therapy. Unfortunately, she went to therapy once, decided it was too tiring, and refused to go again. For a long time after that decision, I was mad at her because I was pompous enough to think that everyone should want to fight to stave off the effects of that kind of disease. In time, I grew up enough to realize that she had to make her own decision. She would spend several years in St. Mary's Hospital, and then the last twenty-six years of her life in the same room in a nursing home. No one that I know of ever remembers her complaining about her lot in life, and I have no recollection of her ever being able to move anything but her mouth and her eyelids. I believe she was in her seventies when she passed away. I wonder if I learned anything from her life.

I'm sure that, by this time, you realize that our community and our family were close; two blocks to the grandparents' house, three and a half to Dad's sister's house, and two and a half blocks to church and school.

As I've suggested, it wasn't easy being born into an Italian family, living in a predominantly Italian neighborhood, being born Roman Catholic, and attending a Catholic church and school. In those days, the community was so close that a kid never thought he could get by with anything. Add being Catholic and attending a Catholic grade school to that, and you felt like, what the neighbors didn't see and report, God would.

My first school, St. Peter's Catholic School, was located in the basement of the church. My kindergarten teacher was Sister Lawrencia, a nun I was sure was seven feet tall. I'm sure the sight of her every morning scared me far more than the sight of my dentist. I used to try and count the buttons on her habit, but I couldn't count that high.

The only thing I remember about kindergarten, outside of Sister Lawrencia, was getting the only unsatisfactory grade I ever received in conduct. I had a girlfriend (Oh, humor me, will you?) who accidentally spilled some paint on the floor one day, and Sister Lawrencia thought I did it and made me sit in the corner. Let's just say I protested loudly.

My first grade teacher was Sister Valeria. The only thing I remember about the first grade has to do with a period of time that I seemed to develop stomach problems every morning when I got to school. (School always did make me sick!) Sister Valeria would always let me go and sit outside for a while. When I think about it now, it was probably depression. I do remember that it had to do with someone's dying because, on one occasion, Sr. Valeria came out and sat on the step beside me. We started talking about death and dying, and then she said something that I've never forgotten. She said that in order for a flower to be beautiful, it had to have older, middle age, and younger parts. I can't remember who it was that died that I was having such a hard time with, but it might have been my Mother's oldest brother, Jim. His is the first death of any kind that I remember.

On the first day of the third grade, one of my assumptions about school was dashed. Much to my surprise, we third graders had two teachers, neither of which was a nun. Sacrilegious, right?

I was also a little uncomfortable having a classroom in the basement of the church and one with bluestone for walls. If the walls

4

did anything for my feeling safe from a possible fire, the furnace being across from the classroom did not. There was also only one way out.

When I got home and got the first volley of questions about the first day of school, Mother hit the roof when I told her my classroom was to be in the basement, right by the furnace. As it turned out, that was my last day in a parochial school. The next day, I was enrolled in the public school system and Emerson Elementary School, three and a half blocks from home. How quickly things can change!

New School, New Friends, New World

Now, one would think that kind of trauma would be, well, traumatic, and you'd be right. Emerson Elementary was a lot larger than was St. Peter's. I don't remember much about the first day, but I was scared. I don't think I knew any of the kids in the school. And then, some help came along.

One of the kids in Miss Olson's third grade class was Marty, the kid that would become my best friend for the rest of my life. And then there was Mike, the kid to whom I give credit for planting the seeds for my interest in mental health and delinquent/criminal behavior. It was also the teachers at Emerson who planted the seeds of interest in the possibility of teaching. But Marty was to become one of the biggest influences and sources of support in my life for the rest of my life.

We really got to know each other when we discovered that we lived a block apart. He passed my house everyday on his way to and from school. And so, we began to walk to and from school together every day. More on Marty, school, and me a little later.

There's one more colorful personality I want to mention on my Dad's side of the family – Aunt Lizzie, Dad's aunt and Grandma Scandin's sister. As I said, Aunt Lizzie was a colorful personality. She was married to Uncle Billy who, I believe, had died before I was born. He, too, was a colorful character. I seem to remember hearing stories that he used to disappear occasionally to take in a boxing match, in Chicago, or a horserace in Florida. Aunt Lizzie grew to become quite an independent lady and developed her own interests. One of those interests was playing bingo, and she was darn good at it. I remember her playing as many as ten or fifteen cards at a time.

She also took my brother, Jack, and me to the Tri-State Fair once or twice. I remember pleading with her to take us on the roller coaster. I don't think we ever believed she would be willing, but she was. When we got off, Jack and I were both barfing our shoe soles up, but Aunt Lizzie was just fine and ready to go again.

Mother and Dad were married in 1940. They were introduced to each other by Mother's sister, Laura, but I don't remember the circumstances. Remember to ask questions.

I suspect there must have been some tension in Dad's family over the fact that he married a non-Italian. Basically, I think that meant trouble for Mother because she had a mind of her own and wasn't the kind to bow to male-dom. I suspect that the women in Dad's family looked at Mother out of the corners of their eyes for quite a few years, feeling that she was somewhat of an outsider in the family. I don't remember feeling any of this if it was operating in the family.

In my family, Dad wanted everyone to believe that he ruled the roost, but we kids knew the head of the family was the parent who carried the biggest stick and was willing to use it, and we all knew that was Mother. Dad was the "yeller," but Mother was the woman of action. As a matter of fact, Jack stole the hairbrush Mom used to make her points with, and he only told her that a few years ago, (as if she couldn't find another one!)

I suppose we were a rather typical working-class family. Mom and Dad seemed to work well together. It was understood and agreed that Mother stayed home, kept the house and raised the kids, and Dad went to work and earned the family income. Both of them were very good at what they did, and both centered their lives on the family.

Mother's Family

Now, Mother's family was just a bit different from Dad's. Mother's mother and father were married when they were age 15 and 25 respectively. They had a total of seventeen children together, the first and last being stillborn. The other fifteen were a mixture of boys and girls, and no, there were no multiple births.

I have very fond memories of my maternal grandparents and those of the aunts and uncles that I was lucky enough to have met. As I look back on my life in retrospect, I'm truly sorry I never met some of these aunts and uncles, to say nothing of the cousins, because as I've said before, I think that everyone a person meets during their lifetime adds to the tapestry of a person's life. If that's true, then it's worth mentioning some of those I did know.

Mother's family, my grandparents and some of the kids, lived in and around Staples, a small town in Central Minnesota. Grandma and Grandpa's home was a small farm. They didn't raise any kind of farm animals, at least, not during my lifetime. They did raise corn, but that's all I can remember. They got where they needed to go in their old Model A Ford with a rumble seat. The house seemed very old to us city-slicker kids, and we all thought it had some nifty things about it, like a toilet in Grandma and Grandpa's bedroom closet. It also had an oil stove in the living room. The living room ceiling had metal grates so the heat from the oil stove would help heat the upstairs where all the kids always slept. When we were sent upstairs to bed, we would put our ears to the floor and listen to the adult conversation going on in the living room below us. That gave us the great, exciting feeling of spying on the adults.

When the city slickers visited the grandparents, a ritual seemed to develop. Grandma would always send us to the store for groceries. Jack and I would jump in the rumble seat and we'd head for town. But Grandpa would always forget one important item. On the way, we would always stop at Grandpa's favorite "watering hole" for what he used to refer to as "a snort." After all, he was Irish! When we'd get home, he would empty the grocery bags on the kitchen table and Grandma, of course, would discover that he'd forgotten at least one important item and would order him to go back to town and get it. We'd all climb back into the car, drive back to town and get the item and, on the way home, we would, once again, stop for another snort. I never found out if Grandma ever figured out Grandpa's little scheme, but I suspect she did. This little scenario occurred with far too much regularity for her not to know. But it's one of those things I'll never know for sure.

I think that what attracts me to most people is a sense of their gentleness. If that's the measure of a human being, then I've been very lucky to know many and to have recognized them. Let me mention some of those who fit this description in my Mother's family.

First would be Aunt Laura, one of Mother's older sisters. Aunt Laura and Uncle Ted lived in Duluth also. Aunt Laura was a registered nurse, but Jack and I both thought she was a registered saint. She died of cancer when she was fifty years old. My mother was with her when she died. As I remember the story, Mother was talking to her when, suddenly, Aunt Laura told her that she had to go, or, "It was time to go." Mother asked her where she had to go. Aunt Laura pointed to the ceiling, telling Mother that, "The angels have come to get me." She lifted her arms to the sky, and she was gone. I'll mention this angel again a little later.

Aunt Nellie and Uncle Joe lived on a farm a dozen miles from Grandma and Grandpa. These people typified the American farm family. Uncle Joe and Aunt Nellie raised a rather large family. The kids went to the local school and did chores after school. And the family went to Mass every Sunday at St. Michael's Catholic Church.

One of my favorite memories of going to Mass at St. Michael's was, first, the smell of the church. It smelled like the farm. Secondly, I used to love watching all the farmers walking into church with their Sunday "go-to-meeting" suits, and wearing boots that had two inches of manure caked on them. For me, it all exemplified the simple life; communities that were close, neighbors that were close, and families that were close. God, I loved those people!

At some point, Aunt Nellie developed cancer of the spine. Her spine kind of turned to mush, and she had to wear a brace to, literally, keep her top half from collapsing into her lower half. And then the cancer went into remission for many years.

Both Aunt Nellie and Uncle Joe were gentle people whose only interests were their church, their neighbors and their children. My favorite memory of them and the farm is waking up in an upstairs bedroom to the smell of bacon and eggs and coffee wafting up the stairway in the morning. I would run downstairs, hoping I could make it before I froze to death during winter visits, and be greeted by heaping stacks of bacon, eggs, sausage and toast on large platters. I could never figure out how so many fried eggs could stay on one platter. And the toast was always stacked about ten high in two stacks on the plate. I don't remember the particular circumstances of their deaths, but it makes me feel good to know they're together again.

And then there was Uncle Tony and Aunt Dorothy, tenant farmers in Iowa. Uncle Tony has been dead for years, but Aunt Dorothy is still very much alive at 93 years of age. These were truly two more gentle souls in my family.

Many years ago, my Mother and Dad went to Iowa for a visit. The atmosphere was a little tense, Uncle Tony seeming to be nervous, restless and upset about something. Dad asked him what was wrong, and Uncle Tony told him he was worried about the condition of the house. He wanted to get it painted. Dad offered to paint it for him. Uncle Tony was very relieved.

A short time after Mom and Dad got home from that trip, Uncle Tony died of a heart attack. A "goodbye" letter was found from Uncle Tony and meant for Aunt Dorothy. Apparently, he sensed or, possibly even knew, the condition of his heart and wanted to get some things done quickly.

Lest you think I have everyone in my family tagged as angels, I don't. Or maybe some were angels with dirty faces. For example, there was Uncle Bill. Now, Uncle Bill wouldn't have struck anyone as a Ph.D. candidate, but he was another gentle soul with a huge heart and toothy grin. He also looked like an Iowa version of Foster Brooks. In other words, Uncle Bill liked his booze.

We had a family reunion at Grandma and Grandpa's farm one summer. Everyone was having a good time, and, of course, the adults were, in some cases, drinking a bit too much. In Uncle Bill's case, it was a LOT too much! There came a time when someone noticed that Uncle Bill was missing, and a general alarm was sounded. Literally everyone was looking for him, including some of us kids who were walking up and down the rows of corn. Eventually someone thought of the outhouse, and, sure enough, that's where we found him—pants down, out cold, and sitting on the hole!

I want to mention one more colorful character in Mother's family, my Uncle Mike. Uncle Mike enlisted in the Army when he was seventeen years old and was a veteran of both WWII and the Korean War. Apparently, he was one of those guys who liked excitement, because he liked to volunteer for dangerous missions. As I recall, he was bayoneted several times, shot once or twice and was captured by the enemy a time or two.

The last time I remember seeing him was at Grandma and Grandpa's. He gave me a leather pouch containing all sorts of foreign currency and coins. I often wish I could remember the conversation that I'm sure took place at the time, but I can't. But I still have that pouch and the currency and coins. One of those coins contains a bullet hole, one a swastika and several are over two hundred years old.

Uncle Mike held the rank of sergeant. I've been told that he had at least several opportunities to be promoted, but his men liked him so much that they set him up in various ways so that he would lose the promotion. I never heard that he got upset about it.

He spent most of his life, from the time of his enlistment, in Germany and had, I believe, a German girlfriend for a long time. I think he died after Grandpa but before Grandma. In any event, he died of a heart attack in a small room in a Bavarian hotel. He was buried in an American cemetery in Germany, in accordance with his wishes.

In My Beginning

From what I've heard, my autobiography really started at birth. REALLY! A few years ago, Mother told me the story of my birth. Just to give the reader some perspective on things, I was born in 1947. I sometimes refer to the state of medicine today as the "practice of medicine." Well, if that's the way I sometimes feel today, you can imagine what I would have said in 1947!

Anyway, Mother got that itchy-twitchy" feeling and decided that I was on my way. The doctor was called and met Mother and Dad at the hospital. The doctor told them that I wasn't ready and went home. Shortly after he did so, I must have decided to pull the first stunt of my life and enter the world. Apparently, the nurses didn't like the idea of delivering a baby on their own, so one of them actually held her hand over the "baby chute" until the doctor could get back to the hospital. So you see, I was a pain in the butt very early in life!

My Sister and Brother

My sister, Peg, struck me, until recently, as having had a very normal and successful life. And that included her childhood and adolescence. But I was wrong; at least about her adolescence. Mother, especially, kept a very tight rein on her, maybe a little too tight. I suspect her parents raised their girls the same way. In defense of perception, however, I think she's turned out to be a very lucky lady, having married a great guy and having three kids who would make any parent proud. I sometimes tell people that my sister's family is the most disgustingly normal family I've ever run into, and that I can only stand being around them for a few days. Then I have to get back to my own planet. Later, you'll understand what I mean.

Jack, my brother, on the other hand, had it rough, and I was always aware of it. He was always being compared to Peg and/or me. Expectations were pretty high, especially in school. I've thought many times that there wasn't a reason in the world that my brother shouldn't have hated me when we were young.

St. Peter's Catholic Church

In thinking back on it, the Catholic Church seemed to govern its flock through intimidation and fear and, for us children, that intimidation took the form of the nuns and, especially, Monsignor John Zarilli. Fear of the nuns was greatly reduced, of course, when we were transferred to Emerson Elementary School. But the fear of Monsignor Zarilli was intense and widespread. For us, Monsignor Zarilli was God's personal representative in our neighborhood, and he was apt to show up at your home at any time.

I remember going to confession on Saturday afternoon (What a way to spoil a perfectly good Saturday.) How we shook at having to walk into that box, confess to our many and mortal sins and waiting for Monsignor Zarilli to ask which school you attended. I remember being so mad that he asked these questions that I had to ask myself if I needed to go to confession a second time to confess to my anger.

One Saturday afternoon, I found myself walking to confession with a neighbor girl (the same one who spilled the paint on the floor, by the way.) We were probably eight or nine years old. She was very upset because she had kissed a boy. In those days, that was very close to having sex, you know. You can understand why she would be afraid of having to confess this mortal sin to Monsignor Zarilli.

When she couldn't put it off any longer, she went into the confessional, knelt down and tried to prepare for the window to open between her and the Monsignor.

The process of going to confession involved a ritual that began with the words, "Bless me, Father, for I have sinned." When the window finally opened, she said, "Kiss me, Father, for I have sinned."

She may still be living that one down.

Emerson Elementary School

My third grade teacher at Emerson was Miss Olson. The Principal was Agnes Gallagher. This grade, of course, was where I met those who would become friends, some for a very long time, and some for far too short a time.

Fourth grade featured my teacher, Mrs. Laura Pribble. She was kind of short and squat, but her teeth scared the hell out of us, or most of us anyway. When we had given her a hard day, she would take the last few minutes of the day to warn us about our behavior the next day. When explaining the options for the next day's possible consequences for the same kind of behavior, she would reach into her purse and produce an Emory board and pretend to be filing her canines. We usually got the point.

Outside of Marty, one of the kids I remember most clearly was Mike. Now I met Mike in the third grade, but what I really remember about him happened in the fourth grade.

Mike had a thing about wearing his glasses. He didn't want to wear them, but Mrs. Pribble insisted that he wear them. Mike would painstakingly take the screws out of the bows and throw them out the window. Mrs. Pribble would make him go outside and find the bows on the lawn, bring them back, put them back on for him and make him put them back on his face.

Another time, Mike stuck the glasses in a can of green paint. Mrs. Pribble made him stick his hand in the paint, go wash them off and put them back on. This kind of behavior continued the whole year, and I began to wonder what made the kid tick. Mike became of even more interest to me when I found out that his father had gotten his sister pregnant. My reaction wasn't disgust, at least not completely, but fascination and curiosity.

There were other kids who became important to me, as friends and/or as kids who, for one reason or another, fascinated me. Among these were Lee, Leeann and her brother, David, Bruce and Gene, who were identical twins, Darrell and Greg. I only mention these people now, but some of them may come up later.

December, 1957

Around the middle of December, 1957, the next and possibly most significant phase or event of my life began. I developed an unexplained high fever. I was taken to the doctor, Dr. Bill Spang, and he ordered me into the pediatrics department of St. Mary's Hospital. For the next eight days, all I remember is needles and more needles and various sizes and shapes of Dracula, who were constantly flying into my room trying to suck my blood. I managed to strike a few blows and fend some of them off for short periods of time but, eventually, they managed to strike and leave with their vial of blood. After eight days, the fever suddenly broke, and I returned home, just in time for the Christmas holidays. But it wasn't over.

MS Or Guillaine-Barre?

One morning in 1958, shortly after the first of the year, I awakened with a right foot that seemed to be asleep, only it never woke up. Over the course of the next few hours, the foot still wouldn't function, and so I found myself sitting in Dr. Bill's office again listening to him tell my parents, again, to take me back to the hospital.

The first thing I remember about this trip back to the hospital happened after Mom and Dad had gone home. I remember looking out into the darkened hallway and asking myself what all of this was the beginning of. I was once told that the definition of the phrase, "peace of mind" was not having to know what's going to happen next. Well, I was a long, long way from having any peace of mind. I was absolutely scared to death.

And then along came an angel in white. Filling the center of the open doorway was a white form with a soft face and an even softer voice. This was one Dr. Floyd Westendorp. He was the first person I met at the hospital that didn't scare me or want my blood.

He asked me to get out of bed and walk down the hall. I remember getting out into the darkened hallway and managing three or four steps before falling. Dr. Floyd picked me up and put me back in bed. Those were the last steps I took for many weeks.

Two main things happened during the first few weeks at the hospital. One afternoon, while Mom and Dad were both with me, I began to have excruciating pain in both legs. I'd never experienced pain like that before. I was very much aware that whatever was going on was not good. I was screaming with pain, and Dad was approaching me to somehow comfort me. I remember watching him approach me as if I were looking through a camcorder. It seemed like the pain increased with every step toward me that he took. I screamed at him not to touch me. Somehow, a decision was made to put me in a bathtub full of warm water and see if that helped. I don't remember if it did or not, and I don't remember how long the pain lasted. The doctors eventually told us that the pain was probably caused by the closing of the blood vessels in my legs.

Probably as a result of this, my doctors decided to contact the Mayo Clinic in Rochester, Minnesota. I remember praying harder than I'd ever prayed that they wouldn't want me. Hell, as far as I knew, Rochester was located somewhere near China. I had no idea how far Rochester was from home.

As it turned out, the Mayo Clinic told my doctors that there was nothing they could do for me that my Duluth doctors and St. Mary's Hospital staff couldn't do. I was very thankful for this huge act of "divine intervention." At least I was going to be able to fight this problem at home where, I thought, my family and friends would be available.

Over the next few weeks, my body systems began to shut down. Bladder and bowel function slowed and then stopped altogether. I began to get numb in the hands and legs and, eventually, my vision was also affected.

Rituals also began to develop. A neurosurgeon, Dr. Bill Pollard, usually showed up every morning to check me over and to follow, or track, the numbing of my body. Dr. Floyd also usually showed up every day and became the "front man" when they decided to perform a procedure I wasn't familiar with.

The first sales job Dr Floyd had to do was to sell me on the idea of being catheterized. He explained the process to me and even showed me a catheter. I didn't know whether to laugh or cry. How the hell did he think he was going to get that thing in there? But the look on his face didn't suggest that he was joking. Over the weeks and months, I got very good at interpreting the looks on his face, and he became one of the few people I grew to trust implicitly.

Another tough day in the trenches was the day he had to explain the need and process for taking spinal fluid. I want to tell you that this was a lot harder to sell than was catheterization. I thought that sticking needles anywhere in the body was obscene, but sticking one in your spine?

As it turned out, there were two uncomfortable things about my first spinal tap. The first was Dr. Floyd's continually telling me, "Don't move!" Of course, every time he said it, I wanted to jump right out of my skin. The second thing was the squeak! Yeah, you read it right. I said, the squeak! The sound of the needle going into the spine made a squeaking sound as if the needle were being shoved into a bratwurst or something. Eventually, it was over, and I realized I had survived the experience.

Eventually, someone decided that I should be moved into a four bed ward. During the next few months, I occupied both Beds 1 and 4. Bed 4 allowed me to see out into the hallway and into the room across the hall. It also allowed me a few seconds warning when a doctor, nurse, lab tech wanting another vial of blood, or Mrs. Arillio, my favorite pain in the ass, was heading in my direction. It made me the ward scout, if you will.

As I recall, the hospital administrator, Sister Marybelle and Mrs. Arillio were sisters. It's nice to know that God likes to keep nasty genes in the same family and not spread them out. Mrs. Arillio was the head nurse on the night shift, and for some reason, we grew to dislike each other. And things never got better between the two of us.

Spending three and a half months in a hospital tends to make some permanent changes in a person, maybe especially in a child. They experience things that others wouldn't normally experience, see pain being experienced by kids too young to experience much pain, kids dying who haven't had much of a chance to live, to see the trust kids put in caregivers violated and to see the cruelty that people with power can inflict on people who have none. Kids can also be pretty cruel and inconsiderate toward others, even other kids.

I've already mentioned the experience of being catheterized. Because all bodily systems closed down below the waist, the catheter became a rather permanent ornament. With the passage of time, my spine also became quite stiff, so the doctors developed a plan to loosen it up.

Part of that plan involved physical therapy. Another part was a contraption devised for my bed that would allow me to exercise my legs while I lay in bed. It involved placing a piece of plywood at the foot of my bed. Someone found a pair of roller skates, and attached two small straps of leather to either skate so they would be able to strap them to my feet. Then a pulley was attached to the frame of the bed so that the end result was that, by operating the pulley with my hands, the legs would bend and rise at the knees, and the skates would glide over the plywood.

All of this worked very well for a while. And then it began to hurt when the skates were put on. In time, it hurt badly enough so that I didn't want to put them on at all.

One morning, Mrs. Arillio came in to put the skates on me before she went home. It was mid-morning. I wasn't in the mood for her, and I certainly wasn't in the mood for the skates, and I told her so. We argued, she insisted, and she tried to force the skates on my feet. I got mad and threw a glass of ice water at her. She, of course, got mad and left my room. But in a few minutes, she was back. She didn't mention the skates, but she said she needed to take a look at the catheter, which she removed. Then she left for the day. Of course, I had no idea as to the possible consequences of having the catheter removed, but this act would become one of the biggest lessons of my young life.

Somewhere along the way, I had taught Dr. Floyd how to play cribbage. He got in the habit of stopping by my room every night before he went home to play a game. Thank God, that night was no exception. When he walked in, I was crying loudly enough and was physically agitated enough so that I couldn't answer when he asked me what was wrong. When he pulled down the sheets, he saw my swollen tummy, and, of course, saw that the catheter was missing.

He called for Mrs. Arillio, who was, by this time, back on duty. When she came into the room, Dr. Floyd demanded to know how the catheter got taken out. She told him that she had taken it out. He asked her why, and she told him it was because I refused to put the skates on that morning. When he heard that, he hit her, knocking her into my locker and onto the floor. I was shocked that this gentle man could actually get violent. He quickly ordered another catheter kit and relieved my discomfort. Although I never remember mentioning the incident to her in any way, it seemed to permanently put me on the defensive. I guess I realized that even though she was trained to help people, she was also capable of hurting them. I didn't like feeling unsafe in a place that was supposed to heal people and relieve pain.

The second part of the plan to deal with my body's problems was physical therapy. That's when Millie, Tillie, and Henry Engler, the physical therapist, entered my life. Millie and Tillie were the two PT department aides who would come and take me to therapy every day. They were very nice, and if I didn't always look forward to the work and pain involved with the therapy, I always looked forward to seeing these two ladies every day.

The day I met Henry Engler, my therapist, I knew I was going to like him a whole lot. He was gentle, had a very soft voice and a fairly thick accent. I was to find out that Henry was born a Swiss citizen and had come to the United States as a young man. In order to thank the United States for allowing him to become a citizen, he enlisted in the Navy during World War II.

He was very reassuring in his description of what to expect during the first treatment. The first thing they did was to put a bikini on my skinny frame. Then they put me on a canvas stretcher kind of thing and hooked it up to a hoist. All of this was happening right beside what looked like a watering trough filled with water. Then, much to my horror, Henry pushed a button, and the water began to churn. Then the stretcher started to rise and moved over the churning water. The lower end of the stretcher began to tilt as if it was positioning itself to dump my butt in the water! Another button was pushed, and the stretcher was lowered into the churning water right up to my neck. After the panic subsided, Henry added a little soap to the water, and I began to enjoy the warmth of the water and the stimulation of the bubbles.

What I didn't know at the time was the doctors had diagnosed my condition as MS, Multiple Sclerosis. I also didn't know that the doctors had told Henry that I would probably never walk again. I also didn't know that Mom and Dad had been told that there was no reason to believe that, given the fact that all body systems were shutting down, the respiratory system would not also shut down. That fact, as I found out many years later, was the reason that an iron lung sat outside my door for the entire length of my hospital stay. I'm very grateful that no one ever told me any of this because, as they say, "Ignorance is bliss."

17

Sometimes I still wonder how I would have reacted had I known the facts concerning that ugly yellow machine. Maybe a little more divine intervention?

When I mentioned not particularly liking the work involved in physical therapy, I'm referring mainly to the work that Henry performed on me. The whirlpool treatments were, in part, a means of getting my spinal column to relax in preparation for the "hands on" part of the therapy session.

As my spine was very rigid, part of what had to be done was to loosen it up by bending it. Bending it took the form of Henry's placing his left arm under my shoulders and his right arm under my knees and forcibly bringing the knees up toward the chest. That hurt! As I would yell in pain, I would often look into Henry's face and see teardrops falling from his cheeks onto my chest. Maybe that was God's way of letting me know I wasn't the only one that was hurting!

In time, I began to ask Henry, "When are you going to walk me?" For quite some time, his answer was, "Do you really want to walk?" He would tell me to pray and ask God to help me walk.

One day after a treatment, I went back to the sixth floor and had some aides seat me in a chair in the hallway. As I sat there, I watched staff people walk past me with seemingly no effort at all. I can't describe how I envied them!

I started to wonder what it would be like to stand on my own two feet! Then I decided to find out. I stopped a few nurses and asked them if they would lift me to my feet just to find out what it felt like. To my surprise, they grabbed me under both arms and lifted me to my feet. I remember looking down and feeling like they were about twenty feet away, and I felt like I was twenty feet tall. After a few breaths of fresh air, the nurses sat me back down in the chair.

When I got to therapy the next day, I could hardly wait to see Henry and tell him about being on my feet. Needless to say, when I did tell him, he was very surprised. The smile on his face went well with the tears rolling down his cheeks.

When he got over the shock, Henry looked at me and said, "You'd really like to walk, wouldn't you?" Then he rolled the gurney over to the parallel bars. He picked me up in his arms and put me on my feet at one end of the parallel bars.

I took a few steps that day, but from that day on, there was no

18

turning back. Whether or not I was ever going to walk again was never a question for either of us. When I think about it now, I wonder how long it would have taken for circumstances to bring me to those parallel bars, had those nurses not been willing to put me on my feet.

I've already spoken about events that contribute to one's development. Keep in mind that a ten-year-old boy is experiencing these events. Let me mention a few more teaching events.

I've already mentioned Mrs. Arillio, Dr. Floyd, and the catheter incident. Well, I got a certain amount of revenge on the Saturday before Easter, 1958. The ward was full, and we were kind of bored. Suddenly, there was Mrs. Arillio with one of her painted on smiles. She asked us if we wanted to have a little fun by painting Easter eggs. She was going to hide them for her young son, Joey. Of course, we didn't believe in turning down a chance to have a little fun, especially when I had a little idea for having a little more fun at Mrs. Arillio's expense.

She gave each of us a dozen hardboiled eggs, each in a carton, and the coloring materials we'd need to accomplish the task. She said she'd be back late that afternoon to pick them up.

As we were coloring the eggs, I suggested to my three roommates that we should hide the eggs on Mrs. Arillio and make her find them. They all thought that was a great idea, so we set about the task of coloring the eggs.

When Mrs. Arillio returned to get the eggs, we were ready for her. When she asked for them, we told her to find them. She got angry, so I told the others to "Give them to her." We all reached behind our pillows, produced the eggs in their cartons, opened the cartons, and dumped four dozen hardboiled eggs on the floor. She, of course, was furious! She walked out the door and we, of course, told ourselves that she deserved it. But it didn't take long for me to realize that Joey didn't. I guess every action has its consequences. It's very uncomfortable to feel that guilt and shame when you're ten years old.

Speaking of shame, one of the worst days of my life was actually one average day when Mother showed up with my usual bag of Snyder's popcorn, and Dad showed up after work, again as usual. For some reason, I wasn't feeling real well. I was kind of short-tempered and ornery. They were both being good at being patient, loving parents. Eventually, I lost my temper and raised my voice at them. I knew what I had done immediately, but I was too embarrassed to apologize. They smiled, said they thought it was time to go home, hugged me and took their leave. The next twenty-four hours were some of the longest of my young life. I wish that I had known then what I know now – that shame is one of the most useless emotions a person can feel, because it prevents a person from doing whatever he can do to quash the feeling.

More Learning Experiences and the People Who Taught Them

If part of the reason for writing this autobiography is to show how people and incidents mold character and personality, I should mention some other people and incidents that had quite an effect on me during that hospital stay. And always remember that you have undoubtedly contributed to the development of someone's personality and character.

One such little guy was another patient, Joey. Joey was a six or seven year old leukemia victim. Of course, in those days, leukemia carried a death sentence. I don't remember how the two of us met. It was probably his father's putting him in a little red wagon and taking him from room to room to talk to the other kids on the floor. Joey and his dad stopped in my room every day for weeks or months. Eventually, he got weak enough so that he couldn't, or wouldn't, speak, and then, there were no more visits. Joey's dad came to the ward one day and told us that Joey had died.

Ray, who arrived in the ward sometime after I was moved there, became my closest friend in the ward, and in fact, on the entire floor. Ray was a little older than me and had been involved in a car accident, which resulted in a broken left leg and right knee. The knee had a stainless steel pin through it. I don't remember a great deal of medical attention being given to Ray. He seemed to be there to mend, but I'm also sure he was sent to keep me company.

But all good things must come to an end, and as the saying goes, the time came for Ray to go home. It was a sad Saturday morning for me, because after Ray's parents took him home, three out of the four beds in the ward were empty. Long experience had taught me that things wouldn't stay that way for long.

I was watching a baseball game on television that afternoon when I heard ambulance sirens. There was nothing unusual about hearing ambulance sirens in a hospital, so I blew them off and continued to watch the game. After all, my Yankees were playing!

In a few minutes, I heard a commotion in the hallway, and it sounded as if it was heading my way. A few seconds later, they wheeled Ray back into the ward. He was wincing in pain, flailing his head from side to side and was throwing up. He wasn't coherent enough to talk, so I just had to lie there and listen to him moan and groan.

As the hours passed, things didn't get any less frightening. Ray quit being able to throw anything up and was well into the dry heaves. I heard his parents talking about a high fever and pain and swelling in the right side. Of course, at this point, "Dr. Scandin" had everything figured out. Then I made my mistake. I told Ray's mother that I thought Ray had a ruptured appendix. She ran to tell the doctor who, rightly, stormed into the room and "ripped me a new one!" Several hours later, the doctor walked in, looked at me, looked at Ray's parents and announced that he thought Ray's problem was a ruptured appendix and that they were going to take him down to surgery and remove it. Ray was well on his way to recovery the following day.

There was a little boy in the room across the hall from the ward that I'll never forget. He was probably about four years old. I only remember a few things about this kid. First, he was in isolation because he had some sort of growth on his butt. Secondly, no one but medical staff was allowed in the room, and that included his parents. But the third and worst thing I remember is the doctor's going into the room, making the kid stand on the bed and then lancing the growth with a scalpel. Sometimes the parents would be at the window of the door, watching the procedure, and I could see a look on the kid's face that asked why they couldn't come in. At some point, I asked a nurse if that procedure shouldn't be done with the benefit of anesthesia. To my surprise, instead of telling me to mind my own business, she agreed that it should have been done under some sort of anesthesia. The boy survived to go home.

Eventually, Ray recovered and went home, and I again found myself alone in the ward. But as I said before, that was always a condition that didn't last for long.

One afternoon, a nurse brought in a six year old kid. The nurse told me that he was going to have a goiter removed the following morning. As I recall, his neck was swollen. The nurse told him that I had seniority rights on the room, and that if he didn't behave, I could have him removed. Then she left.

This kid never said a word. He had a toy car that he would wind up and release, and when it hit something, it would explode. Every time the car flew apart, the kid would look at me with the queerest look on his face. I wasn't feeling too well that day, and I really didn't appreciate the noise or the queer looks. I really got mad because the look on his face made me laugh so hard, my stomach hurt. He didn't respond to my warnings to stop, so I called the nurse and had him removed. End of story, right? Not quite.

The next day, the same nurse happened into my room. I asked her how the boy's surgery had gone. She told me that he died on the operating table. They opened him up and discovered that they weren't dealing with a goiter. The boy had two lungs full of cancer. Whenever I think of those days, I think of that kid. I hope his family thinks about him as often as I do. You just never know, do you?

I mentioned that I never looked forward to physical therapy sessions, other than the fact that I got some time with Millie and Tillie and, of course, Henry, my therapist. What I haven't mentioned is the fact that, due to some remodeling, the road to therapy led directly through 4-North, the psychiatric ward. It always made me a little uncomfortable knowing that I was in the psych ward of the hospital, but I never felt really unsafe because Millie and Tillie were always there.

But one morning, we were delayed on the floor, and the girls had to roll me over to the wall and leave me for a few minutes. While I lay there, I glanced into the rooms as any ten-year- old might do, trying to locate the source of the occasional screams that could be heard reverberating through the halls. I heard what sounded like an older man yell and then another voice curse. It was coming from a room located close to the foot of my gurney. I looked into a room in time to see a well-known psychiatrist hit an older patient who, as I found out later, was refusing a shock treatment.

As I slowly made progress in getting my spine loosened up, I gained more access to the pediatric floor as well as other floors, because I was able to sit in a wheelchair. Believe me, it gave me an entirely new perspective on things.

During most of my hospital stay, there was one special little girl in the girls' ward. I'm not sure I ever knew her name, nor do I ever remember her speaking so much as a word. Every time I went past the ward, I would find her sitting on a rocking horse, just rocking back and forth for hours, just staring blankly out the door into the hallway. I would guess that she was four or five years old.

One night, I was sitting out in the darkened hallway between the elevator, which was always spitting out new and interesting faces, and the girls' ward. My attention moved to the ward when I realized that the rocking horse was still in sight of the door, but the little girl wasn't sitting on it. I could hear people talking, and I recognized the voices of her parents.

Suddenly, I heard a lady crying. In a few minutes, the girl's parents walked out of the room, and I knew the little girl had passed away. After a few minutes, I decided that I'd had enough of sitting in the dark hallway and began wheeling myself back toward my room. As I passed the girls' ward, I had to take one last look at that rocking horse. I think that this was the night that I realized how hard it was for parents and for the families of these sick and dying kids.

Breaking the Rules

Speaking of the stress on family members, it's been nice to see attitudes change toward visiting patients in hospitals. Back in the 1950's and later, the attitude seemed to be that visitors under sixteen years of age seemed to contribute to the medical problems of patients. Funny, I always thought that was true of doctors! But regardless of individual opinions, it was hard on a ten-year-old that couldn't see his brother and sister for that period of time. I was thankful that Dr. Floyd seemed to know the importance of family on speeding the recovery process. But the hospital rule said, "No visitors under 16," and that meant my brother and sister.

One day, though, Dr. Floyd sneaked my entire family into what I recall was a large, dark dining room somewhere in the hospital. I was very happy to see them after so many weeks, but I was also wondering what Sister Marybelle, the Hospital Administrator, would say if she ever found out about the clandestine visit. I didn't want to see Dr.

Westendorp in trouble, nor did I want her to make trouble for Mom and Dad. But there was something exciting about pulling one over on the old prude!

Sister Marybelle was like an itch you couldn't quite scratch. She and her twin itch, Mrs. Arillio, appeared in the boys' ward one morning and began ragging on the four of us about the dirty walls and ceiling. We were trying to figure out how she thought we had accomplished the deed as all four of us were bedridden. Maybe she thought we had been throwing bedpans.

The Beginning of another Chapter

One morning, as he did every morning, Dr. Bill Pollard, the neurosurgeon, came into the ward while I was on the phone playing chess with Marty. He would always pull down the sheets so he could see my feet and then tell me to move the big toe on my right foot. He'd been doing this for so long that it didn't even seem necessary to hang up the phone and mess up the game.

When Dr. Bill told me to move my toe, I looked at my right foot and tried to move it as I had done many times before. But this time, I thought I saw the big toe move. When I saw it, I stopped talking to Marty, and I heard the doctor say, "Move it again." Of course, when I heard the doctor, I knew it was no figment of my imagination. I had actually been able to move my toe! Marty and I ended our conversation pretty abruptly. I started to concentrate on making that toe move, not wanting it to quit moving due to lack of use!

By mid-afternoon, I was sitting in a chair outside of the ward, right next to the iron lung, and kicking both legs and watching in total amazement. Within a short period of time, my internal systems began to work again, and it wasn't long before I could hear the word "home" being spoken close enough to be heard clearly. There was a lot of anticipation about going home, but the hospital staff had become my family too, and it was going to be hard to leave Dr. Floyd, Henry, Millie, Tillie and others. And then there was the question as to how things were going to be done, and get done, when I got home. Soon it was time to leave, and a new adventure was about to begin.

Going Home

I don't actually remember the day I left St. Mary's Hospital and going home. I know I went home on the 101st day of my hospitalization, and the first day that I would not be covered by Dad's insurance. The approximate bill came to just over $2500, or, if you do the math, about $25/day, and that included an $8.00 charge per physical therapy session. How things change! Come to think of it, I wonder what those damned roller skates cost? By the way, I forgot to mention that the reason those skates got painful to put on was that no one thought of covering four blocks of wood that were strapped and rubbed against the large bones on either side of the feet. In time, the bare wood rubbed the skin off. All I knew was that it hurt.

The first thing I remember about going home was finding that my bed had been moved to the dining room of the house. It was also great to have my brother and sister around again, and it was great to get some home cooking. I had lost a lot of weight during my hospital stay, as the food truly "sucked," e.g., you could suck it through a straw most of the time. Also, being that most body systems had shut down, I wasn't really too interested in eating.

Another great reason for coming home was Marty. We had had many phone conversations over three and a half months and had played many cribbage and chess games, but we were now going to be able to see each other, and I was really looking forward to that. Sisters are sisters, and brothers are brothers, but a best friend is something a little bit different.

There's not a doubt in my mind that Marty was put in my life to teach me a few things and to give me some stability that had been lacking for the past few years. Marty was—and is—an eternal optimist. At this point in my life, "optimist" was not a word I was familiar with. I was guarded, life was a war that had to be fought and won, and I always seemed to be concerned about what was going to happen next, and how I was going to be able to deal with it. But Marty was always a mellowing factor. His picture rests beside the phrase, "No big deal" in the dictionary.

For the rest of the summer, we spent most of the day sitting on my front porch, playing poker for baseball cards. If I remember correctly, I still owe him several hundred 1958 New York Yankee team

25

cards. Good luck getting them, Marty! We also talked a lot about school and hoping for the day that we would find ourselves in the same school and in the same classes. We were doing all of this while we were watching our friends playing softball, basketball and football in the vacant lot right across the street from my house.

For five decades, we've talked about those days, and I've thanked him for being there for me. He likes to blow it off, reminding me that it was a long time ago. Well, it was, but I'm no less thankful. Sitting with a sick friend, rather than playing softball with a bunch of healthy friends, day after day, is not something one would expect from an average ten-year-old. So, my thanks to Marty, again, and to anyone who chooses to comfort a sick friend rather than do more pleasant things with healthy friends, especially young people.

In time, I was able to get across the street to watch these friends play basketball, softball and football. On one occasion, while sitting outside of harm's way during a rowdy basketball game, I was approached by a kid I recognized as one half of a set of identical twins, and a younger brother of Mike, my classmate, who had the hang-up about his glasses. Remember? He began poking fun about the fact that I was in a wheelchair and vulnerable to anyone who might want to kick my butt! I defended myself with my mouth but, before I knew it, he had jumped behind me, grabbed me around the neck and tipped over the wheelchair and dumped me on the ground. I tried to hold onto him, knowing that if I let go, I wouldn't be able to fight him off. Somehow, I wound up with my jawbone pressed on a rock and the kid's knee pressing on the other cheek. It didn't take long for me to yell, "uncle." By this time, the kids playing basketball had seen the fight and had come running. The kid ran in the other direction. With a combined effort, we were able to get my butt back in the wheelchair no worse for the wear.

Some weeks later, I saw the kid going into the grocery store across the street from my grandparents' house. I waited for him outside the store and, when he came out, I grabbed him and roughed him up a little. A few days later, I ran into him again, and I was informed that I had beaten up the wrong twin and, incidentally, it didn't seem to bother him any. The one I beat up was a pretty nice kid, the Dr. Jekyll half of Dr. Jekyll and Mr. Hyde. Eventually, my brother, Jack, ran into Mr. Hyde and gave him a few reasons why he shouldn't mess with someone in a wheelchair.

Going Back To School

Eventually the summer came to an end, and it was time to start getting ready for school. I was getting stronger, and I was slowly making the transition from the wheelchair to crutches. Of course, I wanted to go to Emerson Elementary for my sixth grade year, but Mom and Dad found out that Laura MacArthur Grade School had a program for disabled kids, along with a nurse and a physical therapist. So the powers that be decided that I should be enrolled at this school, the Kate Barnes School.

As Kate Barnes was located in the West Duluth area, it was necessary for me to ride a school bus to and from school. It was convenient because everyday, the bus would stop in front of the house, and a bus aide would lift me out of my chair and put me in the seat directly behind the driver.

Four blocks from my house and right across the avenue from Emerson Elementary, the bus would stop again, and the aide would go into an old tattered porch on an old tattered house and carry Ralph into the bus and put him in the seat right beside me. Ralph was seven or eight years old and had clubbed feet.

Ralph was one of the most remarkable people I've ever met. He mystified me. He was the sort of person who would find something positive to say about any kind of lousy situation. For example, if it were bone cold outside, Ralph would say, "It's good weather for polar bears." If the temperature was one hundred degrees, Ralph would say, "It's good for sun tans." He used to drive me crazy with his infernal optimism! I liked Ralph a whole lot, but I certainly didn't like his constantly challenging my views on the condition of man. I don't know what ever happened to Ralph, but I sure wish I thought I was going to live long enough to thank him for entering my life for a short two years and planting the seeds for change.

My sixth grade teacher was Mrs. Dorothy Johnson. She was tall and straight and kind of looked like a Marine drill instructor with lipstick. Her classroom had grades six through twelve and probably eight to twelve students altogether. I believe I was the only sixth grader.

All of the kids had medical problems of some sort. Jim was a polio victim and was confined to a wheelchair. By the way, he was the only person who probably would not have called himself a victim. Marie and Dale had heart problems, and I never was able to identify Rod's problem. Of one thing I was sure. This was going to be one huge learning experience!

In addition to Mrs. Johnson and the rest of the kids in my room, I had daily sessions with Mrs. Somrock and Mr. Shabatura, the nurse and physical therapist, who occupied an office just a few feet from my classroom. I was always glad that Mrs. Somrock was around. I was feeling very sorry for myself and very embarrassed, because I still hadn't regained bladder control. Having to wear a pad and have it changed regularly didn't exactly make me feel normal. Mrs. Somrock was very good at taking things into stride and dealing with my physical problems without adding to my embarrassment.

Mr. Shabatura was just as good at making me feel all right about having to get physical therapy at school. I didn't know anyone else in the school that had bladder problems, and I never remember seeing anyone else getting physical therapy from Mr. Shabatura. In my mind, I had the worst problems of anyone in school. And then my education began.

Dale was a 13-year-old who was born a "blue baby." Bottom line was that he'd had a heart problem since birth. The condition gave his skin a blue tint. His family doctor had arranged for Dale to have heart surgery at the University of Minnesota Hospital, in Minneapolis. He was very excited, and we were all very excited for him. The last day he was in school, we had a party for him, wished him good luck and said our farewells.

In those days, a local Duluth television station had a children's program, which seemed to be nicely timed to coincide with my arrival home from school everyday. Dale's parents had told Mrs. Johnson that we could all keep track of Dale's progress by listening to the Captain Q Show. So everyday we'd all go home and turn on the Captain Q Show so we could get a report on Dale's progress and recovery.

One day, I got home just in time to hear Captain Q say that it was no longer necessary to send cards and letters to Dale. My heart sank. I knew Dale had died.

It was a very quiet classroom that we all walked into the next day. As expected, Mrs. Johnson made the announcement that Dale had, in fact, died. She told us that Dale's mother had called her and reported that the surgery, itself, had been a success. Dale had been sitting up in bed, enjoying the new color of his skin and listening to his mother read cards and letters from us kids. Suddenly, he fell back onto his pillow and died, apparently of a blood clot.

A day or so later, the funeral arrangements had been made, and Mrs. Johnson told us that she had made arrangements for any of us who wanted to view the body at the mortuary. I had seen a few bodies in a mortuary before, and I knew something about kids' dying from watching it in the hospital, but I wasn't ready for what I saw when we went to see Dale.

I'd never seen a dead child before. After I had gotten as close to the coffin as I felt comfortable in getting, I took a seat in the front row of the room and watched the rest of my classmates approach the coffin.

And then I watched Mrs. Johnson approach the coffin. She went up to it, stood there for a moment and then began stroking his hair. I was horrified. I thought she'd gone crazy! Then she reached in her purse, pulled out a comb and began combing his hair! I was just short of frightened.

I guess what really made Dale's death hard to deal with was the fact that the surgery had been successful. The problem had been dealt with, and then the unexpected happened. Why would something like that happen? I still think about Dale every time I'm in the West End and drive past his home.

Jim was another interesting character in my classroom. As I mentioned, Jim was a polio victim, a characterization I know he'd disagree with. Although he appeared somewhat withered physically from the waist down, he was built like the Incredible Hulk from the waist up. No, he wasn't green!

Jim wasn't the best student in the school, but he certainly was the most confident and self-assured kid I'd ever met, with the possible exception of Ralph. Two things amazed me about this kid. When he was late for a class, he would wheel himself down a hallway with the speed of a cheetah and turn around corners on two wheels. I also saw him go up and down steps many times.

I know what you're thinking. This was a very old school, and the steps were very wide from back to front, and very shallow. Jim would tilt his chair back on the large wheels and use enough force to be able to skip UP the steps. He could come down a flight of steps almost as fast as the other kids could walk or run. I guess what I was looking at and admiring so much, was a kid who had adjusted so well to his disability that he didn't know he had one.

Now Rod was kind of an unusual kid, but we clicked immediately. I never did know what Rod's disabilities were, but somehow, it didn't matter. He was a nice kid, and that's all that mattered to me.

In a school situation like ours, there was a lot of free time because classes weren't conducted as in the normal classroom. Mrs. Johnson divided her time between seven grades, and there were no more than ten or twelve kids in all seven grades. Therefore, we all had ample time to complete any homework assignments. When we did have free time, we usually played cards, like poker, hearts, spades, smear, etc. Rod was particularly adept at playing cards.

He had at least one other major talent. He was an accomplished bowler. Rod and I managed to maintain our friendship for several years after Kate Barnes and West Jr. High School. I'm probably the only guy alive who can claim to have had three perfect games bowled against him by the same guy. Disabilities?

West Junior High School

Seventh grade was a whole lot different than the sixth grade. Although Ralph's eternal optimism continued to befuddle me, and Jim continued to amaze me, things got even more frightening because, in the seventh grade, I had to fight my way up and down steps using crutches, and all of my teachers were nice enough to put my desk right next to the blackboard to compensate for my poor eyesight. Instead of being grateful, I felt like they were forcing me to sit in the front of the room with no clothes on. Apparently I felt important enough to believe everyone was looking at me. No one, by the way, was ever unfriendly or unhelpful; nor did anyone ever make me believe they were avoiding me. It was all in my attitude, and everyone probably knew it but me! So far, I wasn't making much progress in growing up and adjusting to my life the way it was. Instead of noticing the kids around me, I was still feeling like I was being picked on. I even managed to forget that my friend, Dale, had died just a short time before.

As I've already mentioned, Mrs. Johnson was kind of an intimidating person. I believe she had been an English teacher in a former life, because she had a thing about English grammar and, in particular, diagramming sentences. Every weekday for two school years, at 2:30 p.m., Mrs. Johnson would line all of us up at the blackboards around the room and have us diagramming sentences out of the 12th grade English grammar book. I thought she should have done prison time for making me, a sixth grader, do English grammar out of a senior English book. Man, I hated the ground she walked on! But this last hour each day did give me a lot to combat Ralph's infernal optimism during the ride home. But eventually the school year ended, and I realized again that I had survived.

Another Change of Schools

My progress in recovering was steady, and during the summer between seventh and eighth grades, Mom and Dad and I talked about where I should go to school in the Fall. I still wanted to go to Washington Jr. High as that's where my friends were going, especially Marty. But my eyes still weren't very good, and it was thought that we should look for a school that might have a program for the visually disabled. We found such a program at Ordean Jr. High School, which was located in the Lakeside community of Duluth.

Like West Jr. High, I would be based out of a classroom with others who were visually impaired. The program had an instructor/advisor by the name of Lawrence Jahn. He was well versed in both Grade-1 and Grade-2 Braille, and would translate Braille-written homework into "typewriter English" so we could hand it in. All of us were capable of walking to classes, so the eighth grade was about as close to a normal school experience as I'd had for several years. But the process of learning was far from over.

I should mention that there were only four of us in the program for the visually impaired. Beside myself, there were Sue, Barb and Peter. We all rode to school together with an Ordean science teacher by the name of Jim Wolff. As you can imagine, we got to know each other very well, and very quickly. And we got close, given the fact all five of us were riding in a Volkswagen!

Sue was my age. She was a straight "A" student and had been blind since shortly after birth. She had been born prematurely and had been incubated. As I recall, the oxygen supply in the incubator was too rich and robbed her of her sight. She played the organ and piano, softball, and she even skied! Another message maybe?

Sue and Barb were best friends and had gone to school together all their lives. Barb was also totally blind. I don't remember the story of her blindness, but she was an above-average student and also played the piano.

Peter could see light but couldn't read written material. He also was very adept at both Grades 1 and 2 Braille. Peter had a friendly relationship with Sue, Barb and me, but he never struck me as being overly interested in a close relationship.

I only remember one eighth grade teacher clearly. That was my math teacher, one Mr. Calvin Marx. Behind his back, we referred to him as "Karl." Well, at least we were paying a little bit of attention in history! His daily ritual was to walk in the door, slamming it, of course, walk up to his desk, and drop a load of books on the table so that he got our attention, and deliver the message to "SHUT UP!" It rarely failed to get our attention.

On the first day of class, he would call to our attention the eight dented lockers outside the door of his classroom. He would also point out that the dents were approximately head-high! The kids rarely had trouble interpreting his warnings.

But despite his direct and indirect warnings about behavior, there always seemed to be someone who was determined to test the water. Pat was the kid in my math class. Pat was a kid who, like Mike back at Emerson Elementary, always needed to have a daily dose of attention from at least one teacher. And one who always seemed to be willing to give it to him was Mr. Marx. Pat never got mean or seriously misbehaved, but I was always curious why he seemed to have to push Mr. Marx, almost on a daily basis, until Mr. Marx would motion to Pat via the forefinger of his right hand, to come with him. Pat would get out of his seat, always with a smile on his face, and march out the door with Mr. Marx following. The door would close and, within a few seconds, we would hear a crash coming from right outside the door. This would be followed by five or six more. Then the door would open, Pat would walk in, still with a smile on his face, and return to his seat. Again, I always found myself trying to understand "Why?"

There were teachers whose classes just about every kid eagerly anticipated going to everyday. One of those was the science class taught by Mr. Wolff. Mr. Wolff was a nice guy, a great teacher and had a heck of a sense of humor.

At the end of the school year when everyone was getting a little nervous about finals, Mr. Wolff stood in front of the class one afternoon, told us to go home and NOT study for the final. When someone asked him why he didn't want us to study, he said, "Because the more you study, the more you learn; the more you learn, the more you know; the more you know, the more you forget; the more you forget, the less you know, so why study?" I'm not sure how many of us took him seriously. I know I didn't! I don't remember how I did on that exam, but I didn't like science anyway. But I did like Mr. Wolff, and I never saw him again after the last day of school.

One spring day, Mr. Wolff was lecturing, and one of the large windows was opened for air. Kids were walking around outside and getting pretty loud. Finally, Mr. Wolff went to the window, looked out and yelled, "Hey, you guys, what do you think you're doing?"

We all got up and ran to the window. One of the kids yelled back, "We just thought we'd move your car!" They had literally picked the Volkswagen Beetle up from its parking spot, carried it to a spot right beside the flag pole, and put it down on the lawn. Mr. Wolff closed the window and resumed his lecture.

By the end of the year at Ordean, the general consensus was that the following year, my freshman year in high school, would be a good time to try a regular school program. Finally! This was going to be my chance to take normal classes in a normal school and be with my friends. It was a very long summer.

By September, I was more than ready for school, anticipating renewing old friendships with friends from Emerson Elementary. My plan, of course, was to walk to and from school with Marty.

But, as they say in the movies, "All is not as good as it seems or as bad as it feels." I don't remember having even one class with Marty, or with anyone else I knew at Emerson during the entire year. So much for wasting much time thinking about what might be!

What I do remember is the strangest school year in this normal school that I'd ever had. Washington Jr. High School was an inner city school, and Central High School was located right across the avenue. Both schools came with more than their share of tough kids. They also had their share of unusual teachers.

On the first day, I was wandering around trying to locate my classrooms. I rounded a corner, looked up, and there was Mrs. Dorothy Johnson, my teacher from Kate Barnes and West Jr. High School. After making with some small talk, I asked her if she had been aware of how much I'd hated her and her diagramming sentences. With a smile on her face, she said she was aware of it, and then she asked me if I was having any trouble with English grammar. When I answered in the negative, she responded with, "I rest my case." Believe me, I've thanked that woman many times since then for the things she taught me.

After the ninth grade, an assessment of the year concluded that it had been the wackiest school year with the wackiest teachers that I'd ever had. For example, one older and alcoholic female teacher drowned in her bathtub one morning before school. Another female teacher kept her booze in a Windex bottle in her classroom locker. There were some good teachers at Washington Jr. High though, and I was lucky enough to get several of them.

The most unusual teacher I had during my ninth grade year was my Mechanical Drawing teacher. Walking into Mr. Wilman's class was like visiting a zoo. At any time during any class, a person could walk into the room and find three or four kids doing chin-ups from the pipes on the ceiling with three or four more kids standing below them with lengths of 2 X 4, waiting to give the kids doing the chin-ups a whack when they could no longer do anything but hang from the pipe. One might also find Mr. Wilman chasing a kid from tabletop to tabletop. Do you know how hard that is to do on a mechanical drawing table?

Before I go any further, I have to make it clear that Mechanical Drawing was far from my favorite class, and Mr. Wilman was not my favorite teacher. But I was always amazed to see the eagerness, almost joy, on the faces of some kids when they would enter that room!

The Mechanical Drawing classroom was on the basement floor of the school, a few feet from a one-way street. My class had a student by the name of Larry (no, not me.) Larry was a big kid, far from the brightest bulb on the tree, and his desk was right next to the window that looked onto the street. One spring day, Mr. Wilman had the windows open, and Larry was yelling at the girls walking out on the sidewalk. Mr. Wilman had told Larry to get his head back inside and get to work, but Larry ignored him and kept on talking to the girls on the sidewalk. Mr. Wilman started walking toward him, unnoticed only by Larry. When he got behind Larry, he grabbed him by the neck of his shirt and the seat of his pants, and literally threw him out the window onto the lawn.

On another occasion, the kid who sat behind me incurred Mr. Wilman's wrath. I remember the kid's being very tall. Mr. Wilman grabbed his paddle—actually, a breadboard—and started his familiar walk of retribution toward his victim's desk. Now, Mr. Wilman was about 5' 7" and the kid was something like 6' 2" to 6' 4" tall. He looked up at the kid and told him to bend over. Much to the amazement of the rest of the class, the kid's response was, "Not until I know that you know what it feels like to be hit with that thing!" Mr. Wilman looked at him for a moment, and then handed him the paddle!

When the rest of us saw that, we bolted from our seats and took cover behind our desks. In a few seconds, we heard, "crack." When I dared peek from behind my desk, a saw a very red-faced Mr. Wilman, complete with tears in his eyes, looking up at the boy, spitting in his hands and saying, "Now, it's my turn!" The kid handed Mr. Wilman the paddle and then bent over. Again, we all took cover behind our desks. Within a few seconds, we heard another "whack," and I saw a piece of the paddle fly past my desk. The kid's face was red, but there were no tears, and he said nothing. Mr. Wilman just turned and walked toward the front of the class and resumed his teaching.

Mr. Wilman's favorite target in my class was Mick. Mick was short and thin, and the only homework he ever did was figuring how he was going to irritate Mr. Wilman the next day. One morning while we were lined up and ready to leave the Mechanical Drawing room, Mick was messing around, and when the bell rang, Mr. Wilman picked Mick up by his hair and carried him up three flights of steps before he ever touched the ground.

Do you remember Mike at Emerson Elementary and Pat at Ordean Jr. High? Well, Mike and Pat and Larry and Mick all fascinated me. I think it was obvious, even back then, that these kids craved the attention, and I sometimes wonder how they're getting that attention today. I do know what happened to one of those kids, and I'll get into that a little later. And it's important to remember that Mr. Marx at Ordean, and Mr. Wilman at Washington Jr. High were a couple of the best-liked teachers by the students at their respective schools! Why? At any rate, I was glad when the school year was over. Washington Jr. High School had not been what I had thought it would be.

The New Neighborhood

In January of my sophomore year, my family decided to move out of the old neighborhood. I have no recollection of why my parents decided to sell the house and move, but they got no argument from me. The only negative was that Marty wouldn't be living a block away anymore. We would see each other in school every day, but as long as his name began with "O" and mine with "S," we probably wouldn't be close enough alphabetically to be in classes together. That would have to wait for the university.

The first new person I remember meeting at Central High School was Doug. Doug sat directly in front of me in Homeroom. Somehow he found out that I had moved to the Duluth Heights community of Duluth, all of a city block or so from his house. I remember his telling me how much fun we were going to have with other kids in the neighborhood. Neither one of us had any idea just how true that statement was going to turn out to be.

For me, the last three years of high school pretty much centered on school, my friends, and my new neighborhood. But it was also the decade of the sixties. Things, and attitudes, were changing.

I'm going to mention three families that became very, very close to me over the next several years. These were like three more sets of parents and three more sets of brothers and sisters. I don't remember how I met any of them initially, but I guess that really doesn't matter. What is important is that I grew to love these people like they were family.

First was Doug's family. There was Vi and Phil, his parents, and Mark, his younger brother. One thing I loved about this family, as well as the others, was that the kids' friends were always welcome, and they always had the coffee on. Thank goodness, Vi, and especially Phil, Doug and Mark, loved to just sit around and talk, and at times, argue.

When Doug was in his late teens, he developed schizophrenia. Vi was empathetic, but I think Phil had a hard time dealing with it. Both before and after the diagnosis, my sense of things was that the relationship between Doug and his dad was strained, and, I suspect, remained so until Phil's death. This left Vi to be the mediator up to the time of Phil's death. Mark was a good kid and a good student, and he was the apple of his father's eye. In some ways, it must have been hard to be a member of this family, but I liked them all very, very much.

And then, there was Helmer and Joan and their two kids, Cheryl and Randy. If Doug's family enjoyed having their kids' friends around, well, Joan and Helmer's house was a 24/7 convention hall. Joan was a clerk at a department store and she was, as they say, "full of the devil." One day when I was in the store, shopping for something for my mother, an older clerk came up to me and asked if she could be of some help. After attempting to help with no success, she looked at me and said, "Well then, shove it up your ass and nail a board over it!" At the same moment, Joan appeared from behind a rack of clothes almost breathless from laughter.

One night, I was at the house watching Joan get ready to go to school conferences. She was very upset, and I asked her why. She said it was all Cheryl's and my fault! By way of explanation, Cheryl and I both had a teacher whose name rhymed with "feathercrotch." Over the course of the year, the name was altered to include "leathercrotch," as well as several other not-too-complimentary names. Joannie's big problem was that she was sure she was going to make a mistake and call her by one of these names. We sent her out the door with a "Don't worry about it." A few hours later, the door burst open, and there was Joannie, spewing all manner of cuss words. She had referred to the teacher as Miss Feathercrotch! If Joan was embarrassed, Cheryl and I didn't particularly love the idea of going to school the next day.

Helmer was much more involved with the community than with his household. This doesn't mean that he didn't love his family, because he did. I think he found his sense of self-respect in the work he did in the community. I think Joan spent their entire marriage waiting for Helmer to come home and do some household chores, like clean up the basement and paint the garage.

One Saturday morning, Doug and I and two other neighborhood kids decided that we'd been listening to Joannie complain about the garage's needing a painting long enough, so we offered to paint it for her. She gave us the money to buy the paint, and we spent all weekend painting that garage. When Helmer got home, he quickly got into his painting clothes and supervised the four of us. Yeah, that was Helmer!

Randy became a second younger brother to me. He always seemed to live in his sister's shadow, but he was his father's pride and joy. He graduated a few years after Cheryl and me and then went on to a local vocational school. After graduation, he accepted a job in the State of Massachusetts. This was around 1972, and I was working in Southern Minnesota.

One day I received a call from the family telling me that Randy had been killed in a hit and run accident in Massachusetts. Of course, I went home for the funeral. The family wanted me to go to the services with them, so I went to the house a few hours before.

When I got to the house, Cheryl pulled me aside and asked me if I would go to the church with her to see the body before anyone else got there. She said she wanted to show me something. I agreed, so we got in my car and went to the church.

The coffin containing Randy's body was in the front of the church. Somehow it didn't seem right that he should be there alone. As we approached the coffin, Cheryl warned me that what she wanted to show me might upset me. She swept Randy's hair away from his right ear to show me that the ear was missing. She also asked me to touch his right eyelid. I'm sure I must have looked at her like I thought she was going crazy, but I did as she asked. His left eye was missing. As we stood there, I remembered Helmer and Joan telling me that when the authorities found Randy, he was still sitting on the motorcycle, which was propped against a tree. His helmet was still strapped to his head, and there was no damage to the helmet. He was still gripping the handlebars.

The family had been told that Randy had been at a party and was on his way home when the accident took place. Supposedly a car with Iowa license plates hit him. Cheryl and I believed then, and I still believe, that a more reasonable explanation is that someone at that party murdered him. Of course, we never shared our feelings with Helmer and Joan. Both are dead now, so I guess my feelings are safe.

Two doors down from Joan and Helmer's house was the home of another friend, Wayne, and his family. Wayne's parents were Daniel and Burnell, and there were six kids in the family. Wayne was the oldest, followed by Greg, Tim, Colleen, Bryan and Janell. If the previous two family homes were my hangouts, Dan and Bernie should have tried claiming me as another deduction on their taxes.

I've always said that the probable reason I never became a delinquent was because I didn't like the taste of beer. I think another reason was because my life up to that point had all but precluded taking any obvious risks. For example, there was no way I was ever going to get in a car if I knew someone in the car was in possession of liquor. Noble, wasn't I? But that attitude put a little damper on my adolescence. I never wanted to become a delinquent, but some of my friends seemed to me to be more normal than I was.

As Wayne told me some years ago, "You always offered me a safer alternative to my more exciting friends." What did he mean? He meant that we found sitting around his kitchen table, just talking, playing smear, and drinking coffee by the pot was also a lot of fun and a whole lot safer. Besides, doing those things gave me a chance to get to know the family a whole lot better.

Getting to know someone well is always a mixed bag because you've got to take the bad with the good. Sometimes the bad isn't easy to deal with, especially when you're barely out of your teens.

I don't think life was ever easy for this family. Dan worked hard to support his family, and it got hard for me to see him come home from work so tired, especially when there were issues involving the kids to deal with.

Around the early part of 1967, Daniel developed kidney problems. I think life got even harder for the family as Dan was in a lot of pain. Eventually he wound up in the University of Minnesota Hospital in Minneapolis, and it was decided that the kidneys should come out. I remember Bernie's telling me that the doctors had said that Dan's kidneys were the size of two good sized walnuts. For some reason, the kidneys were removed and transplants inserted in such a way that he was cut all the way around his thin frame.

Daniel also had to undergo dialysis. In the mid-60s, there were very few dialysis machines in the entire country. I seem to remember a doctor testifying before the Congress and asking for the price of just one jet fighter for the purpose of manufacturing more dialysis machines. It's important to keep in mind that at that time, there were committees that decided who, and who would not, have access to a dialysis machine. I assume Daniel got access because of the size of his family.

I don't remember how long Daniel was in the hospital, but it seemed like it was forever. And it seemed like he was always in pain.. Periodically, the doctors would let him come home for a weekend, always making sure that he had written instructions concerning foods to be strictly avoided. Specifically, the substance to be strictly avoided was potassium.

I guess it never dawned on me to leave the family alone when Daniel was home. One day as I drove into the driveway to say Hi to Daniel, some of the kids walked past me with looks on their faces that told me that they had just had some kind of altercation with their father. When I went into the house, Dan was sitting at the kitchen table alone and crying. He tried to smile, but he was in a lot of pain. Then he looked up at me and said, "If you weren't such a good friend, I'd ask you to take me out in the woods and shoot me."

Sometime after Dan had his kidneys removed, Wayne, Doug and I drove down to the University of Minnesota Hospital to see him. Bernie always told everybody how wonderful the hospital staff was when it came to Dan's care. Judging from what I'd seen, I was a lot more skeptical.

We entered the room one at a time. When I went in, Daniel was in the bathroom. In a minute or two, the bathroom door opened, and I found myself looking at a frail looking, shivering man who was wincing in pain with each step. It also was impossible not to notice that he was leaving a damp trail behind him as his dressing was unraveling and dragging on the floor behind him. I got up to help him get into bed. When I got him seated on the bed, I took a seat beside him and found myself smack dab on a soaking wet bed. Absolutely everything was wet; the mattress, the top sheet, the pillow, everything including the seat of my pants. I asked him how long it had been since the dressing had been changed. He said that both the bed and his dressing had been changed the previous day. Even if I left room for the possibility that he was confused, or lost his sense of time, both the dressing and the bed were far too wet to have had a recent change.

And then, one day, a nurse was prepping him for a dialysis session. She approached him with an injection. Dan asked her what it was, and she told Bernie and Dan that it was potassium. Daniel told her that there must have been some mistake, as he'd never been allowed to have anything with potassium in it before. She told him that it was doctor's orders, so he allowed her to give him the injection. A minute later, he looked up at Bernie, told her that he was dizzy, and died. In shock, the nurse dropped the syringe and it broke on Dan's transistor radio. (Yeah, and I don't know what a 'twitter' is either). It was New Year's Eve, 1967.

Some weeks after Dan's death, I walked into the house and found Bernie crying at the kitchen table. She had just gotten the hospital bill for Dan's care. As I recall, the bill came to $38,000. I remember thinking that that was a lot of money for the "great care" he had received. I told her I didn't think she should worry about a bill for $38,000. I would worry had it been $3,800. I also took the opportunity to ask her if she still had Dan's transistor radio. I suggested that she think about taking the radio to a lab of some sort and have it tested to see if it had any trace of potassium on it. I was thinking that she might have grounds for a lawsuit, but she insisted the hospital had given him excellent care.

In the spring, we buried Daniel on a little hill, under a tree, by a river, in a little town in Northwestern Wisconsin. Once and for all, the pain was over for him, but I'm sure the entire family felt his absence. It's always been my contention that it was probably Tim that missed his father most. I can only imagine how hard it must have been for Bernie to take complete charge of a family of six. She took a job as a clerk at a local department store, which had to be a mixed blessing. The kids continued to grow, of course, and became, ugh, teenagers!

But I'm a little ahead of myself. Daniel died on New Year's Eve, 1967. That would have made me about twenty years old and a sophomore at the university, just to keep things in perspective.

A few more things about my last few years of high school should be mentioned. One of those things would be the junior class play. To this day, I still wonder who the jackass was that convinced me to try out for a part in the first place. The play, by the way, was

"Harvey," a story about an invisible rabbit. Anyway, some damned fool convinced me to try out, and another damned fool agreed.

The play director was an odd-looking little man by the name of Dale. He wore a thin, gray crew cut, had little beady eyes, and ears that stuck out like the elephant in the cartoon. But his biggest problems were his ego and his mouth.

On the night of tryouts, I was praying that I would NOT get a part. After we each had a chance to read, Dale announced his decision for each part. Just as I was telling myself that God had heard my prayers, he announced that the part of Judge Omar P. Gaffney was going to...you guessed it...me. He also announced to the group that he gave the part to me because I looked and behaved like a judge, whatever that meant.

We were all given a copy of the rehearsal schedule and went home to celebrate our victory in getting a part in the play or mourning the decision to try out in the first place. I was definitely one of the latter, but I set about the task of learning my part for the first rehearsal.

The first night found Dale to be very nervous and ornery. I remember thinking that if he was that cantankerous on the first night of rehearsals, what the hell was he going to be like on the first night of the play?

The part of the taxi driver was played by a big kid also by the name of Dale. Dale was a nice kid, but he struck me as neither an intellectual giant nor a thespian. He also wasn't real good at memorizing his lines.

One night, Mr. Dale the director got particularly frustrated with Cabbie Dale and got in his face. He got tired of the coach's nagging, so suddenly he reached out and grabbed him by the shirt, picked him up off the floor, kicking and screaming, and carried him behind the curtains of the stage. We all looked at each other in amazement, and then found the courage to go behind the curtains, only to find Coach Dale hanging by his belt on a coat hook and laughing his head off.

A part of being in the play that I rather enjoyed was getting in the make-up chair. We were introduced to the make-up chair on the first night of rehearsal. He wanted us to get comfortable with the make-up and thought it would help if we looked the part during rehearsals. As he was slapping my face with the powder puff, he said he wanted me to leave the gray hair coloring in through the last day of the play. It made washing my hair just a little difficult, but I managed to reach a compromise between my mother and the coach. It was fun getting on the city bus every morning and listening to the old ladies making comments about "that poor young man with the gray hair."

I've already indicated that Coach Dale wasn't exactly of a personality type that I appreciated in a teacher. Nothing I ever saw or heard during the entire period of the rehearsals, and the play itself changed my mind about that. And then one night I walked into a darkened make-up room, flicked on the light and saw him making love to one of my female classmates. This wasn't the first time I'd witnessed a teacher's behavior straying over the line, but this was the first time I ever saw a teacher taking advantage of a student. I was glad when the play was over and, no, I didn't try out for the senior class play.

Another thing that sticks out in my mind about my high school years is November 22, 1963, the day President John F. Kennedy was assassinated, in Dallas, Texas. They say that everyone remembers where they were when they heard the news of the assassination. Well, I'm no different. I was in my afternoon Study Hall, which was in the school auditorium. Suddenly I became aware of the fact that I was hearing a radio. Then it came to me that I was listening to a radio that was blaring through the public address system. Walter Cronkite had just announced that, "The President is dead." What was strange about this way of finding out about the assassination was the fact that no one made any kind of announcement about it. They just turned on a radio and turned on the PA system. Naturally, everyone just kind of stopped doing whatever he or she was doing and just started to listen to the comforting words of Walter Cronkite. I can only imagine that the reason no announcement had been made was that the Principal, George Beck, was probably as shocked as we were.

After Study Hall, I proceeded to Miss Nethercott's English class. Fifteen hundred students were moving through the hallways of the school in silence, like monks in a monastery. When I walked into the room, Miss Nethercott was sitting at her desk with her head in her hands.

Suddenly, one of the more "brilliant" students in the class burst in the room and yelled, "Bang, bang!" With that, Miss Nethercott bolted from her seat and attacked the kid, grabbing him by the shirt and

43

the hair and throwing him out of the room. We sat in silence for the rest of the hour and went home. It was going to be a long weekend.

I don't remember any conversation with Mom and Dad about the assassination. What I do remember is a very long, surreal weekend involving little else other than watching history unfold on television, watching a little boy saluting his father's coffin, and a flag-draped coffin being pulled down Pennsylvania Avenue followed by a white, riderless horse with boots turned backward in the stirrups.

I also remember collecting things like the local paper dated November 22, 1963, photos and magazines featuring the assassination. I think I knew, even then, that I was probably clinically depressed. Anyway, they say that time heals and, with the passage of time, the impact of the assassination lost its edge, and things returned to normal.

New Church, New Friend

When my family moved to the Duluth Heights neighborhood of Duluth, we actually quit going to St. Peter's Catholic Church and started attending the neighborhood church, St. Joseph's Catholic Church. It almost felt like the divorce from the old neighborhood was complete. Not long after we joined our new church, we had a change of priests – from Father Faith (yeah, would you believe it?) to Father CROSSman (no, I'm not kidding!)

I don't really remember how I met Fr. Crossman, but he would prove to be a lifelong friend and the person who "set me up" with my initial opportunity to work with kids. I suppose my first taste of working with youngsters was teaching Sunday school, only Sunday school in those days was held on Wednesday evenings, at least at St. Joseph's. My first experience was with high school seniors, and that wasn't too bad except for the fact that I wasn't much older than the students.

For the next few years, I taught junior high school-age kids, and this was interesting because just about every Wednesday night, I wound up throwing someone up against a wall and removing some sort of weapon from someone before letting them sit down. Eventually some of those kids and I wound up in a professional relationship that had nothing to do with church.

My Feelings About School

I want to mention a few more things that happened during my high school years that might be of interest. I've said before that I never liked school, and it's true, I didn't. Even though I hated school, I did pretty well. Most people that knew me at the time would probably have told you that it came easy for me, but it didn't, although I don't think I knew it at the time. I was one of eight juniors to be invited to join the National Honor Society out of a class of five hundred eight. I seriously considered rejecting the invitation, as I was very sure that high school had not adequately prepared me for work on the college level. And as I was soon to find out, I was right.

Know Your Government Tour

One thing I had always enjoyed learning about was history and current events. During the summer of 1964, my folks decided to let me participate in the YMCA's Know Your Government Tour of Washington, DC, New York and other cities, government institutions, national monuments and historical sites on the East Coast.

There might have been thirty kids who made the trip. To the best of my memory, we had exactly three chaperones: Mr. and Mrs. Orlich, a pair of teachers, and Norbert Voigt, the tour bus owner and driver.

Before we left on this trip, I talked to a few people who had traveled to the East Coast. One thing that was said stuck out in my mind. I was told to expect that from Indiana east, I would find that white people seemed to have an attitude, and minorities seemed to be very friendly. Now, keep in mind that this was 1964, civil rights was the hottest issue in town, and the Civil Rights Act was being debated in the United States Congress.

I'm not sure we were out of Duluth before we lost our air conditioning. We didn't miss it much until we hit Indiana, and then it turned very hot. As if to emphasize the temperature, Norbert got lost and wound up making an illegal U-turn, and of course, getting caught by the Indiana State Patrol. He was driven into Indianapolis to appear before a judge and pay a fine. Then the trooper drove him back to the bus where thirty-two very warm and wet people were waiting for him to get the bus back on the highway.

One of the first stops was Philadelphia, Pennsylvania. We stopped at Independence Hall to see the Liberty Bell. I am still a history buff, but for those poor souls that are not, actually seeing the Liberty Bell might not mean much. For me, it was like having coffee in the Oval Office. Unfortunately, I don't think today's young people have an adequate appreciation and knowledge of American history that they should. Just my opinion, of course.

Finally, we arrived in Washington, DC, where we spent a couple of days at the Diplomat Motel. The weather was absolutely beautiful, as was the city. We were able to cool off and relax beside the motel's swimming pool. Then we took a tour of the city's historical sites and monuments. One of the things that stuck out in my mind was that all of the police officers I saw on the streets were heavily armed, carried riot sticks, and were leashed to police dogs. Undoubtedly that was the reason we were warned not to stray off by ourselves.

The next morning, we were scheduled to have breakfast in the House of Representatives cafeteria with Congressman John Blatnik of Minnesota. It was very warm—108 degrees, as I recall. Naturally by the time we got to the House cafeteria, I had sweat through my suit, and there was no way I was going to have breakfast with a Congressman looking like a drowned rat and smelling like limburger cheese.

I caught a white waitress and asked her where I could find a washroom. She gave me this "get lost' look and told me she didn't have time. I was pressed for time, so I looked around for another waitress. The first one I saw was a very large African American lady who was balancing serving trays in both hands.

I asked her for the location of the washroom. She told me to "Go out the door, turn left, and go up the stairs to the second floor. At the top of the steps, turn left again and go to the end of the hall and turn right. The washroom is on your left." Then she asked if I understood. I wasn't sure but I told her I did. I thanked her and started for the door. I had only taken a few steps when I heard her tell me to wait a minute. I turned in time to see her give her trays to another waitress and start to walk toward me. When she got to me, she said, "Follow me." I started to protest, not wanting her to get into any trouble with her boss. She smiled but ignored me and led me out the door and up the steps, down the hall and then waited outside the washroom door.

When we got back to the cafeteria, I thanked her, offered her a tip that she refused but thanked me for, and she walked away. I think I was so taken by this woman's actions that I don't even remember the breakfast with Congressman Blatnik.

Although this event was one I'd never forget, another event was to follow that afternoon, which would make us youngsters feel like we were a small part of something very big. We found ourselves in the United States Senate gallery listening to the 1964 Civil Rights debates. I don't think anyone knew just how historic an event this was going to be, but it turned out to be one of the most historic and far-reaching pieces of legislation every passed in the entire history of the United States.

On this particular occasion, the Republicans were filibustering. As I was to learn, during a filibuster, only one member of the opposite party had to be present. On this afternoon, Sen. Eugene McCarthy (D), Minnesota, was supposed to represent the Democrats, but when President Pro Temp Ted Kennedy called for him, he wasn't there. Kennedy ordered the Sergeant At Arms to locate him and bring him to the Senate Chamber. The next day, after arriving in New York City, the day's edition of the New York Times indicated that Sen. McCarthy had been found—in Hawaii.

Before we left Washington, DC, we walked the street surrounding the White House, although we didn't tour it. As we stood by the gates looking into the windows for any sign of the President, President Johnson appeared in a window and waved at us. For a bunch of sixteen and seventeen year olds, I'm sure it crossed our minds that we were waving to the most powerful person on earth. It was quite a feeling!

And then the *coup d' gras* – Arlington National Cemetery. Arlington National Cemetery was probably the main reason that I wanted to take this trip. Here I was, walking up a hill past President Kennedy's grave and that of his infant son, Patrick Bovier, and the Eternal Flame. I remember thinking about just how much American history was buried in that little plot of ground.

We left Washington, DC and headed for The Big Apple. This was supposed to be one of the high points of the trip, as New York City was hosting the 1964 World's Fair. Actually, I could have cared less about the World's Fair as the weather was still scorching hot, something in excess of 100 degrees, and very humid. I was about to find out that New York City had much more interesting things going on than the World's Fair.

For some reason, we went from the Diplomat Motel in Washington, DC, to the White Horse Inn in New York City. This was like going from a Lexus to a Yugo. Remember them? When I got to my room, I found a sliding divider door caving into a crack in the floor in the middle of the room.

When we arrived, we were all very tired and very hot. I crashed on the bed, opened the window, and then threw the drape over my head so I could catch every whisper of air that I could find. It didn't take long for me to fall asleep. When I woke up, I was watching a young couple in the building next to me, how should I say it, "he'n and a she'n" on a bed that was almost close enough for me to touch. I was afraid to move, so I was just forced to watch to climax, so to speak!

They tell me that no trip to New York City would have been complete without taking in a little culture. One night we took in a Broadway play, "How To Get Rich Without Really Trying." I remember absolutely nothing about the play, but the walk home sure was interesting.

As I was walking back down Broadway, marveling at the people, buildings and lights, I noticed a crowd gathering in front of a very posh-looking hotel just across the street. There was a white stretch limo parked in front of the hotel. As God built me close to the ground, I couldn't see who was getting out of the limo, so I did what any young Midwesterner would do. I straddled a fire hydrant. From that vantage point, I could see that it was Liz Taylor who was getting out of the limo. Well, I've never been a big fan of Liz Taylor's, so I decided to lend a little balance to the scene by yelling, "Boo, Liz" from atop my perch. As I did that, one of New York's Finest, on horseback, came up to me, the horse reared up, and I fell off my hydrant. I didn't know New Yorkers felt so strongly about Liz Taylor!

I mentioned that I was very interested in politics and world affairs, a condition that hasn't been reduced in intensity over the years. That's why some of us decided to go to the United Nations instead of the Fair. I was able to sit in on a General Assembly session, the subject of which I can't remember. What I do remember was having a lot of fun playing with the earphones that allowed you to dial up any one of six or seven languages for a translation of the Council proceedings.

Interesting as all of this was, leaving New York City turned out to be even more interesting and exciting. As I was walking across the heliport, I heard some explosions. People began looking around and then started running in every direction. When I picked up a copy of the New York Times the following day, I found out that the explosions were from shells being fired from the harbor by Cuban refugees who were trying to make a point with the Security Council. They wanted the Security Council to do something about a guy named Fidel Castro. Obviously, it didn't work.

Two more things happened before we left New York City. First, a man about three floors above me was pushed out of a window of my hotel the night before we left New York. It didn't even rate mention in print that was big enough to read, to say nothing of making the front page. Welcome to the Big Apple!

The other thing involved patrons of the hotel itself. Over the five or six days we were in New York, I heard a lot of loud conversations taking place in the room next to mine, and all of them were in Spanish. They were playing speeches of Fidel Castro. During the course of the speeches, the occupants seemed to get very excited and loud.

One morning, I was sitting in the lobby of the hotel, waiting for a taxi. The lobby was filled with a number of Spanish-speaking men who looked quite nervous, as they kept looking out on the street. Suddenly, a stretch limo pulled, and a beautiful blonde lady got out, hurried into the lobby and yelled something in Spanish. With that, the lobby quickly emptied. They all got into the limo and sped away. .I always wondered where they went and who they were.

The trip finally ended and we arrived home very tired, but excited about what we had seen, and maybe even a little honored at having visited places like the Smithsonian Institution, the United Nations, United States Senate and House of Representatives, most of the national monuments, in Washington, DC, Gettysburg, Arlington National Cemetery, the US Supreme Court, the US Capital, Radio City Music Hall, Broadway, Niagara Falls and, oh, yeah, the World's Fair! If we didn't learn anything else, I think we learned that there are some beautiful and interesting places to visit in America, and if one can't actually visit them, I think they should learn about them.

But now, it was time to rest up and get ready for my senior year of high school. Actually, I don't remember much about my senior year. I do remember doing a lot of talking and planning with Marty about the university. Marty seemed to be excited, but I was scared. I knew that high school had not prepared me for the university, and I was very concerned about it.

The only thing I really remember about that year was my English teacher, Jewel P., and in my opinion, she was a jewel. She was the perfect picture of self-doubt. I thought she was a great teacher, but she didn't. She tried to quit teaching on a couple of occasions, but she was always driven back by what I believe was a little divine intervention.

She had decided that what she really wanted to do was to become a professional Girl Scout leader. Sometime after entering her new career, she took a group of girls to a basketball game. During the game, she took a fall in the bleachers and broke an arm. Apparently she developed some kind of complication that wouldn't allow her to continue, so she returned to teaching.

Sometime later, she quit teaching again and returned to her Girl Scout career. She took another group of girls on a winter camping trip, but somehow, she froze one side of her face. As a result, she went back to teaching.

She told us all of this on our last day of school. She asked if we had any opinions we'd like to share about what she'd said. I asked her why she thought she was such a bad teacher, and I suggested that she hadn't been getting the message. She did end her teaching career.

During my senior year, I took the ACT Test, the test that was supposed to give you an indication as to what direction you might want to pursue in an institution of higher learning. It supposedly measured one's abilities in such subjects as math, English, history, and chemistry.

One day I received an excited message from my counselor, who asked me to come to the office. When I got to the office, he told me that he had the results of my ACT Test. When he handed me the graph, he asked me to notice that I had one particularly high score. I saw the peak immediately and then looked across the page to find out what subject was involved. I was shocked to see that the subject involved was chemistry.

The counselor was excited about the high score in chemistry, but I was disappointed, and it showed. He asked me why I wasn't pleased with the score. I told him that I had spent an entire school career trying to avoid the natural sciences, and that if he checked my transcript, he'd find I'd never taken a chemistry class. It didn't seem to make any difference to him. Apparently, the score was going to produce some interest in my spending twenty or thirty years developing recipes for jams and jellies for Betty Crocker.

Somewhat miffed at my indifference and lack of enthusiasm, he asked me what I was interested in going into. I told him that I was interested in some sort of social work or counseling. He suggested that I might want to give some thought to school counseling on some level. I told him I didn't think I'd be interested because I couldn't see myself helping some student decide whether to accept a scholarship to Princeton or Harvard while another student was walking past my office having decided to quit school altogether.

Graduation night finally came, and I was forced to go through the graduation ceremony, along with five hundred seven other reluctant (I believe) classmates. It was a warm night, and that made me physically uncomfortable, having to dress in a suit and cap and gown. But the ceremony eventually ended with our getting our proof that we had completed the first twelve years of our education. Unfortunately, I had another four years to look forward to.

The University Years

I mentioned before that, for all of the time between the fifth and twelfth grades, I'd hoped for the opportunity to be in classes with my friends, and especially, Marty. Well, that never happened in all of that time, but the years at the university were a different story. Whether or not two people could take a class together depended entirely on a sufficient number of openings in the class. In high school, it had to do with which of the twenty-six letters of the alphabet your last name began with. "O" and "S" always seemed to be too far apart for Marty and me to be able to take classes together in high school.

At the university, there were sixty General Education credits that were supposed to be completed by the end of your sophomore year, and because of this, many of the classes were huge in size. They were always offered in auditorium-size classrooms. So, because freshmen

51

Larry Bauer-Scandin

concentrated on those General Education credits, Marty and I found ourselves in the same classes at times.

The first thing the freshmen learned about being freshmen is that they were expected to where beanies that identified them as freshmen. There was no way in hell Marty and I were going to wear beanies!

The next thing we learned was that we were supposed to make appointments with our assigned advisors. As my initial plan was to major in History, I was assigned an advisor in the History Department, one Dr. Maude Lindquist. As a freshman, I was a whole lot nervous about my appointment with her, but it would remain in my memory for another reason.

When I knocked on her office door, the first thing that I could tell, by her voice, was that she was old. Old then, a lot older now. She had her back to me when I walked in. When she turned to face me, she had a surprised look on her face. She looked at me and said, "Scandin—I had your father in my class, mmmm, thirty-four years ago!" My first thought was, "Let me out of here so I can drop my History major!" There was no way I was going to spend the next four years dealing with one of my Dad's old high school teachers.

Well, as it turned out, I not only never took a class from Dr. Lindquist, I also never laid eyes on her again. She taught classes in Minnesota history only, and at that time, I saw such a course as being as interesting as watching my toenails grow.

As I had anticipated, I did not find my first year at the university to be easy. Thanks mainly to Marty, we developed a sort of ritual when it came to studying. We would stay at school well into the evening and study in one of the study rooms available to students. When the rooms closed at 10:00 p.m., we would pile in my car and drive down the road to the old Shore Drive Drive-In Restaurant where we would order a few Momma Burgers and a couple of Swamp Waters and two waitresses with nothing on them. At times, you could spot other cars sporting a condom with a dab of shave cream in it (not my car, of course) and tied to the antenna. But mainly, we'd just sit and talk about school, our futures, and the war going on in Viet Nam. Then I would drive him home. This ritual in part kept me somewhat interested in school. Eventually, our first year at the university came to a thankful end, and it was time to figure out what I wanted to do with the summer.

At some point in a person's life, one comes to the realization that he should take responsibility for things such as the gas, upkeep and insurance on his car. Therefore, work was on my agenda for the summer of 1966. Dad offered to get me a job at the steel plant. That was as appealing as a case of the mumps. Instead, I decided to take a job as a camp counselor for the YMCA. The motivation for taking this job may have been a young lady I was fond of who was going to be working at a girls' camp across the lake from the YMCA camp. This was to be the next step on the developmental ladder toward a career.

Some people like being trained, and some don't. I don't like to train, but I like to learn. The camp counseling experience involved some training that I was to be grateful for during the course of the summer. The training we received was concerned with the safety of the campers and staff.

One of the things we had to learn was a procedure for searching the entire camp in the event of a missing camper. Thank God, we got quite good at it. One of the critical places to keep safe was the beach, but I'll come back to this.

The Camp Staff – Another Experience

First, let me introduce some of the staff of Camp Miller. The Director of the Camp was Dick C. Dick was a great boss and I think he made all of us feel valued and supported. But there was a dark side to this man. More later.

And then there was the camp nurse, Holly Kost, who, of course, we called "Holocaust" It was just too inviting! Holly was a great nurse and had a great sense of humor. Her mannerisms reminded me a whole lot of Carol Burnett with blonde hair.

Kim was the counselor who supervised the cabin next to mine and also worked with eight and nine year olds. Kim was also the organist for Sunday morning chapel services.

The chapel services were presided over by a staff person who intended to attend the seminary and become a minister. His name was John. He was, by the way, the son of my ninth grade algebra teacher. But there was a dark side to him also. And last, there was the assistant chaplain...me! The only reason I can think of for winding up in this position was probably because I expressed an interest in it in the job application.

This was a great job. On top of all the educational experiences, there were the other benefits like the pay, about 11 cents per hour, and a 160-hour workweek. And then there was the knowledge that several of us would probably wind up with mononucleosis by the end of the summer. Then there were the kids who wouldn't go to sleep, who had nightmares, and of course, there were the bedwetters. But it was worth it. Experiencing the behaviors of kids ranging in age from eight to seventeen, with different backgrounds and parental situations and abilities, was quite an education, one that was almost worth paying for.

As I said, the summer was quite an education, and a lot of fun. For example, in the fun department, during the course of the summer, we developed a routine of sorts. When we got the kids to bed and asleep, we staff would get together for a few hours and take break from the kids. Usually this involved having a few snacks, and occasionally going swimming, or should I say, skinny-dipping.

One night, Holly and I were skinny-dipping, and we were caught by a couple of the kids in my cabin. Luckily, it was dark enough so the kids couldn't see us below the neck, and I was able to use my most intimidating voice to chase them back to the cabin.

One night, one of the staff members was complaining about the fact that someone was sneaking into his cabin and using up all of his Jade East cologne. We decided to set a trap to catch the thief. The staff member decided to teach the thief a lesson. He emptied the bottle of Jade East and relieved himself into the bottle. Then we all hid behind the cabin. In time, we heard footsteps. The mystery thief entered the cabin, took the Jade East bottle, splashed some in his hands and patted it on his face. As gross as it was, none of us felt for the thief. He walked out of the cabin toward the office. When he walked into the light, we discovered that our thief was the camp director! For obvious reasons, the owner of the Jade East chose not to confront the thief.

My girlfriend at the time, Kathy, worked at the girls' camp across the lake from us. We developed a routine for visiting each other at the other's camp. She was into horses, so she would ride a horse and sneak into my camp. I would meet her in the parking lot, she would secure the horse, and we would get into my car. In the reverse, I would swim across to her camp and meet her on the beach.

One night, she rode a horse into camp, and I met her in the parking lot as planned. For some reason, she decided to secure the horse in our barn, which was located on the edge of the parking lot. Then we jumped in my car. Just as we were discussing the contours of the local terrain, we heard a commotion coming from the barn. Suddenly the barn door blew open, and all the horses, including Kathy's, were running in every direction, and they weren't being real quiet about it either! Within a minute or two, thirty or forty flashlights were shining on us, including a very perturbed Camp Director.

Without going into detail, I was grounded for a few weeks, and Kathy was fired, until I appealed to her Camp Director. Both of our jobs were saved, but we decided not to run the risk of being fired from our very first jobs, so there was no more sneaking into each other's camp.

A lot of the camp experience emphasized fun. The more serious part of the experience was the nightly vesper service at the Chapel in the Woods, located directly behind my cabin, and the regular Sunday church service conducted by the Camp Chaplain. John liked to play the part, and he did a good job...until the Director notified me one day that I was the new Camp Chaplain. He had caught John with a Playboy magazine! Naughty! Naughty! I think it's interesting that I got the job in light of the incident with my girlfriend in the parking lot.

One day, all of the staff was gone on a staff picnic, and I was designated to stay in camp and supervise the kids. Nobody ever knew how hard I prayed that I would get through the day without any serious problems. But it wasn't to be. The trouble came from the teenage cabins. One of the kids ran up to me and reported a fistfight in one of the cabins.

When I got to the cabin, I found out that the problem was racial in nature. Two kids, one white and one African American, had gotten into it, and the fight was on. Both kids admitted to their part in the fight, and the white kid even admitted to having started the whole thing by making a racial remark.

I told both boys, who were stretched out on their bunks, to hit the deck and follow me. The African American kid had a burr up his butt, and believing I was going to have him terminated from the camp program or something, started throwing racial remarks at me.

I took both boys to the staff office, read the white kid the riot act, and grounded him to his cabin until further notice. After he left the office, I read the other boy the riot act. Not for defending himself from the other kid, but for wrongly anticipating my response to the whole thing. I remember asking him why he thought his comments to me were any less racial than the comments that led to the fight in the first place. I think the look on his face was the first time I actually realized the power of the spoken word. Something I said may have changed this kid forever. What a feeling! I think those two kids resolved their problems, but I don't remember seeing either of them again.

The cabins in camp that were closest to the lake formed a semicircle with the lakeshore serving as the straight edge of the semicircle. There were two cabins in this semicircle that were used to house ten to twelve-year-olds. The cabin closest to mine had an African American kid who was a sleepwalker, and talker! Most of the staff was aware that he was a sleepwalker because, at one time or another, he woke most of us up.

One night, some of the staff decided to congregate around the outside of the cabin in the hope that he would do his thing. In time, he woke up with a start, got to his knees and started to preach a real "Hellfire and brimstone" type of sermon. It was great, and he was good! I never heard Martin Luther King, Jr. do any better. The preaching got louder and more animated, and the louder and more animated he got, the more we laughed. I think we were all sorry when this kid went home. I wonder if he's still preaching?

On a sadder note, we had two brothers whose parents boarded them out to Camp Miller for the entire summer so they could travel. As I recall, dad was in the Armed Forces. They were a constant pain in the butt because they got bored with the repetitive nature of the program from one camp session to the next. These two kids would tell the other kids all about the events of the week and at least dampen the experience for new campers. As much trouble as these two were, we all felt sorry for them and wished their parents had been a little more tuned into the needs of their own kids. I wonder where they are today?

A part of the daily routine at Camp Miller was swimming. We operated on the buddy system. Each camper was assigned to a buddy, and for the time you were in the water, each swimmer was to keep an eye out for his buddy. Also, before the kids went into the water, they were to take a numbered tag and put it on their wrists so that staff knew who was in the water and, God forbid, who was missing.

The day came when I was thankful for the pre-season training that we had. One afternoon, we were calling all of the kids in from the water, and as they were putting their ID tags back on the rack, we discovered that we were short one tag. That meant someone was missing.

The alarm went out and the training kicked in. My job was to swim under the three-sided dock that enclosed the beach's swimming area. We all did our jobs as quickly as possible, but we came up with nothing, and no one. We found ourselves sitting on the beach waiting for reports from other areas of the camp, but the three minutes that the doctor warned us about in terms of brain damage caused by a lack of oxygen had run out, and we were now concerned about finding a body. As we sat there with our heads in our hands, undoubtedly trying to figure out how we were going to live with the fact that we lost a kid who had been entrusted to our care, one of the staff came running through camp yelling, "We found him! We found him!"

The kid had grabbed a swimming tag out of turn and unnoticed by staff, and then changed his mind about swimming, and instead, went on a horseback ride. Needless to say, we were all extremely relieved, and the young man involved found himself with very little to do for a while.

As the summer wore on, we all got tired, and some of us got sick, something we were also warned about during our pre-season training. Naturally, I was one of them.

One morning, I found myself being awakened by Holly, the nurse. She escorted me to the Nurse's Station and took my temp. It was on the whoops side of 102 degrees, so she grounded me to her office to rest. After sleeping for a while, I awakened feeling better, so I sneaked out the window of the Nurse's Station and went back to my cabin. Naturally, I just knew the camp couldn't do without me!

The next morning, I got up to lead morning exercises. I was so tired and weak that I found myself doing one-legged jumping jacks. I sent the kids off to breakfast, and I went back to bed. The next thing I knew, Holly was standing over me again, only this time with Dick. He wasn't looking too happy and announced that he was relieving me of my duties until I saw a doctor.

I made the arrangements to see my doctor, and he told me that I had an inflammation of the voice box. He told me I could go back to work "as tolerated." When I got back to camp, I discovered that I had been relieved of duty until further notice. I went to see Dick, and I wasn't very happy that he had relieved me of duty without having heard what the doctor had said. I walked into his office and started to climb all over him like ugly on an ape. I went on and on until I was out of breath. When I finally shut my trap, Dick looked at me and asked, "Are you through?" I said I was, and he said, "You're still relieved until further notice." I couldn't figure out what to say, so I rolled up my wagging tongue, turned around, and walked out of the office. I came to appreciate and admire the way he handled me in that situation. In the end, the CIT (Counselor-In-Training) who was assigned to my cabin got sick before the end of the day, and I returned to my duties.

I mentioned that each cabin went on an overnight camping trip as part of each session's activity schedule. For most of the summer, each cabin went camping on its own. This made the camper/counselor ratio about ten to one. But by the end of the summer, we were going on these overnights two cabins and two counselors at a time. In the event that one of the counselors got sick, we didn't want the kids to panic. The camp truck would also come and get us at the campsite rather than our having to walk the few miles back.

One of my best staff friends, Kim, and I took our twenty kids camping one night. I had been fighting with one of my kids, John, to keep him from calling his parents and going home because he was homesick. He was an unusual kid in the respect that it was uncommon to meet a lad, perhaps nine or ten years old, who was as other-oriented as this kid was. I wanted him to have a fun experience for that reason, if for nothing else.

The evening had been uneventful, involving the campfire, marshmallow roast and the Hateful Hannah stories. When we'd all had enough, we went to our tents and went to sleep.

Early in the morning, Kim and I were awakened by the sound of several of the kids yelling our names from outside the tent. Kim and I bolted from our sleeping bags and unzipped the door on the tent. The kids told us that my little homesick kid, John, had been throwing up all night long. I was more than a little irritated that they hadn't notified us earlier, but they said that John told them he didn't want to wake us up.

58

When we got to the tent, I found John lying in his own vomit. I pulled him out of his sleeping bag, cleaned him up and gave him some water. In a short time, he seemed to come around and was even interested in taking a little food. Luckily the truck showed up a little early, and when we got back to camp, I turned John over to Holly. This incident made me more determined than ever to find some way to keep this kid from going home early.

I checked my log to find out what activities John had been involved in since his arrival at camp. It appeared like he had taken part in just about everything, but I noticed he had not been on a horseback ride. For some reason, he had skipped his opportunities at the horses, so I came to the conclusion that the horses were going to be my last chance to turn John on to something so he would finish out the week. I spoke to the staff person in charge of the horses and asked him if he would schedule John for a ride with the next group.

John was still asking me if he could call his parents and have them come and get him. I told him I'd make a deal with him. I told him that, if he'd agree to one horseback ride, I would let him make the call when he got back. He agreed.

The next horse session was the following day after breakfast. John seemed well, ate his breakfast, but seemed unexcited about the horses. Breakfast came to an end, and the horseback ride was announced. Those who were signed up, including John, left the dining room, and I crossed my fingers.

The group rode back into camp a few hours later with John riding right up front with the staff. I think that sight was one of the highlights of my summer. The look on John's face told me that he might still want to make that call home, but it wasn't going to be to ask them to come and take him home. As a matter of fact, I began to have trouble with the Chief of Horses, as he began to want John along on just about every riding session.

When the camp session ended and John's parents showed up to get him, they gave me a gift of a blanket, and their thanks for taking such good care of their son. Over the next thirty-five-plus years, I would find that this kind of experience would be the real measure of my satisfaction with any job I ever had.

As I've already indicated, by the end of the summer, we were all very tired. Part of the deal we agreed to when the summer began was a final week of dealing with a local church youth group. As they had their own staff and we didn't have to leave the comforts of camp, we assumed the last week would be a piece of cake. Well, don't let the phrase "church youth group" fool you. These kids were straight from hell! They made me dream of sitting on their chests and sewing their lips shut with fishing line. The hostility got so open that both the YMCA supervisors and the church supervisors were concerned about open conflict between the two staffs.

Actually, the only outward act of aggression committed during the week was perpetrated by our staff. We collected all of the urinal soap we could find, put it in socks, and beat the socks on the walls, floors, trees (we kind of relieved ourselves, so to speak) and then sprinkled the pieces in their beds, clothing, pillows and any other of their possessions that we could get access to. Both supervisory staffs were very upset with us, but we were far beyond caring. The summer ended with no homicides and no camp staff additions to the Minnesota penal system.

So now it was time to go home, reflect on the camp experience, take stock of the new friendships made, and (yuck) get ready for school again.

When I took stock of the summer, I decided that the experience had been worth it. Dealing with the kids taught me a lot, and I made another good friend – Kim. Kim was kind of an unusual guy, certainly a free spirit, and how he could keep me gasping for air!

My friends and I were quite the card players when we were kids. One weekend, some friends and I, including Kim, were playing cards at his apartment. As we played, we noticed a number of cars going into and out of the garage of a church across the street. We also noticed that only women were getting out of the cars. I mentioned it to Kim, and he told us that the church was a stud house. I had a hard time believing this. After all, this was Duluth, Minnesota! Kim kept on challenging me to call the church and find out what time their services were. Finally, I got up enough courage to look up the number and call. A male answered and told me their services were "anytime." It was probably in the area of 1:00 a.m.

Kim also attended the university, so we got pretty close over the next four years. I probably attended more parties at his apartment than I had ever attended in all of my life. You just never knew what to expect from Kim, so being around him was always interesting and full of surprises.

I was the first person to show up at one of his parties. When I walked in, he was sitting at the kitchen table dissecting something. As I approached the table, it became clear that whatever he was cutting up was some sort of large fish, or something that formerly resembled a fish. When I took a closer look, I was shocked to find out that it was a baby porpoise. When I asked him where the heck he got a baby porpoise, he told me that he stole it from the aquarium at the university. I couldn't believe he could get by with doing such a thing, but it was far too late to save the porpoise.

Anyway, the guests began to arrive, and the partying and the drinking began. I didn't drink beer, so my imbibing was strictly limited to Coca Cola. In time, I needed to use the bathroom, and I became aware of the fact that I hadn't seen Kim in a few hours. I walked upstairs and located the bathroom. The door was open, so I walked in, did my thing, and as I turned to leave, there was Kim, lying naked in the bathtub with a 6-pack of beer sitting on a chair beside the tub. Use your imagination!

Kim started at the university as an Elementary Education major. Somewhere along the way, probably around our junior year, he got the bright idea that he wanted to be a mortician. He switched majors, got involved in the Pre-Mortuary Science program, and in due course, it was time for some hands-on experience.

He was assigned the graveyard shift (how appropriate) at a local mortuary. He was instructed on what to do if a fresh body was brought in during the night. And then he was alone with a building full of stiffs, the radio on loudly, and lots of prayers to ward off any new arrivals.

But what would a night in a mortuary be with a fresh body being delivered? So here he is, in a building full of bodies and the radio on and a fresh body lying on a table in front of him. Now to get the body ready for whatever!

As he was moving around, nervous and whistling, he must have touched the sheet-covered body at some sort of major reflex point because the body sat up, and the sheet dropped into its lap, Kim looked into the corpse's face, turned white (his description), and ran like hell, apparently leaving the body literally sitting there. If you haven't guessed yet, Kim dropped the Mortuary Science major and re-entered the Elementary Education program the following morning.

The Sophomore Year

My sophomore year didn't go a whole lot better than did my freshman year. I still saw myself as a History major, but I was finding good history grades were hard to come by. And then, a message.

In my day, many university classes gave a student two opportunities at generating a good final grade. One was a mid-quarter exam and the other, the final exam.

I was taking a history class that I enjoyed, even though I couldn't say the same about the professor. I put a total of forty-four hours into studying for the mid-quarter. For some reason, Marty and I decided to take seats in the front of the auditorium, in the second row, on the day we were to get the test and grades back. When the bell rang, the professor started to hand out the tests and grades.

When Marty passed my test to me, I had my eyes closed. I held it in front of my face for a few seconds and then opened them and saw an "A" in the upper right hand corner. I almost jumped out of my chair!

As I wallowed in the warm sunshine of an extremely huge success, my thoughts were interrupted by the instructor's beginning what I thought was his lecture. Instead, he started talking about the test. He mentioned how the test was graded and said that it appeared, based on the grades, that it was a very difficult exam. He said that after having given it a lot of thought, he had decided to throw out the test and, with it, all the grades. Practically before he got the last word out of his mouth, I kicked the chair directly in front of me hard enough to crack the back right up the middle.

For a while after that day, I walked around trying to understand why it seemed like the message I was getting was that I was not supposed to be a History major. That feeling didn't soothe the feeling I had about school in general.

One day, I found myself sitting alone in the Ven Den, a student lounge, sipping on my morning cup of Tab (Ish!!) and pondering what I was going to do. History didn't seem to be working, and nothing else I had taken in the way of classes had succeeded in turning my crank.

And I wasn't done with required General Education classes that I was pretty sure I wouldn't do well in, especially the math/science requirement.

As we were getting close to ending one quarter and beginning another, we were all considering what classes to register for during the next quarter. I had been carrying around a school Bulletin and Class Schedule that described various majors, requirements, etc. I picked up the Bulletin, closed my eyes, and opened the book. I opened it to the Psychology section. I began reading the description of the introductory course. It was taught by Robert J. Falk.

Psychology 101 involved learning about various psychological schools of thought developed by Freud, Horney, and others. Of course, I had heard of Freud, and I thought that studying about a nut like Freud might be interesting. So I decided that I was going to sign up for Psychology 101.

Throughout the university experience, Marty and I and a few other friends made sure that we had enough fun to sort of balance out the time we were spending studying. We played a lot of cards—smear, to be specific—and it was particularly fun because, in those days, playing cards on campus was a "no-no." We would play in the evenings, during the day, and in some cases, even during classes. But in almost all cases, it was after study periods.

These card games carried a risk with them, and in some cases, we just weren't very smart about where and/or when we played. For example, we were playing in the university radio station, KUMD, with a friend who was a disc jockey for the station. Someone had some alcohol, probably Bali Hai at $1/gallon or some other fine wine, and the party was getting loud. The language was also getting a little raw. After a few drinks, I needed to find the washroom, so the disc jockey gave me directions...directions into the girls' dorm. So I find myself walking down a hallway until I spot a girl coming out of a room, dressed only in a towel. I'm sure she was as surprised as I was, but she handled it well. She allowed me to leave without calling Ole, the campus cop.

On the scholastic front, things didn't improve much during my second year. I had taken Geology during my freshman year in order to satisfy five of the fifteen-credit General Education requirement in Science/Math. Given what I've said about my lack of interest in the natural sciences, passing the lecture part of this class was one of my larger scholastic achievements, even though I passed with a "C." But I want to mention the first day's lecture.

The professor walked into the packed lecture hall, approached the lectern, dropped a half dozen books on the table beside the lectern to get our attention, and said, "My name is Dr. Munson, and I'm going to flunk eighty-five percent of you." A lot of us, including Marty and me, looked around the auditorium, and if we didn't say it, we were surely thinking, "Sure you are." There had to have been four or five hundred students in that room.

Well, at the end of the quarter, Marty and I found ourselves standing in a line outside of Dr. Munson's office doortrying to get prepared to see our final grades. Marty was behind me. I looked at the grades and the percentage of students getting each grade, turned to Marty, and told him that, "Munson lied. He flunked eighty-seven percent of us!"

But the lecture part of the class was the easy part of the five-credit course when compared to the laboratory part. The 2-credit lab class was the part that really frustrated me. I had failed this course during my freshman year, and I took it again during my second year with the same result. My fault? I think so!

The class material was divided into three sections. The first concentrated on identifying minerals, the second on identifying rocks and the third on topographical maps. For me, this class was as interesting as watching paint dry.

I managed a little interest in the first section on minerals, a lot less on the second section, and no interest in the third. I managed to get myself to class for the section on minerals, and I even got there most of the time on most of the days we were discussing rocks, but I'll be darned if I could get there for the section on maps.

The end result was that I always got a good grade on the first section and failed the last two, resulting in a failing final grade. Finally I went to the professor and pleaded color blindness. He bought it!

Now, obviously, this was not the right way to handle any class, and it was a definite reflection of a lot of immaturity on my part. Even though this was surely the case, I found out years later, unfortunately, that color-blindness and my eyes in general were probably the reason for my lack of interest in education. Where this particular class was concerned, identifying a rock had to do with being able to identify mineral specks in a rock. I found it impossible, for example, to distinguish between black specks and dark blue specks, so I guessed, with the usual result.

Before I leave this "quarry," I have to mention the one fun experience I had in this class. My lab partner in this third time taken class was a young freshman kid. In front of each of us on the first day of class was a tray of minerals. The instructor began the class by verbally naming the minerals we were going to be studying. As he named each, I would take it out of my partner's tray and place it in front of him. Every time I did so, his eyes got bigger. At the end, he asked excitedly, "Are you a geology major?" I turned to him and said, trying not to laugh, "No, this is the third time I've taken this damned class!"

By sometime in my second or third year, I had had enough success in my psychology and sociology classes that I planned to declare them as my majors when the time came to do so. And after having dropped Dr. Lindquist as an advisor, I had been re-assigned to Robert J. Falk, in the Psychology Department. I was prepared for a slightly easier second half of my university career, but I decided to try something before I entered my junior year.

The Salesians of Don Bosco

I don't exactly remember how I was taken with an interest in entering the seminary. I know it had a lot to do with my admiration for Father Jim Crossman and the strong feeling that all of the events in my life were a part of some kind of divine plan for my life. I wasn't sure about my decision to try the seminary, and I don't think Dad was real excited about it, although he didn't directly oppose it. Although I don't ever remember his pushing me in the direction of teaching, I always seemed to know that that's what he wanted me to do with my life. And teaching history is what I intended to do, but that didn't seem like what the "Man upstairs" wanted me to do.

Probably because of the hospital experience and the YMCA camp experience, I was getting a pretty strong feeling that I wanted to work with kids. I'd also developed the idea that God had gotten me through life so far, and I kind of felt like I owed Him something. I

65

discovered that an Order of priests worked specifically and exclusively with young people on the streets, in correctional institutions, etc. So I applied to, and was accepted by, the Salesians of (Father) Don Bosco, an Order that had the reputation for being the second strictest Order in the Church, next to the Jesuits.

At that time, there were two Salesian Seminaries, one in San Francisco and the other in New Jersey. I was to report to the seminary in Newton, New Jersey, but because I was entering in the summertime, I was to report to the summer seminary in the mountains of Northern New York. Mother and Dad drove me out there and got a bird's eye look at my new digs, and they surely were not as comfortable as I was used to. The closest town was Ellenville, New York, a town of 8,000, 7998 of whom were Jewish.

Mom and Dad left, and there I was, about 1200 miles from home and everyone and everything I'd ever known. Homesickness set in immediately, but it was tempered by the routine and the studies. And there was something else that helped to divert my mind from the homesickness, something they neglected to tell me when I signed up. The place was full of rattlesnakes!

On the first full day, we were all lectured on the rules of the summer seminary, we were issued snake sticks and were made familiar with the borders of the seminary grounds. Anyone found outside the boundaries of the seminary could be made to repeat the entire year of studies.

With regard to the routine, we were to have three hours of Latin per day, six days per week, followed by an hour of study right after each class period. There were a number of hours per day that required complete silence. There were other rules, but they really didn't bother me. I acclimated to the routine rather quickly and easily, actually.

I only remember three members of the staff of the seminary. The Rector, the boss man, was Father Vincent Zuliani. His residence was referred to as the White Palace and was located on a high spot on the seminary grounds. When a student somehow messed up or wasn't picking up on his Latin, an instructor would undoubtedly threaten him with sending him to Fr. Vince for tutoring. This prospect usually made us want to study just a little bit harder.

Brother Bob Burrows was my Latin teacher. He was also a Rhoades Scholar, a fact that scared the hell out of me. I had taken

Latin as a freshman in high school and, let's just say, it wasn't a banner experience. But I did very well in this class, considering that we were expected to master the use of sixty new vocabulary words every day. I think there was another reason for the push to master this many words each day. Three weeks after our arrival at the seminary, we were told, without any warning, that forthwith, we were to communicate with all students and staff in Latin or not at all. Brother Bob even taught us a few phrases that we could use to express our frustration with the severely restricted level of communication.

There were times when I thought God put rattlesnakes on the mountain in order to balance the fear I had of Latin. Most of the novices expressed more than a little frustration with all the Latin, especially when the English Mass was just coming into being. Staff was fond of reminding us that the Latin was to be followed by Greek. That was usually enough to get us to quit complaining.

Everywhere we walked, we swept our snakes sticks in front of us to keep from scaring or stepping on our slithering friends. We also learned never to make any assumptions about what might be under a bucket or blanket. Beating our beds with our snake sticks was a ritual that took place every night before we climbed in the sack.

One Saturday, we invited a bunch of kids who were attending a camp halfway down the mountain, up to the seminary for lunch and an afternoon basketball game. As kids have been known to do, when they were through with lunch, they would bolt from their seats and fly out the door, down the steps and on to the playing field.

One of these kids got a big surprise as he found himself standing on the head of a rattlesnake. When we heard him scream, we all bolted from our seats and ran for the door. As we all stood there with our mouths hanging open, the cook came out, smiled and shook his head. Then he went back inside and got a broom and beat the snake over the head. Then he picked it up, brought it inside to the kitchen and prepped it for supper that night. Hmmm—it tasted just like chicken.

There were some things about the seminary that bothered me. The second and third year students seemed to be the ones hiding most of the Playboy and Penthouse magazines, and it seemed to be these same people who worked overtime at avoiding both their academic and religious responsibilities. I know that sounds pretty pompous and judgmental, but none the less, it bothered me.

Larry Bauer-Scandin

The homesickness never really subsided in intensity either. As I thought about home and even going home, I began to feel guilty about Mom and Dad's having driven me all the way to New York. And what would Father Crossman say, or at least feel, if I went home?

In time, I made the decision to go home, and the preparations began. Brother Bob did spend some time with me trying to get me to change my mind, but I was determined to get home in time to start my junior year at the university.

I found myself needing money for the flight home. One morning after breakfast, I asked Father Vince how I could get down to Ellenville to a bank. He told me that the cook was just about ready to drive down to Ellenville and that if I wanted to, I could go with him. I told him I'd like to get out of my cassock, the required garb of the Salesians of Don Bosco, but he told me to get to the truck if I wanted to go.

Cookie let me off in front of a bank, and he went on to do some chores. It was well over 100 degrees. Even though it was hotter than a French cathouse on opening night, I think the sweating I was experiencing had more to do with the fact that I was still wearing my cassock in an almost exclusively Jewish community.

I ducked into the bank and walked up to a teller window. I noticed that the nameplate by the window read "Rosenberg." I told her I needed to cash a check. She just stood there staring at me for a while. I asked her if something was wrong. Still, she said nothing and kept on pointing in my direction. I was really hot, and I wasn't in any mood to play a game of fifty questions. Finally, she spoke and said she couldn't understand why anyone would want to be, "you know, one of those."

I hoped she meant a priest. I asked her what bothered her about it, and she said she had a niece who wanted to be a nun. I took another glance at the name plate. I looked up from the nameplate and said, "You're not Catholic?"

She said, "No, I'm Jewish and so is my niece."

"You mean, she wants to convert and then be a nun?" I asked.

She nodded and told me, a little indignantly, that that was the only way she knew of to do it. What a smart aleck! Then she cashed my check, and I beat a hasty retreat to the door.

On the day I was to leave the seminary, I was told that the Greyhound Bus would take me to JFK's Eastside Terminal, then I would have to grab a shuttle and take it to the Westside Terminal to catch my flight. When I got to the airport, I found myself at the Westside Terminal, so I needed to find out if I was in the right place or if I needed to take a shuttle to the Eastside terminal. While I searched for an answer, my plane was flying overhead on its way to Chicago.

I soon found myself standing out on an unfamiliar street, in an unfamiliar city, and it was hot enough to melt the soles of my freshly shined shoes. As I stood there trying o figure out what to do, I heard a voice yelling from a distance away. I looked down the street to my right and saw an African American man standing outside a taxi. He was yelling, "Can I help you?" For a few seconds, I didn't know who he was talking to, but then I noticed he was walking toward me. He walked up to me and asked me again if there was something he could do to help. I told him my sob story about missing the plane. He pointed down the street to my left and told me that a block and a half down the street, I would find a building where I could buy a plane ticket to anywhere in the world. I thanked him, picked up my suitcases, and began to walk down the street.

I only took a few steps when I felt someone tapping me on the shoulder. It was the cab driver. He told me to put the suitcases down. When I did, he picked them up, started to walk down the street and told me to follow him. I protested as we were walking in the opposite direction from his unattended cab, but he didn't flinch.

When we got to the ticket office, he put the suitcases down, shook my hand and wished me good luck. I noticed there was a restaurant in the building, and I invited him to join me for breakfast. He politely told me that he didn't "think I'd be welcome in there." I guess the 1964 Civil Rights Act still had some public relations work to do.

Somehow, I made it to Chicago, but the closer I got to home, the worse I felt. I really wasn't excited about seeing Dad or Father Crossman. Eventually I did go home, and I was pleasantly surprised by the reaction of both of them. I was glad to have had the seminary experience, but it was now time to put that behind me and get ready for my junior year at UMD.

Larry Bauer-Scandin

The Junior Year

By my junior year, I had fought my way through most of the General Education credits that should have been completed before the junior year. I, however, was not part of the normal group. I just want to mention a rather unusual experience I had in one of those General Education classes, an English Literature class.

English grammar was my strong suit, not English Literature. A student in an English Literature class, who happened to sit in the seat directly on my left, had been acting like a juvenile delinquent during the entire class period. He was talking just loud enough to be heard by everyone in the class, including the female instructor.

For most of the period, she apparently had made the decision to ignore the jerk, but I was getting mad enough to drop a bowling ball in his lap. Finally, near the end of the period, the instructor threw him out of class. When the bell rang, ending the class, she dismissed everyone but asked me to stay. Naturally, I was asking myself, "What the hell did I do?"

When the last student walked out the door, she closed it, turned to me and asked, "Well, was I right?"

I said, "Were you right about what?"

She said, "For throwing him out."

I thought about it for a moment, still curious as to why she was asking. I told her I thought she was right and wrong, right for throwing him out, and wrong for waiting so long to do it. She smiled and thanked me, and I hurried out the door for my next class. I don't think another word was ever exchanged between the two of us.

I had another interesting learning experience during that year. Every Psychology major quickly became aware of the fact that his/her nerves, if not determination, were going to be tested at the point that the psych department's "bogyman" course, Psychological Statistics, was taken. Psych Stats, as it was called, was the requirement that seemed to spook everyone including me. I was one of those who ran from the course based on rumor and the sight of Stats students lined up at the water fountain taking their Valium. I even went so far as to sign up for the class at the University of St. Scholastica, a college located some quarter mile from UMD. Too late, I found out that their statistics course didn't meet UMD's requirement, as St. Scholastica's course was

70

a three-credit class, and UMD's was five credits. I was forced to bite the bullet and take the class at UMD.

On the first day of class, I made the decision to sit in the first row so I didn't miss anything, and I could see everything. As I was waiting for the bell to ring and the professor to walk in, an older female friend of mine, probably forty-five or fifty years of age and a straight "A" student, walked up to me and told me that she had just dropped Psychology as one of her two majors. She told me that she was so petrified of Statistics that she decided it was worth dropping one major in order to avoid it. One class! I was shocked and disappointed. I was nervous also, but I thought that there was no way I was going to let one class change the direction I wanted to go. I told her I thought she was making a mistake, but she had made her decision.

Eventually, the professor walked in and introduced himself. I didn't know him, and he wasn't a member of the Psychology Dept. staff. He told us that he was not a psychologist, but rather a statistician. I didn't consider that to be good news.

He began to explain his philosophy of education. He believed in open book exams, for example. His belief was that in the real world of a statistician (I wondered whether there could be such a thing,) there would be ready access to research materials, including statistical formulas, etc., but you would have to know which formula to use to solve your problem. In short, he didn't think there was any sense in requiring that we learn formulas. We would be better served by learning which formula to use to solve which problem.

In the end, I got a grade of "C," in the class, and I was satisfied with it. During and after this class, I wondered how my friend Virginia's future plans were affected by her fear of that single class. I hope I was learning not to let fear of failure keep me from pursuing a goal.

Another Little Bump in the Road

Sometime during the school year, I took a job as a desk clerk at the best hotel in Duluth, the Hotel Duluth. I thoroughly enjoyed relating and working with the staff, but I never quite got comfortable using the machines and electronics of the day. Actually, not much has changed to the present day! I plodded along each day, knowing that this wasn't the kind of work I wanted to do. But it offered enough in terms of satisfaction to make me stick with it until something better came long.

The Beginning of It All

Even after the seminary experience, Father Crossman and I managed to maintain our relationship, both as priest/parishioner and friend/friend. What my mother had always said was still true. "If I wanted to find you, all I ever had to do was make four phone calls, one to Doug's home, one to Cheryl's, one to Wayne's, and one to the rectory." Obviously, I wasn't known as a social butterfly.

One spring afternoon, I wound up making a stop at the rectory. Fr. Crossman, or "The Chief," as I'd come to call him (and still do), told me that he was on his way to a meeting in the basement of the church, and why didn't I come along (said the spider to the fly). At first, I answered in the negative, but then, remember, there's a picture of a priest beside the word, "Sneaky" in Webster's Dictionary. So I agreed to go to the meeting. After all, I had nothing better to do.

When we got to the church, I found several men milling around the front of the room behind a conference table. I was surprised to see the Mayor of Duluth, Ben Boo (yeah, I know, I know!) There were three or four others, but I recognized none of them.

Fr. Crossman started the meeting by introducing everyone, starting, of course, with the Mayor. Also introduced was the director of the county's probation department, a member of the Duluth Police Department's Juvenile Aid Bureau and a member of the Minnesota Department of Corrections, one Merle J. Micheau.

As I looked around the room, I realized that I knew some of the attendees in the room. Some of them were parishioners of St. Joseph's, some were local business people, and some were involved with the Duluth Heights Community Club.

Of course, the first speaker was the Mayor, and he introduced the central reason for the meeting. That reason was a loosely organized group of local kids who called themselves the Sewer Rat Gang, or the SRG. They were causing trouble in the community by committing thefts and vandalism to property, etc. What to do about it?

The police, probation department and Department of

Corrections were all familiar with these kids. Those present were invited to give input or share ideas as to what might be done to try and re-direct the kids' energy into more positive activities.

There was some trading of ideas as to how to handle these kids, and there was an attitude among some that nothing should be done as the "What are we doing for the good kids" section of the peanut gallery was also represented—and vocal. For those that held that attitude, I suggested that the answer might be Little League/Babe Ruth League baseball, organized sports teams sanctioned by the Community Club, local hockey teams, etc. Someone even suggested that he would be willing to show films of his many "adventures" traveling in Europe. I had a picture of these kids coming to the Community Club and watching travelogues a few hours each week.

I threw out the idea of opening some kind of drop-in center that would serve to get these kids off the street and give them somewhere to hang out. Others asked about the cost of opening such a center. I suggested that we could start with some chairs, perhaps a radio and someone to staff the place and work with the kids. Ultimately, the goal would be to do some mentoring and problem solving with them.

After an hour or so of discussing these kids and what to do about them, Mayor Boo looked at me and asked if I might be interested in taking on the job of manning such a drop-in center. My first reaction was to say, "No," but then I decided that this was my chance to get out of the hotel job. After a little more discussion, and not just a little shaking on my part, I agreed to take the job.

By the time the meeting ended, it was decided that we would open the center in the garage of the Duluth Heights Community Center. The whole experiment, of course, would take place under the auspices of the Community Club Board, but I would be supervised by Merle Micheau of the Department of Corrections. I would also keep in touch with a representative of the county's probation department as several of the kids were under its supervision. During the next few weeks, I also met with members of the police department's Juvenile Aid Bureau to talk about how we could best support each other in working with the SRG.

One of the specifics we discussed was how to handle a situation in which someone showed up with alcohol, weapons, drugs, stolen goods, etc. The general agreement was that if any of these things happened, I would contact the JAB as soon as I could safely do so.

We also agreed that when the police came to the Center in response to a call from me, and if they took someone into custody, they were to take me into custody also. When we got to the police department/courthouse/jail complex, we would be questioned in different departments. While the kid was being questioned at the JAB, I would report to the probation department.

Actually, this arrangement worked quite well, for when the kids saw me being put in handcuffs, they believed that their behavior was damaging my credibility, and therefore, their Center. And it didn't take long for the kids to get attached to the Center. It was a place for them to be with friends, and to be with people who knew how to relate to each other without being judgmental.

But this summer was about the kids, so let's get to it. Before we do this, I needed to quit my job at the hotel. I made arrangements to see the hotel manager, Bob Heideman. I told him about the new job, thanked him for the opportunity to work at the hotel, but I had to admit my lack of understanding of the business side of the hotel business. He said he'd been trying to think of what to do with me also. He told me that I had been a good employee, but he knew I wasn't happy and that concerned him. Obviously, things turned out well, as he didn't have to confront me, and I didn't have to continue in a job that I hated. It's funny how things work out.

The Sewer Rat Gang

As the Center was about a gang, I guess I should start my discussion of it with its leader, Dan. Now, Dan was kind of a big, lumbering kid who, because of his unkempt appearance, intimidated the other kids. Dan was fond of wearing engineer boots, tattered jeans, greasy black hair, and an unshaven face.

Dan also had a younger brother, David, who was also a member of the gang. David had a good head on his shoulders, and over the course of the summer, he gave me ample reason to believe that the SRG was going to be a transitory thing for him. I couldn't see him developing into a certified delinquent.

Of course, Dan showed up at the Center the first day to scope out the supervisor, and, of course, he put on his best gang leader act and gave me every indication that, at some point, we were going to have to "get it on" in order to find out who was going to be the top banana at the Center.

His pushing over the next week or so got to the point where I knew I was going to do myself more harm than good by trying to avoid a confrontation. So one cold, rainy Saturday night, we drew the battle lines. We could have sold tickets to this event, as just about every kid who was remotely associated with the SRG was there, and as I recall, the list the probation department gave me contained about thirty-five names. I guess it was at that point that I realized what was going to happen. I had to win, or I wouldn't have much influence with these kids, and the experiment would be over before it started.

Dan suggested that we settle things by wrestling rather than the use of fists. I think we both wanted to avoid blood, and I like to avoid pain when possible. I also decided that I had to trust him when he told the others not to interfere.

So there we were, standing out in a cold rain, stalking each other, ready to get it on. To make a short story shorter, I quickly found myself with Dan's head in a headlock. I put my wrist bone to his jawbone and squeezed hard. It took about five seconds for him to give up. As soon as he did so, it struck me that I couldn't react by beating my chest. That wouldn't let him save face, so I stuck out my hand instead, which he took. The unexpected result of all of this was that Dan kind of became my enforcer.

The second in command was Davy. Davy would soon become the kid I would become most concerned about, as he seemed to be the closest to a card carrying delinquent as I had met up to that point. I also discovered that Davy was awaiting a court appearance for having vandalized a bus stop/shelter in the neighborhood.

Jerry turned out to be the most frequent visitor to the Center, and one of the kids I got closest to. Jerry had several brothers and sisters, and I think he more or less got lost in the crowd.

Jerry liked coming to the Center. I think the biggest reason was because he thought he was being heard. And somewhere along the way, Merle, or "Mich" as he was called, also befriended Jerry. And Jerry didn't seem to mind being befriended by a man who was 6' 8" tall! He also didn't seem to mind all the pizzas and cokes Mich and I bought him over the course of the summer. Being identified with Mich also helped me get and maintain some status with the kids as they saw him as being both friendly an powerful.

Although I liked Jerry, he could irritate like an inflamed hemorrhoid. One night, the kids kind of tied me in a chair, put a straw hat on my head and lit it on fire. Their panic buttons were pushed before mine, and they knocked the hat off my head.

I stopped at Jerry's home a few times during the summer. I thought that maybe Betty and Homer could tell me something about Jerry that would help me deal with him. I knew Betty was worried about Jerry, but I think she had so many things going on in her own life, that she didn't have the energy to give Jerry the attention he needed.

After the summer ended, we all went our own way. I re-attached to some of the kids in a different way a short time later, but I'll get into that in a bit.

One thing I learned about very early in my career was that one "should never believe anything one hears about a kid and only half of what they see, because the behavior of teenagers often has a different meaning than what seems obvious.

The SRG's leader, Dan, was one of those kids. Several times over the course of the summer, Dan showed up at the Center showered, shaved, and wearing dress slacks and a dress shirt. On one of those occasions, Dan and I found ourselves alone at the Center. He dropped the gang leader façade and started talking about people making judgments about other people based on appearance. Specifically, he mentioned the different ways people seemed to view him depending on whether or not he was wearing his leathers, engineer boots, etc., or his dress slacks and shirt and was shaven. I told him I thought most people made judgments about people based on outward appearances. I also suggested if he found that to be so true, it would be rather simple to change peoples' minds about how they viewed him. He would simply have to make a choice. Well, he did, a few years later. He got himself involved in a rape and ran.

I heard that he was in Denver in about 1971, and the law was still trying to find him. I spoke to his father once, and I was told that he was still missing when his mother passed away. Sometimes, I still wonder where he is.

The biggest pain in my rump during the entire summer was a

kid by the name of Kevin. Kevin was the kind of kid that made one absolutely positive that God made rear ends for parents to beat on. The smirks that Kevin could produce could make a person want to re-arrange his face.

One night, he came riding into the Center on a stolen bike. He skidded to a halt, jumped off the bike, picked it up and threw it against the wall, bending the frame.

I lost it! I bolted from my chair, charged him like a bull moose and backed him up against a wall. I grabbed him by the long hair, turned my back to him and threw him over my right shoulder, bouncing him off the concrete floor.

He looked up at me with tears in his eyes and said, "Now what good did that do me?"

I looked down at him and said, "It may not have done you any good, but it sure as hell did *me* a lot of good!"

Years later, I saw Kevin sitting in his car. I approached his open window and noticed that the top of his head was bald. When he noticed me looking at his balding head, he said, "No, it grew back." To my knowledge, the Sewer Rats were as close as Kevin ever got to serious legal trouble. Sometimes they fool you!

There's one more family associated with the SRG that I'd like to mention. The family consisted of Marge, the mother, Dick, Bobby, Tom, Linda, a daughter with Muscular Dystrophy, and another daughter whose name I've forgotten. The three boys were marginal at best, members of the SRG. As a matter of fact, they were probably tagged as members because they lived in close proximity to some of the more visible members and may have become guilty by association.

These three boys were always hanging around the fringe of things and making me believe they wanted no part of delinquent behavior, but needed someplace to be. It may also have had something to do with the pressures at home.

When that feeling got too strong to ignore, I decided to visit the boys' home. I really wanted to meet their mother, Marge. As I recall, Marge had been a very young widow. There was no doubt in my mind that this woman loved her children very much, but I was just as sure that she was very worried about the boys, especially Dick. Actually, I think her main fear was having enough parental influence over her teenage sons.

77

I stayed close to the boys during the course of the summer, and I did what I could to keep some distance between them and the more active members of the SRG. I kept in touch with the family for some time after the summer ended. I never heard that any of the boys, with Tom being the only exception, ever got into any serious legal trouble.

I did run into Tom about fourteen years later. He looked like Charles Manson, with long hair and a beard that almost totally covered his face. He apologized for his appearance and explained that it was meant to hide his jaundiced skin. He said that he had been such a heavy drinker that he had developed liver problems that, he said, were terminal.

Sometime later, I thought I heard that Tom was killed in a car accident. From what I was told, there were three people in the car— Tom, a friend who was quite drunk, and, I believe, Tom's baby. With the drunk friend driving, Tom climbed out on the hood of the car, spread-eagled, and the friend began driving erratically down the street, eventually throwing Tom from the hood and killing him. I wish he had thought of a more patented way of killing himself. Jeopardizing a baby doesn't seem to fit the kid I knew, but then, booze can do a lot to change a person.

I've spent some time talking about this summer as if it had been a practicum in social work. But this was an experience not only in the thinking and behavioral processes of the delinquent and pre-delinquent, but also in the humor and dangers of working with them.

During the summer, a lot of the kids showed up at the Center who were obviously drunk, had been drinking, or using some sort of drug. I reported this to Mich, the probation department, and the Juvenile Aid Bureau, but I was never able to find out where they were getting it.

One night, a car pulled into the Center's driveway, and several very intoxicated young people got out. I'd never seen them before, but they knew some of the regulars at the Center. They ignored me like I wasn't there, so I just watched and listened and took a mental note of the license plate number.

As I sat there, the driver lifted the hood of the car and pulled out what appeared to be a straw. They passed the straw between them, each bending over and sipping from (you're not going to believe this) the windshield washer bottle. Very creative! When it was safe, I called the police department, and presumably, they did their thing.

Before going on, I think this would be a good place to mention the drug scene in those days. The Duluth area was experiencing the same troubles with the same kinds of drugs that most other communities were dealing with. But, in those days, people were sniffing airplane glue, shooting peanut butter, mayonnaise and, in one instance I'll mention later, Kool Aid. This added some obvious problems to fighting the drug problem. Just how do you pass a law against Peter Pan?

This summer was full of firsts for me. One of them made me wonder whether this type of work was something I really wanted to give serious consideration to doing. I was at the Center alone one night when a car with three kids drove in. It wasn't hard to tell that they had been drinking, but only one of them seemed to be downright belligerent.

The alcohol was fueling his mouth, and eventually he pulled a pistol from his jacket pocket and pointed it directly at me. I did my best to hide my fear, but I realized just how helpless I was. He kept staggering around the room, always making sure that he didn't get too close to me physically. The scrambled brain in my head was trying to come up with a plan. I decided to try a little shock treatment by turning my back on him and taking a seat. It didn't seem to bother him, and after a little more walking around the place, they all got in the car and drove off. I was on the phone in a shot and reported the incident to the JAB. A squad was sent to the Center to take my statement. I don't remember ever getting word that the police picked up these kids, but I was able to give them a license plate number, so I assume they did.

I knew I was going to have another big problem as a result of this incident. I knew I was going to have to report it to the community club's Board of Directors, and I knew it might mean they would want to terminate the experiment.

When I did report to the Board, there were a few members who thought that kids with guns were more than they wanted to deal with, and I understood that. I pointed out that I had been the one at physical risk and that I still believed in the Center. I also argued that the Center was accomplishing its purpose, which was giving these kids someplace to go, something to do, and someone to talk to about school, home, and some of them were doing just that.

And lest one thinks that the kids are always the culprits, I would like to say something. You may recall that one attendee at the meeting in the church basement asked, "What are we doing for the good kids?" Well, one of the worst of these kids, Davy, had been an altar boy until he made a mistake during a Mass, and was made to feel badly enough by someone that he chose to quit. This same kid was also on a community hockey team, but he was asked to quit because nothing stopped him when he went down the ice with the puck. Both of these stories were confirmed by members of the community club's Board of Directors.

The Start of It All

During the course of the summer, Mich and I became very good friends. I learned to appreciate him both as a friend and as a teacher. We spent a lot of time talking about kids over coffee, his work, and what I was going to do after school. I made no secret of the fact that probation/parole work sounded very interesting.

Near the end of the summer, he told me that there was an opening in his office for an intern, and he offered to talk to his supervisor about me if I would be interested. It didn't take me long to tell him I was.

He arranged for me to have an interview with his Department of Corrections supervisor, Warren Peterson. The position was offered and would be available on January 3, 1969. The position was offered through a program at the university and would be available as long as I was a student.

The First Senior Year

The summer ended, and it was time to get ready for my senior year at UMD. Things had calmed down scholastically, even though I still hated school. The only thing that made it easier was the fact that I had finally completed all of the General Education credits, and I was now able to concentrate on courses relevant to my major, Psychology. Now I felt like I might really make it!

One of the courses I took during the fall quarter of my senior year was a mandatory class called Senior Seminar. I don't remember who the instructor was, but I sure remember the first day.

He announced that we were going to have to commit to working in one of three programs during the quarter. One of the choices was to work in UMD's counseling office. Another choice was to join the Big Brother program, and there was a third choice that I don't remember. I became concerned about the requirement, because the course was a three quarter long sequence course. I was trying to anticipate how I was going to handle the class necessities and an inevitable caseload I'd acquire once I started working with the Department of Corrections in January.

After the first class period, I stayed to talk to the professor about my working with the Department of Corrections. When I mentioned my working with the DOC, beginning winter quarter, he interrupted me and reminded me that "You were the one that was pushing for more practicum offerings. Now you've got them. Choose!"

Anyway, so I could control my own schedule, I committed to joining the Big Brothers. I wasn't really excited about taking on a little brother, but it kept me from any more hours to be spent at the university.

The Big Brothers and My "Little Brother"

I was assigned a little brother by the name of Tony. He was nine years old. The night I went to the house to meet Tony, his mother, brothers and sisters, I found a very attractive, relatively young mother who was trying to raise what I remember as a large family alone. As I recall, the father had abandoned the family. I couldn't figure out how a man could walk out on his family and leave his wife to raise a family alone. Obviously, I had a lot to learn!

I don't remember what Tony and I did that first night, but it didn't take me long to like him. He had a great attitude and sense of optimism. I found out that he loved professional wrestling, so that became the thing we did most often.

I remained involved with Big Brothers and Tony until my Corrections caseload grew to the point where I couldn't handle it, school, and do justice to Tony. I felt extremely guilty about leaving Big Brothers and my relationship with Tony. But he was to show up in my life at a critical time some seventeen years later

The Big Day

I walked into the offices of the Minnesota Department of Corrections on Jan. 3, 1969. As I recall, it was a Monday, and I'm sure I should have been in school, but this promised to be much more exciting. Mich greeted me at the door and introduced me to the staff.

On one end of the rather long wing of offices was Jim. Jim was Mich's partner. He was a nice guy, but he seemed to prefer to work alone most of the time, and he didn't get involved in the office intrigue. Smart man! The only specific memory I have of Jim was the calendar hanging on the wall in front of his desk. He used it to cross off each day as it ended. Each "X" marked one day closer to retirement.

Merle J. Micheau occupied the office next to Jim. I won't try to describe Mich for two reasons. First, he really defies description. Secondly, I'll have much to say about him throughout this book.

Next to Mich was Glen. Glen was probably the quietest of all of us, but he was right up to his five day deodorant pads in the office politics. His relief from it all was the fact that he was "leased" from the DOC by two counties on the north shore of Lake Superior. That allowed him to make strategic withdrawals from the office when necessary.

Next was Maryann. Whether or not Maryann ever believed it or not, and I think she did, she was the usual spark that lit the fire of intrigue in the office, mainly because she was the only female. Glen's wife always seemed to believe that Glen and Maryann had something going on between the two of them, but in my two years in that office, I never saw any such thing.

Next to Glen's office was Maryann's. Maryann handled all of the female cases under the jurisdiction of the DOC, as well as some male cases. We all know, of course, that females can't abuse males.

The main office was occupied by the supervisor, Pete. Pete was a nice guy, and I was to grow to be thankful for his trust in me. But Pete behaved as if he had no knowledge of the intra-office relationships between his agents.

The office next to Pete's was occupied by Fred, another intern, and me. Fred started before me and had already been assigned a number of cases. I don't know Fred's motivation for wanting to work in a correctional atmosphere, but he and I were nothing alike. I think

God even put Fred in my life because, if he hadn't, I wouldn't have met one of the most interesting kids I ever had the pleasure of working with. A little more on this relationship in a while.

And lastly (and the guy closest to the elevator) was Al, our adult agent. It didn't take long to realize that it was Maryann and Al that were fond of each other. Now that covers the professional staff.

Now, who's left? Oh, yeah, the two most important people in the entire office, the two secretaries, Irene and Irene, or Irene and "George." These two couldn't have been more different.

Irene H. was kind of a nasty, foul-tempered thing who found ways of making you pay when you crossed her. She was also the office gossip. No one ever trusted her with anything.

Irene N., or "George," on the other hand, was sweet, always had a smile on her face, and was always willing to stick around and help out in an emergency. As a matter of fact, Mich and I often asked her to interview a client, knowing that she would find out more about what a particular kid might be up to than we could. She simply had a way with young people that made them want to talk to her.

By the way, in case you haven't figured it out, all of us had an obvious problem. Mich came up with the idea of calling one of the girls "George" so that they would know which of them was being called. He knew that "Witchy Woman" wouldn't appreciate the new name, but "George" did. What a lady!

Of course, the first thing I had to learn was office procedure, department policies and regulations, type of reports, etc., etc., ad nauseum. I had anticipated this, though.

Shortly after my experience with the first day on the job, Pete told me that he wanted me to attend a court hearing with Al. The case involved one of Al's cases, a Native American female who had been charged with shining a deer. On the way to the courthouse, Al gave me a little background on the defendant and her rather large family. She pled guilty, and I wondered what Al was going to recommend to the judge, one Honorable Don Anderson.

After the defendant's plea, we recessed, and the Judge, Al, and I, the prosecutor and the defense attorney all retired to the Judge's chambers. The Judge grabbed a tablet and wrote two words on the first page, "Time" and "Fine." He went around the room asking each of us for a recommendation as to a fine and/or jail sentence. When he came to me, I told him I really didn't think it was my place to make a recommendation as I was only an intern and there to learn. When he insisted on an opinion, I told him that, given the woman's circumstances, I'd give her the deer.

I don't think anyone cared for my recommendation, but then I didn't particularly like the idea of sentencing someone based on taking the average number of days and dollars recommended by several people in a Judge's chambers. So much for my first court experience!

In the main, Mich became my partner, teacher, coach, mentor, personal humorist and friend. When there wasn't much to do, I could count on his finding something fun to do, like raid a pool hall to chase school-skippers, or head to the outdoor golf range to smack a few buckets of balls around, always making sure, of course, that he raised the trunk door on the state car, or "Levander Cadillac," as we used to call it, in honor of our then Governor, so no one could take the number on the car and turn us in.

We made our first and only pool hall raid on a spring day in 1969. We knew there were probably a number of kids playing hooky, so we thought we'd keep them a little off balance. The local pool hall was just a few blocks from the office and was on the second floor of the building. The main entrance was on First Street, and there was an exit into the alley between First and Second Streets.

Mich proposed the following game plan. He would go in the main entrance and up the stairs. He wanted me to cover the exit in the alley. He told me that when he got to the top of the steps and the kids saw him, they would take off running for the alley exit, and I'd hear nothing but cue balls and cue sticks and a thundering herd of humanity running down the back steps, headed for the alley exit. He told me to grab one of them as they burst through the door.

He gave me a few minutes to find the alley door and then climbed the steps to the second floor pool hall. I heard his size 14 ½ shoes hit the floor, and as he predicted, I began to hear cue balls and cue sticks and an ominous rumble coming down the back steps. Suddenly the door burst open, and a human tsunami hit me and deposited me in a row of garbage cans. The next thing I knew, Mich's 6' 8" frame was staring down at me and asking why I hadn't grabbed one of them. I was a whole lot embarrassed, feeling like I had screwed up twice within the last few days, but Mich was laughing as he helped me up, and suggested that "They won't be back here today!"

The time came when things had to get serious. Pete told me that he wanted me to go up the avenue to the courthouse and take a young man into custody who had just testified in a trial. This young man was being charged with a violation of his parole, and he was to be held in jail until his parole agent could take him back to prison. The State of Minnesota had issued me a pair of handcuffs, but apparently they didn't feel they had any responsibility for issuing courage.

One of the first things I realized when I walked into the office on January 3rd was that I was the shortest thing in the entire office, including the coat rack. I took a few minutes to look at this kid's file, and as I feared, he was 6" 2" tall and approached two hundred pounds. All of a sudden, my mind conjured up this nightmare of this guy's picking me up while we were walking through the tunnel between the courthouse and the jail, putting me in his pocket, walking out to my car and driving away. So I went to talk to my partner. He told me to just walk into the courtroom, tell anyone who needed to know who I was and why I was there, take out my handcuffs and tell the guy to stick out his wrists. Somehow, this seemed just a little oversimplified! But I knew he was right, so I took the short walk up the avenue to the courthouse, found the right courtroom and walked in.

The Judge, still in his robes, the attorneys, and the subject of my concern were all standing in the front of the courtroom. The Judge asked what I needed. I told him I was there to take the young man into custody on a parole violation. To my amazement, the kid walked over to me and stuck his arms out in front of himself. I put the handcuffs on him, and we walked through the tunnel to the jail. By the way, all the way through the tunnel, he was talking like he was about to go to Disneyland. I couldn't figure it out, but I was to witness this many more times during my career. Another piece of my education.

But let's not forget that I was still in school. Some interesting things were happening there also. I was beginning to really appreciate the fact that I had made the workings of the human mind my educational goal. But I was also learning that people in the "mind business" didn't always make sense.

For example, over the years there've been all sorts of theories concerning behavior and the human mind. In the latter 60s and early 70s, one of those psychological innovations was something called

Sensitivity Training. Basically it involved tearing a person down psychologically and then rebuilding him. It was supposed to teach a person how to take criticism without falling apart. Sensitivity Training was being done on many college campuses. The only problem was that the tearing down session and the rebuilding session was sometimes separated by some period of time, and in some cases, it was enough time that it resulted in students committing suicide.

During this year, my advisor, Bob Falk, embarked on a plan to get his Ph.D. Part of his plan involved some of his students, including me, getting involved in an experiment involving marginally acceptable entering freshmen.

Specifically, we, his senior students, were going to tutor/mentor a group of freshmen who were scholastic underachievers in order to determine whether or not tutoring/mentoring could result in their being successful in the university setting.,

I was selected as the tutor/mentor supervisor. I wasn't particularly interested in the offer, given school and work, but I liked Bob Falk a whole lot, and he did offer me credits as an inducement. Also, the hours weren't set in concrete. So I accepted the offer, based on a maximum 12/hour week.

Over time, this project got to require more than the twelve hours "RJ" and I agreed on. And, as predictable, I started to develop a corrections caseload that also required time.

One day, at a meeting of the tutor/mentors, RJ told us about an individual who was going to be visiting the university to familiarize us with Sensitivity Training. He said we would be required to attend an evening meeting and then would be required to attend a Sensitivity Group. I was furious because I was concerned about having enough time to do all these things. I went to the evening meeting, but I was spittin' mad, and I didn't care who knew it.

During this guy's talk, he told us that we would all have to attend at least one session and, "If you don't like it, you can stand up and tell me to 'go to hell' and leave."

At that point, I closed my briefcase, stood up, told him to "go to hell," and left, with Bob Falk right behind me. He told me to calm down and start thinking about which session I wanted to attend, because we had to sign up that night. I kind of felt like I was back at Camp Miller! Reluctantly, I went back to the room, but I didn't apologize, even tough I should have. My feeling a time crunch wasn't his fault.

On the night of my group session, I was met at the door by the instructor, who blocked the entrance to the room. He wouldn't let me into the damned room! I told him that Bob Falk told me I had to attend, and that was exactly what I was going to do. I brushed past him and took a seat. I sat through the session and never went back for another. The interesting thing about all of this was that every time I ran into this guy in the hallways of the university, I said "Hello" and never got anything in return except a scowl. So much for sensitivity training!

During this school year, I took a class in Criminal Law taught by a professional criminologist by the name of Dick Deming. I enjoyed his classes, but he didn't sell me on a lot of his ideas.

Toward the end of the year, he approached me and told me that the university was going to introduce a major in Criminology the following year. He suggested I might want to consider coming back for a fifth year and taking the three courses I lacked for a second major. My first reaction was to laugh, but then I thought about the fact that I would probably be able to continue as an intern for the DOC. After giving it some thought and checking things out with Pete, I decided to go back for a fifth year. I never would have thought it possible!

Pete was anxious for me to become familiar with the correctional institutions I'd be dealing with and their staffs, so it was arranged for Mich and me to take in all of the facilities in one week-long round robin tour. During the course of that week, we visited St. Croix Camp, Lino Lakes, the State Training School at Red Wing, the Rochester Vocational Camp, St. Cloud Reformatory as it was called then, the Minnesota Home School, at Sauk Centre, and Thistledew Camp, in Togo, Minnesota.

Each facility's program was developed for a certain type of client, e.g., 14-16 year olds who needed to concentrate on school, or 18-21 year olds who needed to learn how to get up in the morning and go to a job. The other institution, the St. Cloud Reformatory, or "Gladiator School," as it was called, was the high security facility for inmates up to age 26.

Eventually, we got to the Vocational Camp in Rochester. We stopped at the Superintendent's office to let him know we were there. Mich wanted to see one of his guys and asked the Superintendent if he was available. He told us that the kid was assigned to the kitchen and that he should be there getting things ready for lunch. We told him we'd just wander over there and find him.

When we got to the kitchen, it was quiet and looked unoccupied, so we didn't just yell out for the kid. We just walked up and down the rows of canned goods and other supplies. As we rounded a corner, we almost ran into the rear end of a body, literally a naked rear end, as a matter of fact! Reflex action made him turn around, and when he did, we saw that he was sprouting an erection and had a wad of bread dough in his hands. When he saw us, he quickly tossed the bread dough and pulled up his pants. He didn't know what to do with his very red face! Somehow, the three of us found a way to assume a more business-like posture, and we managed to finish our business and leave the building without wetting our pants because this was so amusing.

We went back to the Superintendent's office to say our goodbyes, and he asked us if we wanted to stay for lunch. Mich and I looked at each other, and he told the Superintendent that we needed to be on our way. We left without needing CPR. Next stop, the "Gladiator School," the St. Cloud Reformatory.

Now this, for me, was a scary experience. It was also known as the Greystone Castle, as the walls are made of stone and are dotted with guard towers. It makes quite an imposing sight from Highway 10.

When you first entered the facility, you found yourself in a lobby. Then you proceeded to a barred door that had to be keyed open. Then you found yourself between that door and another door that had to be keyed open. That meant that someone spent his entire shift walking between these two doors, unlocking one of them and then the other. Then you found yourself in prison.

Mich took me upstairs and introduced me to some of the caseworkers that were working with our clients. We told the appropriate staff who we wanted to see, and we were invited to use two of the interview rooms to talk to our clients. My list of clients was quite a bit shorter than Mich's, so when I was through, I went downstairs and I sat on a bench and just watched, and listened, and watched as one law enforcement officer after another came through the barred doors with guys in handcuffs, leg shackles and transportation belts. I couldn't imagine surviving in a place like that, and some of these guys were barely more than kids.

As I sat there deep in thought, I heard someone yell my name. I looked up at the second deck and saw a young man talking to a correctional deputy. Then he started to walk down the steps and toward me. I didn't recognize him until he was just a few feet away.

It was Mike, the kid I met at Emerson Elementary, who had the thing about wearing glasses. Remember him? I asked him what he was doing there, and he asked the same. I told him I sure as hell wasn't an inmate. He told me why he was there, but I don't remember the crime.

I asked him if he was still living in Duluth, and he said he was. That led me to ask him who his parole agent was. He pointed up at the second deck at Mich, who was talking to a caseworker but was eyeing Mike and me.

He leaned close to me and said, "You know what? I'm going to kill him when I get out of here." In another minute, a guard called to him, and he said goodbye and took his leave. That was the last time I ever saw him.

In a few more minutes, Mich was done, and we took a very quiet walk out to the parking lot. I was very happy to be out of there and the constant noise of steel doors closing, the sights, and especially, Mike. I couldn't forget the smile on his face when he told me he planned to kill Mich. And would anything but a very sick, or stupid, mind tell one parole agent that he intended to kill another?

When we got to the car and hit the highway, Mich turned to me and asked what Mike had to say. I told him that, among other things, he told me he was going to kill him when he got out of prison. I looked at him and asked him what a person says to someone who says he's going to kill you when he gets out of prison.

He looked at me, smiled and said, "I don't know what you're going to tell them, but I tell them, 'You're number 2375, and the line forms to the right. Get to the back of the line!'" I told him not to discount that threat, as I had known Mike for fifteen years. He acknowledged that he knew Mike was dangerous, and he considered him to be one of two guys he'd ever dealt with that he thought was capable of carrying through on that threat.

The next stop was the State Training School, at Red Wing. As usual, the first thing we did was to check in at the Superintendent's office. As we were walking toward the Administration Building, we were passing a lot of kids going to one program or another. I noticed that just about every kid we passed looked at us, and almost looking like a military salute, began scratching the side of their noses with the baby finger of their right hand. I asked Mich what was in the water that made the kids' noses itch. He looked at me and smiled and informed me that that was the kids' way of giving parole agents "the finger." You can see why this guy was my teacher.

When we got to the Superintendent's office, we also found out that earlier that morning, about thirty kids had run away, and in a short time, there were about twenty-nine cars missing from the Red Wing community.

Our last stop was Thistledew Camp. Now, Thistledew Camp is located in Togo, Minnesota, and is tucked so far out in the woods that only Davy Crockett could find it. When we got there, Earl Gonzales, the Assistant Superintendent, was in the process of strapping six or eight pair of handcuffs around his waist. They just had half a dozen kids run off, and they were about to go out looking for them. They would find one kid, handcuff him around a tree, go on and find the next and do the same until all of them had been found. It struck me that the DOC would be in a heck of a lot of trouble if a staff person forgot where he handcuffed a kid or a bear happened along and mistook a kid for a French dip in handcuffs while they were chasing other kids. No one lost this time.

Eventually this trip ended, but I had seen and learned a lot. Mich and I must have traveled six or eight hundred miles together during this adventure. He did all of the driving, and I asked most of the questions. We also got to know each other a lot better.'

It's probably time to prove that I actually did some work to earn my paychecks. When Pete became convinced that I was catching on to the basics of the job, he began to assign me some of the usual kinds of cases. The first of these was Mike, a Native American kid who lived in a heavily Native American part of Duluth.

Ninety-eight percent of the time, our office got cases that had already been through the county's probation department, and a court had committed the youth to the Commissioner of Corrections. That meant that, under most circumstances, we did our background investigation, and made any institutional recommendations without having met the kid.

Well, Mike was my first case assignment, and I was determined to make a professional impression when I made my first home investigation and evaluation. For some reason, I made that initial visit on a Saturday morning. When I knocked on the door, it was answered by a child about five or six years of age. I asked her if her mother was home, and she told me to come in. I followed her into the living room, where I found three other youngsters, all pre-school age. They were watching their mother having sex on the couch! I knew it wasn't her husband. He was doing time in the work farm. With my best professional demeanor, I said, "Excuse me!" A very embarrassed lady jumped off the couch and invited me into the kitchen. By the way, she knew I was coming. No surprise visit here.

I don't remember anything about the conversation I had with this boy's mother. But nothing could have changed my mind about what I would be recommending to the Youth Conservation Commission (YCC) the paroling authority. There was no way I was going to recommend that this kid come home. I went to the office Monday morning, wrote my report to the YCC, and recommended that after Mike did his time, he should be placed in foster care. Unfortunately the YCC bought my recommendation.

When Mike finished his institutional program, he was paroled to a foster home and promptly ran away. Within a few hours, he was home, and I took him into custody. I returned him to the Reception Center a day or so later. After doing another stretch in an institutional program, Mike was flown to a foster home, in North Dakota, and promptly ran again.

I called his home to tell his mother, and she said she'd call me when he got home. By this time, I had figured out that Mike was a homing pigeon. Eventually she called, and I found myself driving to the house in a cold rainy night to try and take him back into custody. When I knocked on the door, Mike answered it. When I stepped through the door, Mike turned and started walking toward the kitchen. I was right behind him.

Suddenly, he wheeled around and gave me a shoulder butt that knocked me on my butt, and he took off out the front door. As I picked myself up off the kitchen floor, mom looked at me and said, "Aren't you going to chase him?" I suggested that he wasn't going too far, being that he was naked from the waist up. I told her I'd be back in the morning.

I was back at the house early the next morning. I was told that Mike was still sleeping. I climbed the steps quietly, and at the top, got on my knees to peak around the corner into his bedroom. I thought he might be ready for me, and I had no intention of being hit again or losing him again.

Mike was asleep on his stomach. I approached him with my handcuffs open, tapped him on the shoulder and, when he turned over, I grabbed a wrist and threw the cuffs on him. I threw a sweater or something over his shoulders and helped him get his jeans, socks and shoes on. Mom got a jacket, and we threw that over his shoulders. There was no way I was going to take those cuffs off!

As I was driving Mike to the jail, I began to think about my placement recommendations. I was beginning to consider the possibility that the turmoil I'd seen at the house was normal for him, and maybe home offered the best hope for success for him.

While Mike was being held at the Reception Center yet again, mom and I got together to talk about what to do with him. I told her I would be willing to recommend he come home after another institution program, if she would agree to work with me in terms of seeing to it that he abided by the rules, e.g., a curfew, school, etc.

She also told me that she was willing to work with me and that, if Mike were to take off again, she would contact me so I could attempt to take him into custody. She also told me that she would be willing to do all of this on one condition. She was willing to work with me only. She said that if I ever showed up with the police, she would shoot the police officers and me. I agreed, but it wasn't a promise I should have made, and I knew it

One day, I stopped at the house to see Mike. When I got out of my car, I saw Mike's older brother, Steve, one of Mich's parolees, sitting on a Harley-Davidson that was parked on the front porch. He was holding a shotgun on me and sipping out of a pint bottle of liquor. He was very angry and very drunk. For the second time in my young life, I found myself standing on the wrong side of a firearm. He was rambling and threatening to shoot me, but it became clear that it was Mike he was really mad at. And the reason? Mike and Steve's wife had run off together!

We were kind of at a stalemate. Steve was still pointing the shotgun at me, and I was still standing in the middle of the front yard. Where are the cops when you need them? I decided to do what I had done once before at the Teen Center—turn my back on him. That surprised him and seemed to make him even angrier, but I told him that if he was going to shoot, I didn't want there to be any doubt about what had happened. He kept yelling at me to "Turn around!" Eventually, I heard him start the engine of his Harley, roll right down the steps of the porch, across the lawn and west on Fourth Street.

I got in my car and went directly to the Police Dept. I found the two guys I worked most often with in the Juvenile Aid Bureau, Dave Morris and Jim Foucault, told them what happened and asked them what they thought we should do.

Their answer? "Sit down and have a cup of coffee. We'll wait a while and then go pick up the pieces." Several hours later, the PD called and told me they had found Mike and his sister-in-law in a motel in West Duluth. Steve never did find them.

The sum of my experience with this family was that it was totally lacking in any values that I would have been familiar with. This family taught me that my concept of the word, "normal," was not always going to be in sync with that of others, and I was going to have to be careful not to be too judgmental. Mike didn't seem to work real well anywhere when it came to remaining law-abiding, attending school, etc., but he did best when he was home. Another lesson learned.

Mike was one of the last kids I saw before I moved to Southern Minnesota during the summer of 1970. I remember telling him that it hadn't been fun chasing him around for the past year and a half. His reply was, "Yeah, but it sure was fun running from you!"

About two years after I moved to Southern Minnesota, Mich called and told me that the Duluth Police Department called and said they wanted to talk to me. I called Foucault and Morris at the Juvenile Aid Bureau. I jokingly asked them what the heck they could want with me two years after I'd left town. They said they had Mike in custody, and he was telling them I was his parole officer. That was just like Mike.

Charlie's Story

One day, I was sitting in my office, and I couldn't help but hear Fred, my office mate, dictating a Pre-Parole Report. He was recommending that a 15-year-old who was the subject of the report, be continued at the institution rather than be released. This was the second time he had recommended the kid be continued. That meant a third six month stretch, and that was a long time for a 15-year-old to be in an institution in those days. But what really bothered me was that in all that time, he hadn't driven the forty or fifty miles to even meet the kid.

I questioned him about the kid, whose name was Charlie. He got irritated when I asked him how he could recommend a continuance without even having met the kid. He got so irritated that he told me I could have the kid. We both went into Pete's office and talked to him about it, and within a few minutes, the paperwork had been done and I had been assigned one of the most interesting kids I've ever known.

The first thing I did was to make arrangements to meet Charlie at St. Croix Camp. What I found myself looking at when I got to the institution, was a hybrid combination of the Charmin Baby and Dennis the Menace. He had curly, blonde hair and blue eyes, was 5' ½" tall, and weighed eighty pounds. Don't ask me why I remember those statistics because I don't have a clue.

By the time I left the facility, I had decided that it was time to give Charlie another chance at home. When I stopped by the home to meet Charlie's mom, I found a woman who looked as if she'd been "rode hard and put away wet." She looked tired, both physically and emotionally, and it would have surprised me if she could keep up with her son, if my first impression of him was any indication. But the plan for Charlie always was for him to return to his mother's home, so we agreed to give it a try.

Now, Charlie had a little history that strongly suggested that he was going to be a very interesting kid to work with. For example, his reputation included being one of Duluth's most active drug users. At this point in my short career, I was inexperienced enough in working with delinquents in general, but I definitely didn't know anything about drugs. But Charlie was going to prove to be a good teacher about drugs, and about adolescent behavior in general.

In time, I was to find out that when Charlie was feeling like I was ignoring him, or I was just too busy to spend much time with him, he was known to stand in the middle of the intersection of Lake Avenue and Superior Street and yell, "Acid for sale!"

What would that accomplish, you ask? Well, it usually resulted in three or four squad cars descending on him and wrapping him up for the short trip to jail, and a phone call to his parole officer. And if you're asking, "Why didn't you just leave him there for a while?" Well, here's why.

Exposing the St. Louis County Jail staff to Charlie was like exposing them to a flu virus. They told me that they would not lock him up if they ever found him to have no drugs on his body. I would have to come to the jail and search him myself. They were that sure Charlie had been born with a stash on his body.

The police once picked Charlie up and brought him to the jail. They took him to an interview room where they strip-searched him. They found nothing, so they called me.

I went to the jail, and staff pointed me in the direction of an interview room. I walked in, and Charlie stood before me wearing nothing but a smile. I picked up his clothing and checked the linings, pockets, collars and anything else I could think of that he might use to hide drugs. He was still smiling, so I was pretty sure there was something to be found.

I told Charlie to stand up, and I searched his hair, armpits, even between his legs. Nothing. The smile on his face told me he was hiding something, and then it dawned on me. I told him to bend over. The smile disappeared immediately. He refused to bend over, and I told him to bend over or I'd bend him over. When he did, I saw a string. I gave it a not too gentle pull, and out came a balloon containing "acid tabs" (LSD). I dropped the balloon on the floor and told staff they could now lock him up.

Charlie liked to have fun, but he had little use for school or work. When he turned sixteen, I decided not to fight the school problem, but I did tell him he had to find a job. Of course, he tested my patience, but when I told him to find a job or I'd return him to the Reception Center, he looked at me like he might have gotten the point. When he walked out of the office, I was hoping he wouldn't force my hand.

At the end of the day, I took the elevator down to Superior St.

and started to walk the block to my car. As it was rush hour, there were hundreds of people on the street. I found myself at the corner waiting for a traffic light. As I stood there, I looked to my left and saw a familiar form wearing a pair of metallic sunglasses and holding a cup in his hand. I walked over to him and slowly lifted the glasses from his nose. The cup was stuffed with pencils (I wonder where he stole them) and he had about ten dollars in change. I asked him what the heck he thought he was doing. He said, "Working! You told me to get a job, didn't you?"

I said, "Yeah, but I didn't mean panhandling!" I was too tired to discuss it. I put the glasses back on his face and went home. I also told him to have his butt in the office the next morning.

In January of 1970, Charlie absconded from supervision. He was, therefore, in violation of his parole, and the appropriate warrants were issued. He had a few days head start on my warrants, as mom didn't even bother to let me know he was gone. By cornering a few of his friends, I found out that his plan was to head east, but not eastern Duluth. The East Coast! In a day or so, I found out he had been in Quincy, Illinois, and the next thing I knew, I found out he was in Boston. As I was to discover later, when he got to Boston, he cased an elderly lady's home for a while. When he was satisfied that she was living alone, he sat on her front steps and cried until she came out and found him. She undoubtedly thought he was a few years younger than he was, felt all sorts of sorry for him, and took him in. Over a period of a few days, she bought him some new clothes, fed him, etc. When he was no longer tired, hungry or cold, he sneaked out a window and continued his journey.

He headed west and somehow got himself hired as a "band boy," whatever that was, for an internationally known rock band of the time. I remember contacting them by phone, and telling them what I thought of their harboring a runaway juvenile.

In March, 1970, law enforcement finally managed to catch up with Charlie at the University of Arizona, Tucson. He was residing in one of the male dorms and was functioning as a go-fer, or maid. There were things in Charlie's history that suggested that he was capable of doing other personal favors, and that always concerned me when he was on run.

Actually, Pete took the phone call from Tucson authorities that

Charlie was in custody. When he got off the phone, he called me into his office and told me to make the arrangements to go to Tucson. I was elated. How many of us get the opportunity to go to Tucson in March?

There was a plane leaving for Arizona in a few hours, so I got ready and was about to leave the office and drive to the airport when Pete's phone rang. Suddenly, I heard him calling for me, and I knew, I just KNEW, that my trip was going to be cancelled.

I walked into Pete's office, and he told me that he'd just spoken to Tai, the purse strings department of the DOC, and she told him to tell me that she was going to send the Transportation Unit of the DOC instead. Pete told me to call the Unit and give them some background information on Charlie.

When I called, they did a certain amount of teasing about my getting screwed out of a trip to Tucson. I told them that when Charlie saw them instead of me, they were going to wish I had made the trip. They said they'd call when they got him to the Reception Center. All afternoon, I fantasized about throwing darts at a picture of Tai.

When the Transportation Unit folks finally did call, I wound up having the last laugh. They told me they'd never go anywhere ever again to get a kid of mine. I asked what happened. They said Charlie started kicking and swearing as soon as he saw them, and he kicked and screamed all the way home. I told them that I was very sorry to hear that one of my parolees caused them so much trouble, and I'd have a good long talk with him about it. Then I hung up and fell out of my chair laughing.

A few days later, I got a call from Charlie, who was very upset because institution staff was insisting that he have his long hair cut. There was a rule against long hair, and after three months of being on the run, I can only imagine how long it was. I told him that, if the rules said he had to have his hair cut, then he was going to have his hair cut. Then I made a mistake. He asked me if I would be okay with his keeping his long hair if he could get staff to change their minds. I told him that if he could get them to change their minds, it was fine with me. Not very smart of me, but I never even considered the possibility that this kid was manipulative enough to get a bunch of professionals to change policy.

I don't remember ever seeing Charlie again, as I graduated a few months later, and he was still in the institution. I kept track of him over the years, and every rumor I got indicated that he had made a marginal adjustment as an adult.

I want to tell one more story about Charlie before we leave him, or he leaves us to history. It's not a long story or an important story; it's just another story about this amazingly unique and fun kid.

Charlie called me at the office one day. He was very excited, as he usually was. He said he was calling to give me some good news, that news being that he had quit using LSD. I told him that was great news, but I wondered why. He said he'd found something much better. When I asked him what it was, I was almost afraid to hear. He said, "Grape Kool-Aid!" I asked him what he did with grape Kool-Aid. He said, "Shoot it (in a vein)!" I'm sure the only thing that would get him high would have been the sugar, and the grape had nothing to do with it whatsoever. But that was Charlie.

I ran into a friend of Charlie's, a few years ago, and I asked him how Charlie was doing. He told me that Charlie had disappeared in the Alaska wilderness while working as a guide. It was a lonely end for an unusual but amazing kid.

More on Mich

I've already mentioned some of the fun that Mich and I had as partners and friends, but it's worth taking more time to show you why working with this man was so much fun and such an education.

One summer night, he asked me if I would help him corral one of his runaways. I had nothing better to do than homework, so I agreed. We had supper and developed a game plan.

After supper, we headed for the kid's neighborhood in Duluth's West End. A short distance from the kid's house, we passed a home that seemed to be hosting a hell of a party. Mich and I pulled up to the curb. He told me that this party was just the sort of thing his kid would attend. We found a phone and called the Juvenile Aid Bureau and asked for backup.

Mich and I and two officers went to the front door, and two uniforms went to cover the back. We had no warrant, but we really only meant to snoop.

We knocked on the door, and someone answered and invited us into a small porch. As we were talking, I noticed that we were able to see into a living room. Beyond that was what appeared to be a bedroom with a mattress sitting in the middle of the floor.

As we were standing there talking to the young man who let us in, someone tapped me on the shoulder. When I turned around, I found a young man and a young woman, both stark naked, and the man sprouting an erection. He looked at me, seemingly unconcerned, and said, "Excuse me." As I stood there with my tongue mopping the floor, I tapped one of the officers on the shoulder. He, the second officer and Mich all turned, locked eyes on the couple for a moment; then we all looked at each other, and we began to part like the Red Sea, if you know what I mean. The couple walked through the path we formed, through the living room and into the bedroom, where they simply flopped on the mattress and started to...well, you know. We all looked at each other, shrugged our shoulders, turned, and left.

Besides his Duluth cases, Mich also covered the Eveleth-Virginia-Mountain Iron side of the Iron Range. I never got involved in any of his cases, except for an occasional chase. But I frequently went to the Range with him to observe how he worked with his cases, the communities, and law enforcement agencies. I learned that you had to work at developing good professional relationships.

Where the Virginia, Eveleth and Mountain Iron Police Departments were concerned, there had developed a long-standing ritual, long before I dawned on the scene. On each and every trip to the Range, Mich contacted all three PDs, and those officers on duty all converged on the Coates Hotel in Virginia, where the coffee was on Mich. I don't ever remember visiting the Range without paying deference to that ritual. I found that ritual to be extremely helpful in helping me develop positive relationships with people I would need to have good relationships with, including these three agencies.

The Loss of an 11-Year Old Boy

I want to mention another "first," one that served to keep me in touch with the serious nature of this work. I had been assigned an 11-year boy. As usual, he was at the Reception Center when I got the case. I was saddened at the age of the kid and wondered how one so young could already have strained the county probation system to the point of commitment to the Commissioner of Corrections. It should be stated that at the time, the law more or less required that all treatment options at the county level be exhausted before a commitment to the Commissioner of Corrections could be made.

I don't even remember this kid's crime. What I do remember, and will never forget, is getting a phone call from the Reception Center informing me that the boy had hanged himself with his own shoelaces. A staff person had forgotten to take them from his shoes. This was the first of thirteen youngsters I would lose over the next forty years.

Employing Offenders

Back in those days, I don't ever remember anybody's getting out of the Reformatory unless he had a job to go out to. Being that it was just a little hard to apply and interview for a job while in prison, it usually meant the job had to be found for the client by the parole officer. And potential employers didn't flock to your doors to make any job offers either.

But one Duluth company came pretty close to doing just that. That company was Jeno's, Inc. The owner and president was one Jeno Paulucci. His chief assistant was Lee Vann. Jeno had a local reputation for taking on all sorts of marginal employees, usually at minimum wage, but he was a Godsend to our office, because he was always willing to put our people to work. All we had to do was call Lee Vann and tell him a job was needed for a new releasee. His answer was always, "Send him down."

I once asked him, "Don't you want to know what the guy did?"

His answer was, "No, just send him down."

I asked him the question because this particular young man's forte was to walk the streets of Duluth and grab women in the area of the crotch. Obviously, the word, "liability" hadn't entered my mind. Anyway, this guy became a very happy, productive employee, until he joined the navy.

Yet today, the lack of sufficient employment possibilities continues to hamper the possible success of today's correctional releasees. Sufficient housing is a closely related problem. Remember, Mr. and Mrs. Taxpayer, that one out of every thirty American adults eighteen years of age and older is currently incarcerated or on some form of supervised release. We'll either continue to pay for incarceration, or we can shift our attention to helping these people acquire the essentials needed by everyone.

Another Problem in My Own Neighborhood

One spring morning, I received a phone call from the Principal of one of Duluth's grade schools, Lowell Elementary. Agnes Gallagher was my Principal at Emerson Elementary. She said she was having a problem she hoped I could help her with. When I asked her what the problem was, she told me that she thought about eighty percent of the kids in her school were drunk. It was approximately 9:00 am! Of course, I considered for a moment that she was drunk. But I knew her much better than that.

I went to the school and, when I walked in the door, what I witnessed made me feel like I was walking around inside an old pinball machine. Six, seven, eight-year-old kids were literally bouncing off the walls.

I checked in at the Principal's Office and sat with her a while, trying to figure out what was happening. How could this many kids be this drunk at 9:00 am? Where could they all congregate to do their drinking, and where the hell would they get the booze?

After giving it a lot of thought, and knowing that the liquor stores weren't even open yet, I was trying to think of what else these kids could have gotten into between home and school, that would explain what we were seeing. And then it dawned on me. Extract! And I had a damned good idea where they got it before school. I told Miss Gallagher that I had an idea and that I'd be back shortly.

I walked across Central Entrance to the local community market, and I spoke to the owner, with whom I'd spoken on several occasions during my summer with the Sewer Rats. They had managed to squeeze cigarettes from the store clerks at times. I asked him if he'd sold any extract to a bunch of young kids, that morning, and he admitted that he had, adding that he thought it was a little strange for that many kids to want extract. I told him that a large number of the kids at the school across the street were very drunk. He was shocked and promised he'd never sell extract to the kids again. I walked back across the street and told Agnes that the mystery had been solved.

Then I left her to figure out how she was going to handle her school full of mini-alcoholics.

Teenage Burglars

One night, while I was home studying, (yeah, I still did that occasionally) I got a phone call from a kid who refused to identify himself. He told me that he was a member of a teenage burglary ring, but he wanted to get out. He told me that he was in possession of some stolen property and that he wanted to give it up to me, but of course, he wanted to give it to me on the condition of anonymity. I told him I wasn't going to take hot property off his hands and turn it over to the police for him. Then he told me that he had thirty keys. I asked him what the keys were to, and he said, "Just about every school in the city and the Barnes-Ames Building, a building used for storing school equipment." That made me reconsider my decision, but I told him I wanted to think about it and that he should call me at the office the next day.

The following day, I talked to Mich about the call from the teenage burglar. He asked me what I thought I should do. I told him that if what the kid said was true, just about all of the equipment owned by the school system was in jeopardy. I was inclined to accept the kid's offer. Mich said he thought I was right.

Eventually the kid called, and we agreed to meet. I don't think I'd make a deal like that again and I don't know Mich's reasons for supporting my rather questionable deal, but the deal had been made.

We met at the agreed upon site, the kid got out of a car, and opened the trunk. In the trunk were a television, a camera, and a few other electronic items. We put the stuff in the trunk of my car. Then I asked for the keys. He produced two key rings containing about 30 keys. It would have been easy to memorize the license plate number and turn it over to the police department when I turned in the stolen items, but I didn't. What I did do is drive directly to the police department and the Juvenile Aid Bureau, where I found both Dave Morris and Jim Foucault. I asked both of them to come out to the car with me. When I opened the trunk door, Dave looked at it and said, "Holy s---! That stuff's stolen!"

We grabbed the stuff and brought it into the office. Then came the questions, the first of which was, "Where the hell did you get this stuff?" They weren't real happy with me when I told them I couldn't tell them. As a matter of fact, they suggested that they might even charge me with burglary. I was betting that they were bluffing, but believe me, this young pup was shaking in my chair.

Bottom line was that they did not arrest me, and I was very happy to get into my car and drive off. On the morning of the following day, I began to notice a familiar car that seemed to be following me everywhere I went. I was concerned about it until I was able to identify it. At some point, I realized that the car was the JAB's unmarked squad. They had been following me, hoping that I would lead them to the kids in the burglary ring.

A couple of days later, I made an institution run, and as I was pulling back into Duluth, I was listening to a newscast on a local radio station. I heard an announcement that a juvenile burglary ring had just been busted in Duluth. The report went on to say that a lot of the stolen items had been found under the porch of one of the teen burglars.

I decided to stop in at the JAB before I went home. Jim and Dave were both there when I walked in. One of them looked at the other and said, "We've been expecting you!" I told them I thought it was kind of pathetic that they didn't give me any credit for the bust. I was kidding, of course. They asked me how I thought they should have explained that a parole agent brought in a load of stolen items, after taking the stuff from the thieves, and then refused to tell the police where he got it. I guess they had a point.

The Tracey Group Homes

Another part of my education was learning that there was going to be times when we just couldn't work with a kid in his own home. To help out in those circumstances, the Department of Corrections licensed a number of group homes. Agents in my office supervised the DOC's homes in Duluth. One day, Glen brought me to the Tom and Donna Tracey home, which, I discovered, was very near my home.

Tom was a custodian at a local high school, and Donna was a housewife and professional mother. They were licensed for ten boys and had two of their own still at home, a teenage girl and a teenage boy. Tom kind of looked like a caveman and had a voice to go with it.

103

Although he could intimidate kids with his voice, he really was a nice guy and was very much into his own kids and the foster kids. Donna, however, was the one that most of us DOC agents dealt with most of the time.

I used to stop at the Tracey home quite often, mainly because I liked them a whole lot, and their home being close to mine helped. I became aware of the fact that Glen did his share of hanging out at the Tracey home. It didn't take long for me to get invitations to get-togethers and parties at the Tracey's. I didn't have a real active social life back in those days, so I gladly accepted a lot of those invitations.

One of those invitations was to a New Year's Eve party, 1969. Tom and Donna, their adult children, Glen and his wife and I were there. Somebody had what was referred to as an adult Monopoly game with a few twists. When you threw the dice and moved your piece around the board, the instructions on the cards that were drawn might read, "Light up." If your next three moves resulted in drawing cards, all of which read, "Light up," that meant you had four cigarettes hanging from your mouth. Other cards read, "Take a drink." The next few cards you drew might also read, "Take a drink." Well, I think you get the picture. About halfway through the game, the kids, including the foster kids, were making the drinks and probably a few for themselves as well.

I must have passed out. When I woke up, I had a piece of cold chicken in my mouth. If Pete had found out about this party, Glen and I would probably both have been fired, or at the very least, hung by the thumbs.

I want to mention an incident that I heard about one afternoon at Tom and Donna's, that made Tom very angry and taught me something about government bureaucracy. I was sitting at the kitchen table one afternoon when the back door burst open, and a very angry Tom walked in the kitchen. Donna asked him why he was so angry. Tom related that when he got to work that morning, a delivery truck delivered eight hundred pounds of government packaged oatmeal. That school had no meal programs, so the oatmeal was useless to that particular school. Tom's supervisor told him to "Burn it and keep your mouth shut!" Tom threw a lot of it in the trunk of his car and brought it home. He was furious, thinking about how many other schools in the country might have been getting similar deliveries.

Tom and Donna had a son and daughter-in-law, Roy and Marla, who were seriously considering becoming a teen male group home for the state also. Their home was in the process of being built, so they were temporarily living in the basement. It passed the state conditions for one kid. I targeted them for the first kid I needed to place in a foster home.

You might not remember this, but I was still in school at this time, or, at least, I was paying tuition. It seemed like I was never at school, but then, I was never looking to graduate summa cum loud-mouth anyway. As a matter of fact, I cut one class 48 out of 50 times. That might be a record. Actually, I was doing much better scholastically, probably because the classes in my majors were much more interesting and there was less reading. The fact that I had a goal after graduation also helped.

I intended to continue in corrections. All was looking good. But there was still to be a learning experience or two before I left the hallowed halls of UMD.

A Case of Mistaken Identity

During my fifth year at UMD, Duluth found itself very busy trying to figure out the intentions of a new resident who just happened to be a declared atheist. This guy went around challenging anything that smacked of religion, and went very public with his objections.

Unfortunately, one of my psychology professors had the same last name as this atheist. This professor, Dr. Kenneth DeYoung, was never going to win a popularity contest among the students, nor were his classes easy, nor in my opinion, interesting. In other words, he taught the driest courses, was usually kind of ornery, and was always tough. Put another way, he wasn't well liked.

In time, Dr. DeYoung's family became confused with that of the atheist. His kids had been assaulted on their way home from school. As the number and intensity of these incidents increased, he began to change, and I don't mean for the better. For example, he wouldn't allow a student to question a marked wrong answer on a test, wouldn't be questioned in any way, and got more and more aloof.

Eventually a lot of the psychology students became angry and frustrated, and a movement started to have him removed from the department. They decided to circulate a petition among the students in the department. The seniors especially believed they'd have to get my signature on the petition as the senior student in the department.

One morning, several students approached me and asked me to sign the petition. I refused to sign, telling them that they looked like a bunch of vultures circling a dying animal. I wouldn't be a part of trying to take advantage of the man's personal problems in order to get rid of him. They weren't very happy with me.

Several days later, I received a message from Dr. DeYoung asking that I come to his office. I made the appointment, went to the office, knocked on the door, and heard him tell me to come in. When I walked in, he had his back turned to me and said absolutely nothing. I sat down in a chair until he turned around.

When he turned, he said," I heard there's a petition circulating concerning me." I told him the story was true. He also told me that he'd heard that I refused to sign the petition, and he wanted to know why I had refused.

I said, "Wrong reason."

He looked at me for a few seconds and said, "Thank you."

Then he turned his back to me, and I got up and left. I don't think another word was exchanged between the two of us for the rest of the year. I think Dr. DeYoung resigned from the department at the end of the 1971 school year.

I'd been assigned another Native American youngster by the name of Terry. Terry was not the quiet kid that most people describe when talking about Native American kids. As a matter of fact, I don't ever remember having a Native American client who was quiet. Terry was being raised by his grandparents in West Duluth, and they were two people I really learned to enjoy visiting. I felt sorry for them because they simply didn't understand their rebellious grandson, but they loved him very much.

Terry ran away from the Reception Center, and several hours later, he called me at the office. He told me that he was at his grandparents' home. I told him I'd come out to the house and pick him up. He told me not to, that he just wanted to visit his grandparents for a while, and then he'd hitchhike back to Lino Lakes. I thought about it for a moment, and I told myself I would be covering my butt if I went out to the house or sent the police, but I decided not to. I told him I'd call the Reception Center that evening and make sure he got back. He promised he'd be there.

For some reason, I didn't call that night, but I did call the next morning. I spoke to Frank Wood, who eventually became Commissioner of Corrections. I asked him if Terry had turned himself in the previous night. He started to laugh.

I told him to "Shut up and check."

I heard him put the phone down, still laughing as he walked away. Then there was silence, and he picked up the phone again. He said, "Well I'll be a son of a bitch, he turned himself in at 9:00 p.m. last night!"

I said, "Thanks, Frank" and hung up. I sat there for a few minutes and just smiled.

There were three other kids who kept me very busy and who taught me a lot during my year and a half in the Duluth office of the DOC. One of these was 14-year-old Mike.

Mike's parents were Dave and Marge. The family lived in the Lakeside community at the Eastern end of Duluth. As you can see, our case assignments were not made based on geography.

Mike was a handsome kid who looked a few years older than his fourteen years. His parents were good people, and they both made very good coffee. I know; I was at the house in the middle of the night on more than one occasion!

I believe that I had recommended that Mike be returned to his home on probation, e.g., be released directly from the Reception Center without being placed in an institutional program. I had been working with Mike's parents to set some rules of probation that would, hopefully, keep him in line when he got home.

Mike's hearing was scheduled, my report and recommendation was in the hands of the paroling authority, the Youth Conservation Commission) and all we could do was wait to be notified of their decision.

On the morning of the hearing, I received a phone call from caseworker, Eloise Kapsy, who told me that she was no longer going to support my recommendation for probation. She said that Mike had walked away from the facility earlier that morning.

"Walked away?" I asked. I told her that didn't make sense and asked her to put Mike on the phone.

When he got on the phone, I asked him what the heck he thought he was doing. He said he was "afraid to come home to all the girls." I told him that I should have his problem. I also told him that he was coming home whether he liked it or not. I promised him I'd have a solution to his problem when he got home.

I got Eloise back on the phone and tried to convince her to continue to back the recommendation for probation. After some discussion, she agreed. After all, he was going to have to come home at some point—girls or no girls. By lunchtime, I had received the call. Mike had been granted probation and would be arriving in Duluth on a Greyhound bus late that afternoon.

The Greyhound Bus Depot was all of a half block from the office and a block from my car, so picking him up and taking him home wasn't going to take a lot of extra time. When the bus pulled into the depot, Mike got out and walked up to me. I reached into my pocket and pulled out a paper punch and paddle lock and tossed them to him. He got the message. I told him that, short of a murder charge, he was not going back to the institution, so he'd better make up his mind that he was going to make it at home.

I took Mike home and discussed the rules with him and his parents. I emphasized that if he absconded from home, school, or was late for curfew, he might find himself being the guest of honor at the St. Louis County Jail for a weekend.

Of course, I had to be tested. That's what they make teenagers for! For several weeks, Mike put my threats to the test, and in a way, I think he won, because I don't ever remember throwing this kid in jail. The reason I probably never threw him in jail was because he was only fourteen years old. Maybe I thought we could break him by other means, I don't know. But he did indeed test my and his parents' patience!

For several Friday nights in succession, Mike's parents notified me that he was out after curfew, and I'd hop in my car and raid a party at the home of one of his friends and drag his butt home. That's why I know Dave and Marge both made great coffee, because we had more than one butt-chewing session with Mike in the middle of the night.

Apparently there came a time when Mike decided he was being hassled more than he wanted to be, so he finally settled down. I never did jail him, and he never even came close to being returned to the

Reception Center. In time, he made a very adequate adjustment to life on the outside. I was to have one more indirect contact with Mike some fifteen years later.

There was another family I was "blessed" to have on my caseload that had some special features about it. First of all, there were nineteen kids in the family, the first three being wards of the Department of Corrections. When I first came into contact with the family, each of these three kids had a different parole agent. That made for a mess because we were always getting, "Well, Mr. So-And-So doesn't do that," or "wouldn't do that."

I suggested to Pete that he assign all three to the same agent so there'd only be one value system operating in the house. Naturally, and much to the eternal joy of the other two agents, Pete assigned me to this family. And what a family! Boy, some people just don't know when to keep their mouths shut.

I walked in the house one day just in time to witness mother bending over, and literally pulling the rug out from under dad. He got up and ran upstairs. She took off after him, and I took off after her. When I got upstairs, I discovered that he and she didn't even occupy the same bedroom, and that his bedroom door had a deadbolt lock on it. I don't think it was to protect himself from the kids, but then, maybe it was. On another occasion, I walked in the house just in time to watch the Mrs. chasing dad up the stairs with a broom.

Periodically, kids who were institutionalized were allowed short home visits, especially when it was close to their being granted a parole. This gave the kid, the family, and the parole officer a chance to lay down some pre-release ground rules, to re-establish contact with the school, etc.

The normal situation at lunchtime around the office was for Mich, "George" and I to go one way and for the rest of the office crew to go another, except for Irene ("the Grouch"), who went her own way. On one occasion though, we all found ourselves together at a Chinese restaurant right across the street from the office.

During the lunch, I received a phone call from the police department. It was an urgent request for me to get my tail out to this kid's home. David was home for a visit and was refusing to go back. I was told that mom was holding six officers at bay and was refusing to turn him over to the officers.

I bolted from my chair and ran the block to my car. I had never seen a gun in this home, but somehow I could see mom with one in her hand. I was really concerned about "Ma Barker" hurting someone. When I arrived at the house, I saw three squad cars and witnessed six police officers, including two juvenile officers, being held at bay by mom and her broom! I walked over to the juvenile officers to find out what was happening. They asked me what I wanted them to do. My suggestion was, "Why don't you just shoot her?"

Anyway, after soothing mom's feathers for a while, she agreed to turn David over to me. I turned him over to the juvenile officers who locked him up until I could write a report and make arrangements to get him back to the Reception Center.

As you can tell, I did eventually kind of strike out on my own where supervising a caseload was concerned. Pete seemed to trust me, and I did more and more transporting of parole violators and other things on my own, but not always.

Mich and I once found ourselves needing to transport three YOs (Youthful Offenders, 18-21 year olds) back to the Reception Center at Lino Lakes, a distance of some 80-90 miles. We went to the jail and had the guys sprung from their cells to get prepped for the journey, which meant being cuffed. For some reason, Mich decided they didn't need to be cuffed, something I was a little uncomfortable with and something, I'm sure, would never be done today.

We got them in the back seat of the car and started heading out of town. Before we even got out of town, Mich turned to me and said, "I'm bored."

My first reaction was to say, "Give me your TS (tough shit) card, and I'll punch it for you."

Before I could say anything, he said, "Take off your cuffs and throw them in the back." Then he turned to the guys in the back, who were every bit as confused as I was, and told them, "When we get stopped, put those on." They just looked at each other.

We headed down the highway, all of us feeling like Mich was manicuring his toenails in the fan. We were slithering down the highway at a paltry 90 mph and better. It didn't take long before a highway patrol car was on our tail. As instructed, the guys in the back put the cuffs on. Mich pulled the car over and rolled down the window. The officer approached, stuck his head in the window and looked into the back seat. When he saw the three guys in handcuffs, he looked at Mich and said, "Get the hell out of here." This scenario was repeated three more times before we got to Lino Lakes. Never a dull moment! The entire trip couldn't have taken us much more than an hour.

As I've already mentioned, there were times when we got, well, bored, and we always tried to figure out something stimulating to do. That often meant trying to chase down a runaway. On occasions that we were lucky enough to locate one, it usually meant having to take the kid back to the Reception Center as a parole violator.

One beautiful morning, Mich and I had to do just that. We drove to the jail, trussed two kids up in bright, shiny handcuffs, and walked them out the door. Mich had his boy by the left arm, and I had a grip on my boy's right arm.

When the heavy steel door closed behind us, both boys broke from our grips and ran down the street in opposite directions. I looked at Mich and said, "Now what do we do?"

He responded with, "Hmmm—nine o'clock. Time for breakfast. How about Perkins?"

But catching runaways could be a hazardous undertaking. Up to this point, I had been shoulder-butted and knocked on my butt and had been held at bay by a drunk on a motorcycle holding a shotgun.

One day, Mich and I found ourselves in a foot chase of one of his guys. We chased him right into a garage. There we were, standing in the middle of a driveway, yelling at the kid through a closed door. Suddenly, instead of the kid coming out the door, a blast from a shotgun came out the window. Mich and I both did what came naturally. We hit the dirt, or the concrete, to be more accurate.

As we lay there looking at each other from our bellies, I thought about how sensitive I'd been about being the shortest guy in the entire office. But at that moment, it dawned on me that in this circumstance, I was damned glad that I was thirteen inches shorter than Mich. As he was to tell me later, "Some guys will try things with me that they'd never even consider pulling on you, because of your size." Another important lesson learned. I never had another physical confrontation with a client for the next 36 years.

"Pissquick"

Another one of my more enjoyable clients was Patrick, or Pissquick, as I used to call him. I don't remember how I came into contact with Pat, but he turned out to be one of those kids who grew on me like mold. Maybe it was because his parents were so difficult for both of us to deal with. Maybe they were just tired of Pat's shenanigans. You see, Pat had two main problems. First, he didn't have much use for school, and secondly, he liked to drink.

One night in the middle of the night, I got a phone call from Pat asking me to come and get him out of the house. A real war was taking place between Pat and his parents, as I could hear them yelling in the background. I wasn't terribly excited about removing this kid from his home in the middle of a snowstorm, especially since I had no place to put him except in jail, and I really didn't think I was going to be inclined to do that.

When I got to the house, I found that everyone had an attitude. Pat's parents seemed almost excited about Pat's being removed from the house and had a suitcase packed for him. We left quickly, and there we were, driving through downtown Duluth toward I didn't know where, in the middle of the night, and in the middle of a snowstorm.

And then I had an idea. I thought of Roy and Marla Tracey, the son and daughter-in-law of Tom and Donna Tracey, the group home parents at whose home I spent so much time. I remembered that Roy and Marla were considering becoming foster parents for the Department of Corrections, and their home was close to mine.

When I thought about it, I thought Roy and Marla would be just the right foster parents for Pat. So I headed for the house. I thought to myself: *"Ah, what the hell, I'll either scare them into getting licensed or I'll scare them out of getting licensed!"*

When I pulled into the driveway, Pat and I got out of the car and plodded through the snow and up to the front door. I made sure that Pat had his suitcase. I knocked on the door, and in a minute or two, the door opened and there stood Roy, still very much asleep (as I had been hoping.) It was a good thing he was. I kind of shoved Pat in the door, looked at Roy and said, "You're now the proud foster parent of a sixteen year old. His name is Pat. I'll talk to you in the morning!" I grabbed the doorknob, shut the door and ran for the car like my pants were on fire.

I called Roy and Marla from the office the next day and sort of apologized for the rather crude way of asking them for their help, and I told them about the circumstances of Pat's removal from his home. We made an appointment for me to stop at the house on the way home and talk to them and Pat and discuss plans for getting Pat enrolled at Hermantown High School, rules of behavior, Roy's and Marla's expectations, a clothing allowance, etc. Oh, did I forget to mention that Roy and Marla agreed to keep Pat? I was really hoping that this placement would work out, as I was concerned that Marla was pregnant with their first child. A brat like Pat could add more stress to a family than it could handle, but I guess I had to trust that they would make that decision themselves.

By this time in my short career, I had learned that in most cases, there was a honeymoon period, which typically lasted from several minutes to several weeks after yanking a kid from the family home and placing him in foster care. The honeymoon period usually ended when the kid discovered that the foster parents' rules were usually tougher than those of their parents. Was that a plan or what? It was the same for Pat, and his main problems, as I've said, were attending school and drinking.

But where school was concerned, Pat was to meet his match. His match was in the form of one Principal Ray Wero. Pat treaded softly for the first few weeks, both at home and at school, probably testing me to find out how much it was going to take for me to yank him from foster care and return him to the Reception Center, or for Roy and Marla to get tired of his shenanigans, tie the sidewalk to his butt and throw him out. So the honeymoon ended, and "Pat the Brat" showed himself.

At the meeting at Roy and Marla's the day after placement, I had made it clear to Patrick that anytime he was late to school, skipped school, or was a discipline problem at school, he would spend the very next weekend in jail. Period! Of course, I had to be tested.

One day, I checked with the school and found out that Pat was missing. I checked with Marla and found out that he had returned home on the school bus as usual, and at the usual time. What he neglected to tell them was that he hadn't been to school in between. I went to the house, threw my handcuffs on him and drove him to the St.

Louis County Jail. When I turned him over to the jailers, I told him to have a nice weekend and that I would spend the weekend trying to figure out whether or not he was worth a trip to the Reception Center on Monday morning. He was not real happy!

As they were taking him away, I was thinking of ways to really apply the pressure on him to get his stuff together. Then I had an idea. I asked Lud, the jailer and part-time sadist, what was on the menu for the weekend.

He said, "Are you kidding? Bologna sandwiches and jailhouse stew, as usual." I told him that I wanted Pat to get stew for every meal until Monday morning.

Pat was also a kid who liked to take two or three showers every day. I told Lud I didn't want Pat to have any showers, and I'd be back at 7:00 a.m. Monday morning to pick him up. Lud was more than happy to comply with my request.

I was worried about Pat all weekend because I really didn't like locking kids up in jails. But my philosophy was, "Better two days in jail than six months in an institution." Anyway, I was at the jail at 7:00 am Monday morning and found Patrick slumped over in a chair, looking like he'd just chased a fart through a keg of nails. He was slumped over in his chair, had greasy hair, and looked like he could slither right out of his own skin. He looked great!

I looked at him and told him that it was an absolutely beautiful day out there, a perfect day for a ride to the Reception Center. He turned to me and asked if I was going to take him back. I told him that that was my intention unless he could give me a damned good reason why I shouldn't. He apologized and promised to get his act together in school. I decided to drag the discomfort out a little longer by not telling him where we were heading until we got to the car.

I drove him home, told him to get in the shower, and get ready for school. He didn't hesitate for a second. A half hour and a full tank of water later, I took him to school, hoping that the experience would stay with him for at least the rest of the day.

Eventually, of course, Pat forgot the lesson. One morning, I received a phone call from Ray Wero. He told me that Pat was screwing around in school again and was encouraging other kids to follow his lead. I told Ray, whom I hadn't met personally yet, to tie the sidewalk to Pat's back and throw him out.

His answer was, "Make me."

I was surprised and told him that I was on my way to the school. He asked me if I was going to stay for lunch. I told him I hadn't thought about it. He said, "Well, if you do, bring your own stomach pump. We don't provide them." Then he hung up on me.

I went to school and walked into the main office. I looked at Ray's personal office door, and it had a piece of wood screwed to it with the word, "Warden" burned on it. I knew immediately that this was going to be a very interesting first meeting.

I knocked on the door and was told to come in. There stood a short, stocky Principal Wero standing over Patrick, who was sitting in a chair. Ray told me to have a seat, so I took a chair right across the room from Pat.

Ray stood over him and said, "Now Patrick, you've been in my school for a few months, and you've been doing nothing but screwin' off, and it's gonna stop! Do you know why it's gonna stop?"

Then Pat made the mistake of smiling. Ray grabbed him by the front of his shirt, pulled him right out of the chair, got right in Pat's face and said, "Because if you don't, I'm going to break every bone in your body!" Then he dropped Pat back into his chair. I believe Ray made a believer out of Pat that day, because I don't remember having any more problems with him, at least, as far as school was concerned.

And incidentally, if you think this set up a hate-hate relationship between Patrick and Principal Wero, it didn't. I saw Pissquick and Principal Ray having lunch together in the cafeteria an hour later.

As I mentioned earlier, Pat also liked to drink. One Friday night, Roy called and told me that Pat was gone, and he was pretty sure he was out drinking. He wanted to go out and find him. I drove to the house, hopped in his car, and we began making the circuit. Roy and I must have visited six or eight joints known for not doing a lot of ID checking, and whetting our own whistles at each establishment, of course. After all, searching for Pat was hard work.

Eventually, we staggered to the car and drove home, not having found Patrick. When we got home, the door flew open, and there was a very sober Pat, who looked at us two very drunk adults and said, "Boy, is Marla mad at you!"

Roy looked at Pat and asked, "Why?"

With a grin on his face, he said, "Because she delivered the baby a few hours ago!" Like the chicken I was, I told Roy I'd see him later, got in my car and took off for home with a very guilty conscience.

I was really lucky that I had some energy back in those days, because it wasn't at all unusual that I would get a phone call at 2:00 am from one of the Iron Range police departments, have to get dressed and drive fifty or sixty miles to dig a kid out of a jail, drive him back to Duluth and lock him up, and then get home in time to get ready for school.

On one such occasion, I got a call from the Virginia, Minnesota, Police Department and its Juvenile officer, Larry Cuffy. Larry always gave me a boost of confidence, because he was even shorter than I was. He was holding three of my cases and wanted them out of his jail.

I drove to Virginia and pulled into the police department parking lot. Then I realized I only had one pair of handcuffs, but I remembered that Pete had passed out several pair of new experimental plastic cuffs, which amounted to thin, plastic belts which had to be cut off and then thrown away. I put a few of those in my pocket and went inside to get my fill of "Cuffy bologna."

Larry dug the three kids out of their cells, and I did a quick assessment as to who was going to wear the regular cuffs and who was going to wear the others. After making my decision, I put the kids in the car, making sure that the kid I trussed up best was sitting directly behind me.

A few miles down highway 53, the kids asked me if they could have a cigarette. In those days, Mich and I rarely denied such a request, unless we wanted to make someone uncomfortable. Not something I'd do today, believe me! Even though this may not have been the smartest thing to do, I wasn't dumb enough to be other than wary, so I did keep watching them via the rearview mirror.

During one of those spot checks, I noticed that one of the kids in plastic cuffs was leaning over the other kid wearing the plastic cuffs. He was trying to burn the plastic cuffs off the second kid with his lit cigarette.

I pulled over to the curb and threw the car into park. I jumped out and ran around to the passenger side rear door and yanked both kids from the rear seat. I threw one and then the other against the car and emptied their pockets of cigarettes and lighters, throwing them in the gutter on the side of the highway. Then I turned their belts around so that the buckles were in the back and used two sets of plastic cuffs on each kid, one to secure the hands and the other to secure both to the belt. It looked kind of odd, but it did the trick. I got them to the jail in Duluth with no further problems, got them checked in, and got home just in time to see the sun rise.

The stretch of highway between Duluth and the Range Cities had been the road to and from a lot of laughs for Mich and me. And once in a while, even a *client* furnished us with a good laugh.

Late one night, I received a phone call from the Minnesota State Highway Patrol. They were calling from the St. Louis County Jail and said they had picked up one of my parolees on highway 53, "under suspicious circumstances."

The patrolman told me that my client, who had been released from the prison in St. Cloud, had been involved in a car accident with his girlfriend. Neither of them appeared to have been drinking nor under the influence of drugs of any kind. He said the problem was that they were refusing to say how the accident happened. For that reason and because he was on parole, they decided to take him in and let me take a run at him.

I drove to the jail and found the young man in an interview room with his head down on a table. I asked him if he and his girlfriend were alright. He assured me that they were both fine. I asked him what happened, and he told me that he couldn't tell me. I asked him if that meant that he couldn't remember. He said, "No, I just can't tell you."

I told him that the situation was that, if he gave the officer a satisfactory explanation, he'd probably be released, and he could go home. If he didn't, they'd probably hold him until they could put the accident together themselves.

He looked at me and said, "I can't very well tell them that my girlfriend kind of had her head in my lap, and I lost control of the car!" All I could do was shake my head. He wasn't very happy, so I tried to regain my professional demeanor. I told him that I thought he had a limited number of options and that he should think seriously about telling the officer the story, let him have his laugh and go home, or he could get ready to be a guest of the county for a few days. Reluctantly, he agreed to explain the situation to the highway patrolman.

117

I walked out of the interview room and told the officer that the kid was ready to give him a statement, but I wouldn't go in with a full bladder, if I were him. The jailer and I watched through the interview room window as the patrolman sat down at the table and took the kid's statement, periodically looking at us with a smile on his face.

I guess there's no explaining where a guy comes up with some ideas to help him with his work, and there is no picture of me beside the word "creative" in Webster's. I had a young parolee who was unfortunate enough to break out in "zits" when he was misbehaving. It crossed my mind that I could save myself some work if other kids had the same problem or if I could make them believe that I knew something about what they'd been up to since our last meeting. With this kid, though, it was a no-brainer. If his face was all broken out, all I had to do was ask him what he'd been up to, not if he'd been up to something.

I decided to put two chairs next to my desk, one a wooden, straight back, uncomfortable thing, and the other, a swivel, padded, and relatively comfortable thing. I put a sign above the two chairs which said, "If you've been behaving, sit here," with an arrow pointed toward the padded chair; "If not, sit here," with an arrow pointed toward the wooden chair. You'd be surprised at the number of kids who would come in, look at the sign, and take a seat in the wooden chair. Whatever works, I guess.

Making My Decision

I was getting ready to wrap up my fifth year at the university, and I was beginning to plan for my graduation and entry into the wonderful world of full-time employment. I planned to stay in corrections, but I now had to get a full-time position the same way everyone else had to. I had to take the Civil Service tests and go through the oral interviews.

I took the written part of the Civil Service exam, passed it, and was scheduled for the oral part in St. Paul. I was scared to death, but even scary situations can turn out to contain their share of humor.

While I was sitting in a huge hallway waiting for a pair of huge doors to open, I was thinking about what I'd do if for some reason I couldn't find a position in the Department. As I pondered the possibilities, the doors opened, and a young lady whispered, "They're ready for you."

I responded with, "Are they asleep?" She smiled politely.

I walked into a huge room and found myself looking at five people, all with hands folded on a long table. Seated at a small table off to the side was the young lady who had come out to get me. She was the stenographer.

The five inquisitors introduced themselves and began asking questions, in sequence, from one through five. But there was a hitch, one that bothered me. The lady who occupied the fourth chair skipped the first round of questions, and the second, and the third, and the fourth, and the fifth. Finally, the chairman asked her if there were any questions she'd like to ask. She said, "No, but there's something I'd like to tell him. I'd like to tell him that he's the most unusual young man I've ever interviewed."

Now, if I was afraid before I walked in that room, I was really concerned when the questioning began, not because I didn't know the answers, but because of the type of questions that were being asked like, "Which institution in Minnesota do you think is the worst?" Then there was, "What do you think of your supervisor?" They couldn't ask those questions of the average interviewee. The average person being interviewed wouldn't have had any work experience in the Department yet.

Anyway, they really wanted an answer to these questions. I kind of jokingly asked them if they wanted the truth or a lie. They said they wanted the truth, of course. I told them that Pete was a nice guy and that I appreciated the fact that he seemed to trust me, but he wasn't always tuned in to what was going on in the office.

After a 45-minute-long-20-minute-interview, or so it seemed, it finally ended, and we all shook hands and said our goodbyes. As I turned to leave, one of them called to me. When I turned toward them, the chairman said, "Say 'Hello' to Pete for us."

All the way home, I imagined that, as soon as I walked out of the room, they got on the phone and called Pete to tell him what I'd said about him. I was also still concerned about Member #4's not asking any questions. I guess I found out that working a caseload was easier than taking a Civil Service interview.

The next few weeks were agonizingly long. As I recall, persons taking a Civil Service exam had to place in the top three on the list in order to be considered by the Department. Eventually, I was notified that I had placed first on the Civil Service list, and several interviews were eventually scheduled, but only one was a field position, e.g., a non-institutional position. I was smart enough to realize that if I wanted to break into the Department, I might have to take a position in one of the institutions until I could get a field position, but I wasn't enthused about the idea.

Interviews were scheduled at Stillwater State Prison, the Reformatory at St. Cloud, and the juvenile facility at Red Wing, Minnesota. The first two interviews came and went, but the Red Wing interview was kind of interesting.

The superintendent of the facility was Orville Pung, who eventually became the Commissioner of Corrections. I don't remember much about the interview except for one question he asked, that being, "How do you think you'd like working in an institution?"

I remember my answer clearly. It was, "I won't."

He asked me to step out in the hall so he could consult with an assistant. I remember stepping outside and telling myself that I'd blown it. I hadn't taken five steps outside his office door when it opened and he asked me to come back inside and offered me the job. I told him that I had an interview coming up for a field position, which I did, and I asked if I could have a while to get this done. He agreed and we agreed to keep in touch. I drove home trying to figure out what the heck had just happened.

The field position that was open was in New Ulm, Minnesota, a city of about 13,500 people and located in the South Central part of the state. It was a three county operation that was getting probation/parole services from two probation/parole officers.

The day of my interview was extremely warm, and I was extremely uncomfortable in more ways than one. The interview took place in the Chambers of one of the three probate/juvenile judges, the Hon. William B. Mather, Jr. Also taking part in the interview was the probation supervisor, Paul E. Wagner and the judge representing the second county, the Honorable Rick Weiss. I was very aware that a third judge was missing, but no one ever mentioned it. Anyway, the interview went as well as could be expected, and I was glad when the interview ended so I could get in my car, turn on the air conditioning and go home.

As I was driving though, I began to think about what it might be like to work for the people I had just met. I had become comfortable with them over the course of the 45-minute interview, but I was still wondering about where the third judge had been. I also realized that it was beginning to look like it was either going to be this field position or the Red Wing institutional position. The race was on. The clock was ticking.

While all of this was going on, I finally managed to graduate from the university and wrap things up with my friends at the office, my caseload, and especially, my partner, my good friend, mentor, and teacher, Mich. I knew that I would always maintain a relationship with him, and I hoped that I could maintain some contact with "George," as I had really grown to love her over a period of two years. And I even knew that I would probably maintain some degree of contact with some of my caseload, a thought that didn't at all bother me. How could I possibly lose interest in what was happening to Charlie (aka: "Bimbo,") or Patrick, (aka: "Pissquick?")

You would think that graduation and a graduation party would be very pleasant experiences. Well, you'd be right. Graduation marked the end of a long, hard road, and I was anxious to get to work. Ideally, there would have been an opening in the Duluth office, and I would have settled down into a long career in my own hometown. But that wasn't to be.

The Wonderful World of Politics

Orv Pung continued to call from the Training School in Red Wing, and I continued to stall, hoping for a call from New Ulm. Finally, it came. Judge Mather called and told me that he was formally offering me the job, but there was a hitch (naturally!) He reminded me that one of the judges was missing at my first interview. He said that he would like to meet me before he made up his mind. But Judge Mather told me that I didn't have to come back for a second interview as he and Judge Weiss had made up their minds. I decided that it wasn't a good idea to start things out by irritating one of my soon-to-be bosses, so I said I was willing to drive back to Southern Minnesota to meet him. We decided we'd meet in Judge Bull's courtroom. Judge

121

Mather would meet me there.

The day of the interview was very hot, but I didn't know how much hotter it was going to get. I arrived, in Gaylord, found the courthouse and Judge Kenneth Bull's courtroom. Judge Bull was kind of a scary-looking guy who looked somewhat like a concrete slab with red hair.

Judge Mather introduced us, but almost before releasing him from the handshake, Judge Bull went into a tirade about losing his probation officer, my predecessor, Vicki Peiser. He said he didn't think I had her abilities and know-how, et cetera.

I was shocked and not just a little angry, maybe a lot angry. I finally got a chance to say something, and I wasn't about to pull any punches. I said, and this is very close to a quote, "Judge, there's only two things you know about me right now. Number one, I'm not as good-looking as Mrs. Peiser, and number two, I'm not pregnant."

He seemed to get even angrier, although I can't figure out why, but Judge Mather kind of grabbed him and pushed him into his chambers.

I could hear the two of them engaged in a rather heated conversation, and I stared out the window of the courtroom thinking that my smart mouth had pushed me over the line.

When the two judges re-appeared, Judge Bull seemed to have calmed down and welcomed me to his county and said he was looking forward to working with me. Judge Mather and I took our leave and walked out to the parking lot where he asked me to follow him back to his home in New Ulm.

I followed him the twenty-five miles back to New Ulm. He invited me to take a seat at the dining room table, and he broke out a bottle of Four Roses Whisky and a two liter bottle of 7-Up. We proceeded to get very drunk.

On the way to getting very drunk, we talked about some details concerning a starting date, moving date, living arrangements, etc. We decided that August 1, 1970, would be my first day on the job. I would make the move to New Ulm on or around July 28, and would move into the Dakota Hotel until I could find a suitable apartment.

Eventually the next day, I drove home thinking about starting a new career, being away from home for the first time (well, not quite,) wondering if I'd like the new job, the people I'd be working with, leaving family and friends, and especially, trying to make it on my own. Like it or not, it was about to happen, and I was very excited about it.

And So It Begins

To the best of my recollection, Judge Mather made the arrangements for my arrival at the Dakota Hotel. I think all I moved was what I could stuff in the car. I got to town with no trouble and checked into the hotel. I had been invited to the Judge's home and was introduced to his wife, Esther. We had a pleasant dinner, and I began to feel like I was going to enjoy knowing and working with these people.

After supper, Bill, as I was asked to call him, and I drove over to the courthouse where he showed me my office and that of my supervisor, Paul Wagner. Our offices were located directly across the hall from the Probate/Juvenile Court offices. After completing a short tour of the courthouse itself, we adjourned to Ebert's Chalet, a place I'd wind up spending many, many happy hours in over the next several years.

Monday morning finally arrived, and I was excited beyond belief. I was actually able to find the courthouse on my own, where I was greeted by Paul, Bill, Bill's clerk, Florence, Paul's and my secretary, Sharon, and one Mel Schroeer, the courthouse custodian and one of Bill's closest friends.

By the time all of the introductions were made, lo and behold, it was time for coffee! After all, it had been a rough day so far! This was a ritual that was to be repeated hundreds of times and exactly four times daily, seven days per week.

Paul and I hopped in his blue VW Beetle and headed in the opposite direction of the Chalet. We pulled into a tiny restaurant, and I do mean tiny, ten stools around a horseshoe-shaped counter known as Don's Café, owned and operated by one Don Morris, and a smart aleck extraordinaire!

The first thing I learned at Don's Café was that it could be expensive, especially for someone who made $475/month after taxes. The ritual at Don's included shaking dice to find out who was going to pay for four coffees, Bill's, Mel's, Paul's, and my own. I lost my ritual virginity on my first visit to Don's Café. I was really beginning to get a good feeling about these people. Now, it was time to get to business, at least, until lunch.

Most of my first day was spent familiarizing myself with procedural things concerning the Juvenile Court. Don't forget, I hadn't had any experience with juvenile courts yet. There was a lot to learn, and I needed to learn it fast. I was also introduced to other courthouse personnel including the Welfare Department Director, Clark Kellett, and some of his staff.

Eventually, Paul and I sat down and started to talk about the caseload I was inheriting from Vicki Peiser. Don't make the mistake of thinking that my first day was uneventful.

One of the things I was to find out about Paul was that he had an idea about how he was going to assign cases. In time, it became obvious that he liked cases that involved exerting control over a client. If the client was "messed up," somehow, or the family was a mess, it got passed to me.

My first experience with this trend was Jerry, who had been jailed after convictions for rape and kidnapping. Jerry was on parole prior to the offenses and so was looking at a revocation of his parole by the Department of Corrections also.

I awakened one morning to the latest edition of the New Ulm Daily Journal and a front-page story, complete with photograph, about Jerry's conviction. The photo, though, was what I really found interesting and a little scary. He had scratched a death list on the wall of his cell. On it were the names of the trial judge, the Hon. Noah Rosenbloom, the prosecutor, his attorney, two witnesses for the defense, and me as his parole officer. No wonder Paul gave him to me.

Eventually, Jerry was sentenced to forty years in prison. That was the longest sentence ever handed down in Brown County up to that time. Even though Jerry was available for me to meet, as the jail was right next door to the courthouse, I took a pass on that and opted to meet him in prison sometime down the road.

I finally did meet Jerry at the Reformatory in St. Cloud, and I found him to be scarier than anyone I'd ever met except for Mich's friend, Mike. I think it was the rage going far beyond anger that was so frightening. His ideas and attitudes seemed to come right out of a horror magazine.

During the time he spent in prison, he continued to harass people on the outside by sending death threats to people involved in his conviction. I received some very angry phone calls from people who wanted his outgoing mail to be read before sending it out. Unfortunately this couldn't be done, either for legal reasons or because of departmental policy. I can't remember which.

When Jerry was ready to be paroled, I decided that it would be a very poor idea for him to be released to New Ulm. I felt that either he or the City of New Ulm would never survive the experience. So I looked for some help from the direction of Blue Earth County, a more metropolitan county than was Brown County. Blue Earth County had to accept supervision first, so I approached Joe Kubicek, a very experienced probation/parole officer, and a man who would become a close friend over the years. Joe struck me as a man who was particularly adept at dealing with older cons who had been "strained through the horse" a number of times, e.g., cons that had been in the system for some time.

Joe readily accepted the case, and Jerry didn't oppose the transfer. Bottom line? Joe got Jerry a job in a junkyard, and as I recall, he wound up marrying the boss's daughter, and eventually bought a farm somewhere in the area. I don't think I ever heard or saw anything of Jerry again.

After far too much time in the Dakota Hotel (it must have been all of three or four days,) Bill told me that he had located an apartment for me on Front Street. He took me to the apartment where the landlord was waiting. It was a basement apartment with two bedrooms and a large bathroom. The only problem with it was that it was a basement apartment, and all of the windows were glass brick, which, I was to find, would get to be very depressing. But I took it, as the rent was $80.00/month. As my salary was $667/month and about $475/month after deductions, it seemed like the price was right. But I was also to find out that this was the side of town where most of my caseload lived. Thanks a lot, Bill! I love you, too!

Steve's Story

One of those cases who lived too close to me was Steve. As a matter of fact, Steve and his family lived about two blocks from me. Steve's dad, Vern, worked at a local dive known as Hucky's Hideaway.

125

Larry Bauer-Scandin

Vern was a musician and could play the organ stone drunk or out cold. He really was that good. Unfortunately, Vern was an alcoholic who earned ten dollars per night, and Hucky was gracious enough to let Vern charge his drinks against that ten dollars. What a guy! That meant that Steve, his mother, Ruth, his sister and two young brothers rarely had enough food in the house.

To add to the family's problems, their landlord (slumlord) was a very well known local personality with a very big mouth whose name sounded very much like "laughing f-ck-er." And that's exactly how the kids used to refer to him. He was so lax in keeping Steve's home in decent repair that on one occasion, I walked in the house and watched Ruth doing the dishes in the bathtub because the kitchen sink had backed up.

One day, I found myself having lunch in a local restaurant, Eibner's, and I heard a familiar loudmouth, Mr. Laughing F-ck-r, describing the City of New Ulm as being "a city of thirteen thousand Germans, six Irishmen, three Jews and one f-ck-n Pollock, and the f-ck-n Pollock is the mayor of this goddamned town!"

It also wasn't unusual to see Steve's two younger brothers going around the neighborhood begging for food. It was truly sad. Eventually, I believe, both boys were placed in foster care.

I really never had anything to do with Vern. He never seemed to be home even during daylight hours, and he wasn't much help when he was home. Ruth was the glue that held the family together. She and I did a lot of talking about Steve and his problems. One of his more serious problems was school attendance. The principal, Tom Wilson, didn't seem to like Steve very much, and I was to be added to that list of least favorite people. I think he had parolees and parole officers as members of the same class of people.

Steve's attitude seemed to be one of keeping his environment, and all the people in it, sufficiently agitated that no one would forget he was around. I tried everything I could think of with him, e.g., curfews, jail, butt-chewing sessions. Through it all, Steve needed attention, and his parents didn't have the inclination, in one case, or the time, in the other, to give him that attention. And it got even worse when it was discovered that Ruth had terminal cancer.

One Friday afternoon, I stopped in to see her. I knew she was very close to death. I held her hand, and we talked about Steve. She

126

was very worried about him and the other children. She asked me to take care of Steve for her. Then, I left for the weekend. When I returned, I found that she had passed away.

Not all of my relationship with Steve was of a serious nature, and Steve did have some victories in his life. One afternoon, I parked my car in front of Leuthold-Jensen Clothiers. I got out of the car and promptly locked my keys in the car. I stood there cussing for a few moments and then got the idea to go into the store and get a clothes hanger.

As I stepped toward the door, I found Steve standing there. He realized what I had done and offered to open the door for me. I told him to leave the car alone until I went inside and got a hanger. I went into the store and got a hanger, and when I got back outside, two of New Ulm's finest had Steve bent over the hood of my car and were handcuffing him. He yelled at me as they stuffed him in the squad car. I waved goodbye as they drove him off to jail for trying to steal my car! I let him sit in jail a few hours to think about the implications of an auto theft charge, and then had him released.

Steve was also responsible for one of the greatest experiences of my life, but I'll leave that story for a more appropriate time.

Before discussing anymore members of my caseload, I think I should introduce some other characters who had an impact on just about everything I did professionally.

I'll start with the Sheriff, Irv. Now, Irv was neither the kind of person nor the kind of law enforcement officer that I was ever going to learn to like. I just didn't trust him. In time, I found out that the person in the office that I trusted even less was his chief deputy, Harry.

Irv was what I would call the titular head of the office, he sheriff that the people elected, but I think Harry was the guy wielding the power. Harry and his wife lived in an apartment on the floor beneath the Sheriff's Office. There was strong reason to believe that Harry had the office bugged. I can think of at least two deputies who were fired for saying something nasty about Harry, and they both claimed that the statements were made in the office. Of course, I suppose this poses the possibility that there might have been another "rat" hearing and reporting the statements.

A good friend of mine, Steve Ulmen, had a state case who had been sentenced in my county. Apparently, the crime didn't warrant a revocation of the kid's parole, but he was sentenced to jail time in my jail.

This young man had some medical problems, one of them being some sort of heart trouble. The other required the use of suppositories. Because of these medical problems and because of the reputation of the boy's hosts, Irv and Harry, Steve asked me to keep an eye on the kid while he did his time. Of course, I agreed.

I decided to see this kid, I suppose he was 18 or 19 years old at the time, at least twice per day and at different times of the day so that Irv and Harry couldn't detect a pattern to my visits.

Now, this kid sure wasn't the nicest kid I'd ever dealt with either. I think the heart problem scared the hell out of him, and he sure wasn't happy about having to use suppositories. As a matter of fact, that's what seemed to set the stage for the problems that developed between Irv, Harry, and the young inmate.

One late afternoon before going home for the day, I decided to drop in and see the kid. I heard him yelling from his second floor cell. There was also a terrible smell wafting down the steps from the second floor and crawling right up my nose. I ran up the steps and found the kid on his cot, on his back, head rolling from side to side and moaning loudly. The smell was downright obnoxious. I looked around for the source of the smell, and suddenly I spotted an open box of mothballs literally frying on the radiator, located only a few feet from the cell and just out of the kid's reach. I was sure that the box had been placed there on purpose. I grabbed it and threw it down the stairs.

I called Steve and told him about the incident. He took steps to get the kid out of our jail. Quite a statement: to not be able to trust that a person would be safe to serve a sentence in a county jail for fear of the Sheriff and his Chief Deputy. Irv was defeated in the next election, by the way.

The City of New Ulm also had a police chief. Dave, by himself, was a nice guy, and the entire Department was a nice bunch of guys to work with. But every barrel has a rotten apple, and the New Ulm Police Department was no exception.

In time, I came to the conclusion that the locals, including the kids, were just like any others I'd had contact with. Alcohol and the usual variety of street drugs were also found to be readily available. I began thinking about striking out on the drug education speaking circuit. I spoke to Bill Mather about it, and he offered to build me a drug display kit. I took that as his support for the idea, but I was to find out that not everyone was going to be happy about the idea.

I'm not exactly sure how word got out, but one morning I got a call from the Chief who asked that I come down to the Police Dept. When I walked into Dave's office, there was a sergeant present. Chuck could hardly restrain his anger. He was furious as he, unknown to me, had just finished a drug education course, and he had plans to go out on the lecture circuit also. He certainly didn't want any competition from the new kid on the block. He even threatened to arrest me and have me charged with Possession of a Controlled Substance if I traveled around with a display kit full of live drugs, as I had planned. As Chuck was standing there rippin' me a new one, Dave was sitting there saying and doing nothing. You'd better believe, I never forgot this incident. I even suggested that we try and find a way to work together, but he wasn't interested.

I went back to the courthouse and told Bill about the meeting with Chuck and the Chief. He said he'd take care of the problem when he got the display kit built.

Within about a week, Bill had the kit built. It was big and a little heavy, but it was built to take abuse and protect the contents. He also painted a small sign on the front which said, "Property of the Brown County Juvenile Court." He looked awfully proud of himself.

A few days later, I got a phone call from none other than Sgt. Chuck. In his nicest voice, he told me that he was scheduled to give a drug talk locally, and he wanted to know if he could borrow my display kit. I was just a little suspicious.

I told him that I never intended to be separated from my kit, but I told him he could borrow it if he didn't mind my being in the audience during the talk. I also suggested we get together beforehand, as I had some unusual things in the kit that he might want to ask questions about before he got started. He agreed to get together thirty minutes before his talk was to begin, but he never showed up.

A short time into his talk, someone asked him why he had the nutmeg in the kit. He couldn't answer. Some in the audience got a little irritated, and someone finally asked who the hell the kit really belonged to. Chuck didn't have much choice but to introduce me and to invite me to answer audience questions. He wasn't very happy, but he hadn't been very smart either. In any event, I never was able to develop any sort of relationship with Chuck or the Chief, but the rest of the department and I worked very well together.

Selecting My Church

It didn't take long to join a church after my move to New Ulm. There were two Catholic churches in New Ulm, one being St. Mary's and located on the southern end of town, and the Cathedral, located on the northern end. Someone told me that most Catholics living south of Center Street attended St. Mary's, and those living North attended the Cathedral. As I lived on North Front Street, I joined the Cathedral.

I learned that the high school being operated by the Cathedral was in trouble financially, and Bishop Alphonse Schladweiler and Monsignor Joseph Ettel had imported three young priests to re-energize interest in parochial education into the congregation. The three new priests were Fr. Ed Ardolph, Fr. Tony Platte, and Fr. Dick Gross.

Of the three priests, I became most closely familiar with Fr. Gross as I again began teaching CCD Sunday school classes, but I also found out that Fr. Dick was often called into family conflicts by Bill Mather. So I often saw him in the courtroom.

In the main, Wednesday evening's CCD classes were the constant where these three were concerned. But I also gained other friendships as a result of my church activities.

Two of these were Jim and Judy Toth. Jim was a supervisor/manager at a trailer home manufacturing plant in New Ulm. Judy held an MBA degree and taught at Cathedral High School. Outside of Bill Mather, Jim and Judy became my closest friends.

The three young priests did what they were brought in to do, and did it very well. But Bishop Schladweiler and Monsignor Ettel, being representatives of the conservative wing of the Church, eventually took exception to what they referred to as the lifestyles of the three priests. Lifestyles referred, in part, at least, to the fact that they and we, the CCD teachers, got together every Wednesday night after classes, went to Eibner's Restaurant, and shared a light meal and (horrors) a pitcher of beer.

Now, this wouldn't have bothered me so much nor made me so mad except for the fact that I had seen one of the two accusers, on more than one occasion, indulging in a drink in the same restaurant—and alone. I would have settled for simply not liking the man until he and his fellow accuser decided to deport all three of the priests.

The parish was split on the issue of the priests and their lifestyles. In general, the younger people supported the priests, and the older parishioners supported the Bishop's decision to transfer them.

The split within the parish led the Bishop and Monsignor to call a parish-wide meeting to discuss the situation. I would guess that several hundred people showed up on the evening of the meeting. The only items on the agenda were Fathers Ed, Tony and Dick. I don't remember the details of the meeting, but it became clear that the decision to deport the three priests had already been made. There was really nothing to discuss.

Sometime during the course of the meeting, I addressed the Bishop as Bishop Sidewinder. The terms "hypocrisy" and "hypocrite" seem to best describe the meeting and the clergy involved. This was the first time that I ever experienced this degree of anger, frustration and disappointment with my Church.

Within a few weeks, the three priests were in the final process of readying themselves for transfer. Frs. Tony and Ed were transferred to churches within thirty miles of New Ulm, but Fr. Dick was sent to a small town in Western Minnesota, a transfer that he really didn't wind up minding as he was a hunter and fisherman, and his home was in Western Minnesota. His last words to me were, "I'll be back." I wasn't to see him again for about seven years.

I went to Mass as usual on the Sunday following the Rat Pack of Reverends leaving town. When I walked into church, I discovered that Bishop Schladweiler was celebrating the Mass. I became so angry that I decided I shouldn't stay, so I left. I never returned. Over time, I developed other differences with my Church. I decided that I couldn't support a structure or an institution that I didn't think was behaving like it had the best interests of its members at heart.

Roommates

In time, my basement apartment became more than I could deal with. For a while after moving to New Ulm, I found myself going home to Duluth just about every weekend. Eventually though, that got

131

to be a long trip, and I began spending more weekends at home in New Ulm. The lack of natural light in my apartment had been driving me crazy. I began mentioning my wanting to move to friends and acquaintances, one of which was Jim Jensen, the owner of a local clothing store, whom I'd become far too fond of.

One day, I walked into the store, and Jim told me that the two young guys living in the apartment above the store were looking for another roommate. Jim had mentioned that I was looking for another apartment. Arrangements were made for me to meet the guys to look over the apartment. I had already met one of them, Jamie, as he worked for Jim.

A meeting was arranged so I could see the apartment and meet Jake, my other would-be roommate. I thought Jamie would be a fun kind of guy to be around, but Jake somehow gave off signals that he might present some very interesting times. Even though I was a little gun-shy of Jake, I couldn't pass up the opportunity to save $50 per month on my rent, so-o-o, I accepted the invitation to move in.

Now the apartment was certainly big enough for the three of us, but there would prove to be times when the White House wouldn't have been big enough. It had a decent sized kitchen and living room, a small bathroom and three bedrooms, one being very large.

We were average young guys who were out to avoid as much housework as possible. We decided to be very logical in our approach to housework and privacy.

For example, we decided that there was no reason why the three of us couldn't share the same bedroom so we didn't mess up the other two bedrooms. Made perfect sense to us! We even worked out an agreement whereby in the event that one of us had a girl in the apartment, the bedroom was available to them exclusively. Logical, right? Suffice it to say that we really did have an agreement that worked for a while.

New Year's Eve, 1970

By the end of the year, I had become fairly comfortable with my new work environment, my caseload, co-workers, my supervisor, Paul Wagner and, especially, with Bill Mather. As a matter of fact, I got to be kind of a fixture at the Mather's. As a result, I got to know

Bill's wife, Esther, and his daughter, Kris, quite well.

Sometime during the holiday season, Esther asked me if I might be interested in meeting her niece, Peggy, who lived in St. Paul and would be visiting with her mother on New Year's Eve. Now, even if I'd been so inclined, how would I have answered "No" to that kind of question? Bill's comment was, "You'll be sorry!"

I don't actually remember meeting Peg and her mother, but I do remember that first impressions were good. I was fairly comfortable as Peg and I left to spend New Year's Eve with Paul Wagner, his wife, Avis, and their two kids. It was unusually warm for New Year's Eve.

We spent a pleasant evening with the Wagners, and dutifully saluted the New Year with a toast. It was time to go home.

When we stepped out the door, we discovered that it had rained and it was very slippery. We managed to get to the car, say our "Goodbyes," and headed for the Tenth St. Hill. When I looked down the hill, it was obvious that the entire street was nothing but a sheet of glare ice. Even through my booze-soaked brain, I was able to make the decision that we couldn't get down the hill safely, so we turned around and went back to the Wagner's.

The distance back to Paul's place was less than two blocks. We pulled into the driveway, but the car wouldn't stay in the driveway. Paul's driveway was in the same condition as the Tenth St. Hill. We actually formed a chain between the front door of the house and the door of the car and pulled the car into a safe position on the street. It was that slippery.

As it was now after 1:00 am, we had to decide whether or not to call the Mathers. In psychology, they call this an avoidance-avoidance problem, e.g., having to choose between two uncomfortable options. We chose not to call. Paul and Avis didn't seem to be concerned, but all I could think of was that I wasn't bringing the judge's niece home on our first date. Even though I wasn't all that concerned about Bill, Esther and, especially, Peg's mother, Louise, was a different story.

I don't remember making a call to the Mathers in the morning. I think we just got up and went home.

When we walked in the door, Bill, Esther and Louise were standing in the middle of the living room floor with arms folded in a rather threatening pose. I took it seriously for a moment, and then the room broke into laughter.

By the time Peg and Louise left New Ulm, I knew that I liked both of them a lot, but I didn't know how much a lot was going to prove to be. Peg and I had also made plans to see each other again.

A Very Memorable Memorial Day, 1971

In the spring of 1971, I met a young lady who worked at the courthouse. She had moved to New Ulm from Marshalltown, Iowa. Her work supervisor introduced us. Patty was a beautiful girl with a soft, sexy voice. On our first date, I picked her up and asked her what she'd like to do. She said, "All I want to do is be with you," and I was sure I was in love.

Our second date was Memorial Day. We, meaning Jamie, his girlfriend, Patty, Patty and I decided on a picnic. Jake was off to the races and places unknown. At about 6:00 pm, we were ready to go home and relax in the apartment.

As we were driving down Minnesota Street we passed the front door of the apartment and discovered it was open, which seemed very strange. For the heck of it, we decided to drive through the alley and take a look at the rear door of the apartment. We found that the rear door was also open, and several people were standing on the small porch located off the kitchen. A lot of loud talking and even louder music was floating into the alley from a story above us. Jamie and I looked at each other, and almost in unison we said, "He's having a party!"

We drove through the alley, returned to Minnesota Street and parked right in front of the apartment. Jamie and I told the girls to stay in the car. He and I decided to get upstairs as fast as possible and close the party down before it attracted the attention of the Police Department.

On the way upstairs, we decided that Jamie would head for the living room, and I would head for the bedroom. The simple plan was to start grabbing bodies and just kind of throw them down the stairs.

Halfway up the steps, I spotted a half-naked guy sitting beside a glass of overturned beer, the beer rapidly finding its way down the last dozen or so steps. I grabbed him by the hair, pulled him down the steps and threw him out the door onto Minnesota Street. I ran back up the steps and headed for the bedroom. I found three couples, one in each of our beds (all naked, of course.) I pulled them all out of the beds and herded them toward the steps. As they all ran down the steps, I threw their clothes after them. I was wondering how many squad cars had come down Minnesota St. and seen the half-naked bodies roaming around. I was sure I was going to find out the next morning.

Jamie was also pushing bodies toward the steps from the direction of the living room and kitchen. As I helped him escort the last of the bodies out the door, I looked up the street, and sure enough, a squad car was going by very, very slowly. It was going to be a long night.

Jamie and I were both furious at Jake, and by the way, where the hell was he? By this time, we had called the all clear, and the girls had joined us in the apartment. We began the hunt for Jake, but we couldn't find him anywhere. We concluded that he wasn't in the apartment.

We surveyed the house. The living room carpet was soaked in beer, and a large picture had been kicked out of the frame. There was a keg of beer in the bathtub. There wasn't two square inches of floor, carpeted or not, that wasn't bathing in beer, and the walls were almost as bad.

As we were looking around the place, trying to figure out how we were going to explain what had happened to anyone who might voice a complaint, the girls suggested that we get busy and get the place cleaned up. The girls stayed home to pick things up as best they could, and Jamie and I went to the store to buy mops, cleaners, etc.

Somehow we managed to get energized, and by the time the sun came up, we had managed to put the apartment back into fairly decent shape. We all flopped in chairs and began to appreciate just how tired we were. And then a terrifying thought crossed my mind.

I looked across the room at Jamie and asked, "James, what's below us?" He looked at me like I'd been drinking.

"What?" he asked.

I repeated. "What's below us?"

Then, he said, "Oh, my God, the store!"

It had struck me that a lot of the beer soaking through the floor was probably dripping onto the clothing in the clothing store below the apartment.

Jamie got on the phone and called Jim Jensen and asked him to come down and open the store. We decided we couldn't wait for the store to open at 9:00 am. Jim wasn't happy about being awakened, but he agreed to come down.

When he opened the door, we saw nothing initially. But on closer inspection, we saw drops rolling down the walls behind the hanging clothes. Luckily the clothing racks were secured to the walls in such a way that the clothes didn't touch the walls. After a short inspection, we decided that there wasn't anything more we could do until later in the day, so we all went home.

Jamie and I went upstairs, said Goodbye to the girls, and they went home. Jamie and I flopped into a couple of chairs. When I looked up, there was Jake standing in the doorway. He looked at us and said, "I need a shrink." He had been passed out under one of the beds in the bedroom.

Suffice it to say that it took him quite a while to recover from the cool atmosphere that developed around the house as a result of this little party. By the way, no one ever mentioned this party to me. But it was a very memorable Memorial Day!

One more thing before we switch subjects. Several days after the party, I stopped in at Patty's office to see her, but she wasn't there. I kept on trying to contact her over the next few days, but no one seemed to know where she was. I was beginning to worry, and it didn't take long for me to conclude that her co-workers simply didn't want me to know where she was. Finally, the lady that introduced us in the first place must have taken pity on me and decided to tell me what had happened. Patty had discovered that she was pregnant by a former boyfriend, back in Marshalltown, and in accordance with the mores of the time, she had returned to Iowa to marry the baby's father. I never heard from her again, but obviously I've never forgotten her.

Wrestling with Mono

In June, 1971, I started running a fairly high fever in excess of 103 degrees. At first, I assumed it was the flu and fought it as though it was, but that didn't work, and the pain was getting hard to deal with.

On a Sunday morning, I called Bill Mather and asked him if he might know of a doctor who might be dumb enough to be in his office on a Sunday morning. He said he thought that his doctor, Cornelius Saffert, might be in his office. He gave me the number, I called, and lo and behold, he was in. He told me to get to the office as soon as I could.

Of course, he took a medical history, some blood, and as I recall, he gave me my favorite thing, a penicillin shot before sending me home with another appointment date. When that day rolled around, I wasn't feeling any better, the fever was still up there, and I was still aching a lot.

Dr. Saffert told me that I had mononucleosis or, as it was sometimes referred to in those days, "the kissing disease." I don't think it had much to do with kissing, although it is passed on through body fluids. I asked him how bad it was. As I recall, he said that the normal unit of blood had between 60 and 100 white cells in it; mine had 2500. I asked him what we could do, and he said he wanted me in the hospital. I told him that people in hell wanted ice water. Of course, my caseload couldn't do without me! He said the real problem was the fever, and if we couldn't get it down, it could take a toll on my heart in time. I knew enough about medicine to know that was true.

Another thing Dr. Saffert wanted to talk about was the medical history that he had gotten from the doctors in Duluth. He asked me what I understood the diagnosis to be concerning the paralysis in 1957. I told him that I had always been told that the diagnosis had been Multiple Sclerosis, and that several years later, the Mayo Clinic concurred in that diagnosis. His response was, "They were lying to you." Naturally, I was shocked. I asked him if he didn't mean they were mistaken. He said, "No, they were lying."

He asked me if I remembered the spinal taps I'd had as a kid. I asked him if he thought any nine year old would ever forget a spinal tap. He went on to explain that one of the absolute necessities for diagnosing MS, at least in those days, was an elevated protein count in the spinal fluid. He said that my medical records indicated that I'd never had an elevated protein count in my spinal fluid. I was shocked and angry, but I knew my first problem right now was the mono itself.

When I left the doctor's office and walked to the parking lot, I sat in the car for a while, trying to think of a way to get and keep the fever down. Those thoughts were being interfered with by the doctor's use of the word, "lying."

Larry Bauer-Scandin

After some thought, I decided to go to the drug store, buy some Niacin, and see if that would help. "Corny" hadn't given me any options outside of the hospital.

I went to the courthouse the next morning like a dummy, and Paul asked how things had gone at the doctor's. I told him it was mono, and he wanted me to go home. I told him that if I were going to hurt, I'd just as soon be doing something. He told me he could order me to go home. I suggested that he could order me out of the office, but not home. He just called me a knothead and left it at that. I told him I appreciated the implications of the problem, but I really didn't want to go home where I could concentrate on how much I hurt.

As it turned out, the Niacin did the trick. I discovered that I could take a Niacin cap, and fifteen minutes later, I was sweating like an Olympic runner, and the fever went down to nothing.

The following Thursday was my regular day in Sibley County and Ken Bull's court. Before going into court, I popped a Niacin capsule and then took my place at the counsel table. There was no air conditioning in the courthouse, but the windows of the courtroom were open. It was a very warm day. The hearing began, and so did the sweating.

As the hearing progressed, I became aware of the fact that my entire shirt was wet as well as the upper two or three inches of my slacks. Even my tie was soaked. Drops of sweat were actually dripping from the tip of my tie and into my lap. You can guess what that looked like, but boy, did I feel good!

As this was going on, His Honor had also taken notice, and the face under his strawberry blonde hair was beginning to turn white. Finally, this rock of composure called a recess and ordered me into his chambers. Almost before he had the door shut, he blurted out, "Are you all right?" I had forgotten that I had taken the Niacin, but I assured him I'd never felt better!

Some six or eight years after leaving Ken's county, I ran into him and his wife, Jeanne, in a restaurant. They invited me to join them. Ken's first question? "Were you on drugs that day you were sweating so badly in my courtroom?" I'm not sure he believed the explanation about the Niacin or not.

In any event, I recovered from the mono, but it would be years before I would get over Corny Saffert's telling me that the Duluth

138

doctors had lied to me and my parents.

Big Brothers of New Ulm

One bright, sunny summer morning, I was sitting at my desk trying to get both eyes open so I could read the mail. I looked up and saw a young man sitting in one of the two chairs in front of my desk. I said, "Good morning" and asked him what I could do for him.

He said, "I'm going to be on probation pretty soon, and I want you for my probation officer." I couldn't help but smile, as the kid told me he was all of eight years old. Charlie told me that he did a lot of drinking. He was one of, I believe, nine boys being raised by a single mother, a registered nurse employed at a local hospital. After a little more talking, I invited my young friend to stop in again. He asked if he could bring a friend.

The next morning, I looked up to see Charlie sitting in the same chair, and his friend, also eight years of age, sitting in the chair across from him. As it turned out, this little guy was also fatherless.

After they left with an open invitation to stop in whenever they were in the neighborhood, I began to wonder how many kids in and around New Ulm were fatherless. I wondered whether a Big Brother-type program would go over in conservative New Ulm.

Several days later, I found myself at the home of Jim and Judy Toth. Jim, as I mentioned earlier, worked for a trailer home manufacturing company, and Judy taught at Cathedral High School. Both were gentle people, very community and church minded, and unfortunately childless.

During the evening, I mentioned my little visitors to Jim and Judy and asked them if they thought there might be any interest in starting a Big Brother-type program in New Ulm. They both thought it was a great idea and said they knew a few people who might be interested in becoming big brothers.

Over the next several weeks and months, Jim and I worked on developing application forms so that we could do the best possible job of matching the interests of both the big and little brothers. Eventually we got a group together that acted as the Board of Directors, and in a short time, we had our list of candidates for both big and little brothers. It was left to me to decide who would be paired with whom.

139

But my choice for Charlie wasn't on the list of big brother candidates. For Charlie, I had a particular big brother in mind, that being Jim Jensen, the owner of the clothing store below my apartment. I was sure that if I approached him directly, he'd tell me he was too busy, so I knew I'd have to get creative.

I decided to let Jamie in on my plan, as it involved his not being around when I approached Jim. One afternoon, I went in the store and began looking around for a new suit, as I had done too many times in the past. I gave Jamie the signal to get lost so Jim would have to deal with me.

Jim did look for Jamie, but not seeing him, he was more than happy to take another shot at selling me a suit. After a little business talk about suits, I mentioned the big brothers and asked him if he might be interested. He hesitated, questioning his qualifications as a big brother to a fatherless kid. I told him the story of Charlie's visits to my office, and I told him that I thought he and Charlie would be a perfect match. He still hesitated, so I played my trump card. I told him I'd buy a suit if he'd become a big brother. He smiled and shook his head, and I wound up walking out of the store with both a new suit and a new big brother.

When all was said and done, we probably had in the neighborhood of fifteen adults and kids wanting to take part in the program. It was decided that the introductions would be made at a picnic. The kids and adults would get to know each other during the picnic, and then we would all take a short walk to a local park and play a game of softball.

After the picnic, I suggested to the adults that they start walking to the park with their little brothers. I wanted to hang back a little, wanting the kids to get to know their big brothers.

As I walked half a block behind the group, I looked up and saw Charlie and Jim walking hand in hand and Charlie with a smile on his face the size of the Grand Canyon. I will never forget the look on that little boy's face! It was another one of those moments that Mich spoke about that would make the kid business worth all the effort.

By the way, Jim Jensen wound up hiring Charlie as a salesman in his store when he was old enough, and the last time I saw him, he was selling cars at New Ulm Ford. Well, no one's perfect! He looked like a happy, healthy young adult to me.

Even though I've spent a lot of time talking about various people who've had an effect on my life in some way, the kids have occupied at least as important a spot in my life as the adults. So I want to get back to them, at least for a while. And I hope the reader doesn't think in terms of what I did for them but what they did for me, the opportunities they gave me to learn, to share, to give, to try to make hurting people feel better.

Bobby's Story

One summer morning during the Brown County Fair, I found a petition on my desk charging a young man, age 15, with Shoplifting. On the surface, this looked like just another delinquent act committed by just another delinquent.

During the hearing, I discovered that this young man had come into town with the "carnies" staffing the fair. Further, it was found that the kid had been on the run for three years. After pleading guilty to the charge of Shoplifting, the Court declared him to be a delinquent child and placed him on formal probation. It also ordered an investigation into the boy's background.

Bobby was a slightly built blond kid, probably weighing between 130 – 140 pounds, and might have been 5' 5" to 5' 6". I also discovered that this kid had been driving one of the carnival semis.

During our first interview, he not only told me that he had been on run for three years but that he was also an escapee from the Indiana State Hospital. He told me that his father was the President of the Indianapolis branch of a large internationally known Protestant religious denomination and was an ordained minister.

According to Bobby, as he preferred to be called, the reason that he'd been committed to the State Hospital was because he used to stand between his mother and younger brother when she would lose her temper and start wailing on the kid. Lest you think I bought all of this, I didn't, until I called the parents and the Indiana State Hospital. The hospital confirmed Bobby's story. When I called the parents, I was told that they weren't interested in getting the boy back, but they did agree to send some clothing. When I received the box and opened it, the clothing had so many holes that a centipede could have worn the stuff. God, I was mad!

141

So, now that the decision had been made to retain jurisdiction of this kid, the problem became one of what we were going to do with him. The first problem was to find him a home. What do you do with a kid who had gotten used to earning a living driving a semi and who hadn't been in school for three years?

Although I don't remember the research I did involving locating a foster home for Bobby, I wound up placing him with a farm family who lived just south of Sleepy Eye. He liked his foster parents, and they liked him, but Bobby was used to being on his own, and that was going to prove to be a problem.

The next problem to be dealt with was getting him in compliance with the State law requiring him to be in school. I didn't have a clear idea of his school history, so the local school experts decided on the grade he would be placed in. But it wasn't the grade or the schoolwork that was to cause the major problem. This kid simply couldn't identify with what he referred to as the childish behavior of his classmates.

Because of his problems with school, Bobby frequently missed classes or skipped school altogether. Naturally, this led to phone calls to the foster parents and then to me. When the pressure built, he would just take off, but he always wound up back in New Ulm. Whenever he was on run, all I had to do was call local law enforcement and tell them to be on the lookout for a kid wearing a white tam on his head. I swear, he never took that thing off!

My favorite memory of this boy was the day he walked in my office, shortly after he was placed on probation, and asked if I'd like to make a marijuana bust. I asked him how much he was talking about, thinking he was going to be talking a few joints. Much to my astonishment, he said, "Eight hundred pounds."

He told me that it was attached to the underside of several of the carnies' semis. I couldn't even imagine 360+ kilos of marijuana, so I asked him if he was absolutely sure. He said he was, so I called Rich Gulden, New Ulm's Police Chief, and asked him if he'd like to get his ugly mug on the front page of the Daily Journal. I told him about the marijuana, and apparently the appropriate warrants were obtained and the bust was made.

Paul E. Wagner

You might have picked up on the fact that, thus far, I haven't said a whole lot about my immediate supervisor, Paul Wagner. From the start, I realized that Paul and I were very different people. We got along well together as long as he didn't think that I was forgetting that I was his assistant.

I admit that there were a few times when I definitely did forget that he was the boss, but in time, I realized that we were going to have problems that were primarily caused by his attitude.

For example, I was once invited by a Mankato television station to take part in a drug discussion panel. Paul was okay with the idea, or so it seemed. When I got back to the office, after the TV appearance though, he told me that, "In the future, you introduce yourself as Larry Scandin, Assistant Probation Officer under Paul Wagner."

One very uncomfortable problem for me concerned the fact that Judge Bull didn't particularly care for Paul, especially at salary establishment time each year. Paul always dictated the Order that established our annual salaries after Bill Mather and Rick Weiss agreed on a percent of increase. Paul always put both of our salary figures on the same Order, and then gave it to me to get Judge Bull's signature. Judge Bull always had a fit as he thought Paul was being overpaid. He didn't like having to approve Paul's salary in order to approve mine. I realized that Paul was using me, but there wasn't much I could do. Actually, Judge Bull couldn't do much either if Bill and Rick agreed to the salaries.

The County Court Act

By about 1972, Minnesota law mandated that Minnesota's Probate/Juvenile Courts were to become County Courts. The duties of the new County Courts would be expanded. Judge Bull saw this as his chance to separate from the tri-county agreement with Brown and Watonwan Counties. It also meant he would need his own Court Services Department. He asked me if I would be interested in the position.

Although I loved living and working in New Ulm, it was

becoming apparent that Paul would be more comfortable with another assistant. I knew that I loved New Ulm, my friends, and even my caseload, but Judge Bull's invitation was just too hard to turn down. And besides, New Ulm was only about twenty miles away. So I accepted his invitation to become his new Court Services Officer. He decided that Sibley County's split from the tri-county agreement would be effective on January 1, 1974.

One of the problems a person in my profession faces when he leaves a position is having to do some separation work with his clients, and separating from Bobby wasn't easy. He couldn't understand why I had to leave. I tried not to forget that he was only fifteen and needed a friendly adult.

After my move, Bobby would call me and complain about having to deal with Paul Wagner, his new probation officer. No matter how many times I told him that he must learn how to deal with Paul, he didn't seem to want to deal realistically with his new situation.

One day, at a regional staff meeting, I asked Paul how he was getting along with Bobby. He said that Bobby had disappeared, and there was an APB out on him. He was never found, and I wouldn't have expected him to be. He had become used to living his life on the run. I've always been sorry that Bobby was never able to become grounded and secure enough to become comfortable in his 15-year-old skin. He is another one of those kids that I'll never quit thinking and wondering about.

The Mathers

When I look back at my life, I'm constantly amazed at what an incredible pain in the butt I must have been to some people. It seems like I've spent more than half my life occupying chairs in other peoples' homes, and Bill and Esther's was certainly no exception.

Even though there were times when I wished I were somewhere else, spending so much time in this house did net me, if not them, a lot of memories revolving around Mather family members I met there including, of course, one Margaret (Peggy) Louise Bauer.

But another was Judge Bill Mather, Sr., or Judge Bill the Elder, as I was known to call him. His Honor had occupied the chair of Judge of Probate/Juvenile Court in Brown County for some 45 years before passing the gavel onto his son, who kept it warm for another 35 years or so.

Bill, Jr. always told me that he never wanted to be an attorney, to say nothing of being "Da Judge." Bill had been in the aircraft design business in California, and was pressured by his father into coming home and entering the William Mitchell School of Law. He always said he regretted his decision to go to law school, but I never got any indication that he didn't like being the judge. I also believe that he was very well versed in the law.

Judge Bill, the Elder, was fond of walking to the courthouse several days per week. The distance was probably a mile or so, and Bill was 95 years old when I met him. I could always hear him coming down the steps to the basement level of the courthouse, and I always knew that his first stop was going to be my office. It was located right at the base of the steps. He would stand in the doorway, and I would do my best to ignore him for a few seconds. Then I would look up and pretend like I was surprised at finding him standing there. I would always greet him with, "Good morning, Your Honor. To what do you owe your long life?"

He would always answer with, and I do mean always, either, "Peanut butter sandwiches" or (my favorite,) "Keep your bowels open and your mouth shut!"

After a little chatting, he would wander across the hall to the Probate/Juvenile Office that later became the County Court office, pull out one of the old probate record books from under the counter, open it to any old page, scan it and then, more often than not, I could hear him yell back to Bill, Jr. "Billy, Sylvia Snodgrass did not die on October 4, 1921; she died on October 3, 1921. Change it!" Bill Jr. would walk out of his chambers, walk up to the counter with pen in hand, draw a line or two through the incorrect date, and change it as ordered. God, I loved that old man!

Old Judge Bill passed away at the tender age of 96. I remember standing in the mortuary with Bill, who was, of course, being bombarded with condolences from every attorney and judge in three or four counties. One of them came up to Bill, expressed his sympathies, and was shocked when Bill responded, "What the hell do you expect? He was ninety-six years old!"

After the guy slithered away, I asked Bill what the heck his problem was. With a very irked look on his face, he tapped the face of his watch and said, "It's nine o'clock! It's time for coffee!" Shortly thereafter, we were on our way to Ebert's Chalet.

Bill, Jr. was also an interesting character. Some things he did on the bench scared me, like falling asleep during a hearing. Thank God, he taped every hearing.

Bill always had the best interests of the kids in mind. I never worried about that. He didn't have a reputation of being a friend to law enforcement. For example, a kid had been charged with Possession/Consumption of an alcoholic beverage, specifically, beer.

During the hearing, the arresting officer was placed on the stand and was being questioned by the prosecution. They had presented an open beer can as evidence. During the questioning, Bill asked the officer why he was so sure the can actually had beer in it. The officer said that he assumed the can had beer in it. Bill asked him if he had tasted the contents. The officer replied in the negative. "Well, then, how can you be sure?" Bill asked.

Then Bill told the following story. He said that a pregnant woman's doctor once told her to come in and bring a urine specimen. She couldn't find an appropriate container, so she put the specimen in an empty, pint-sized booze bottle.

On her way to the doctor's office, she decided to stop at the mall and do some shopping, but she forgot to lock the doors. When she got back to the car, the booze bottle, which had been sitting on the front seat, was gone. The thief, Bill pointed out, had made an assumption also. The case was dismissed.

On another occasion, a young couple walked into my office and asked to see the Judge. They told me that they wanted to get married.

With a smile on my face, I led them across the hall to the Probate/Juvenile Office where Bill was leaning on the counter, flipping through the pages of the morning paper. I told Bill that the young couple wanted to talk to him about getting married. Bill said nothing and continued to flip through the pages of the paper. Once again, I told him that the young couple wanted to get married. He looked up at me, and then at the couple, and asked, "Why?" They looked at each other, turned and walked out of the courthouse. Sometimes, I wonder if that couple ever did get married.

During the trial of one young man, I found myself on the witness stand as a witness for the prosecution. The boy was being defended by Dick Kelly, who eventually succeeded Bill as the County Court Judge. Dick's tactic for dealing with my testimony was to object on the grounds that I was testifying as an expert witness. Every time he did so, Bill overruled his objection.

Finally, Dick accepted the fact that his plan wasn't going to work, so he asked me how long it would take to furnish my credentials, university transcripts, etc., supporting the Court's decision that I was an expert. I told him, after looking at Bill out of the corner of my eye, that it would probably take a few weeks. With that, the hearing continued.

After the hearing, Bill and I were standing out in the hallway talking when Dick walked out of the courtroom. He walked up to us and asked me again when he might expect to receive my credentials as an expert. I reminded him that I had testified that it would take a few weeks, but that I had no intention of getting them for him.

With that, he got very upset, reminding me that I had testified under oath that I would get the material. I told him that I had not said I would furnish the documents, only that it would take a few weeks to get them. He had only asked how long would it take. He was furious, but Bill was trying not to laugh. Dick gave Bill a pleading look, but Bill only shrugged his shoulders.

Dick turned abruptly and walked down the hall and out the door of the courthouse. For the rest of my career in New Ulm, I always made sure that I was wearing my bulletproof Fruit of the Looms when I was in court with Dick Kelly.

One more adventure brings a smile to my face when I think about Bill. There came a time when most of the probation officers in the nine county Mankato District became pretty frustrated with the Department of Corrections. A lot of this frustration had to do with new legislation concerning offenders, but some of it also had to do with departmental policy.

Somebody came up with the idea of opening our own correctional facility, program it the way we wanted it to be programmed, and quit using the department's facilities. We all agreed to canvas our judges, and somewhat surprisingly, there seemed to be a great deal of support for the idea. To maintain interest on the part of my three judges and to keep them interested in the work that was going to have to be done to get the idea off the ground, I got Bill and Ken Bull to agree to a trip to Duluth to tour the Arrowhead Juvenile Center.

I made the arrangements for the tour and the motel, and the three of us headed for Duluth. I don't remember much about the tour except that Bill and Ken were impressed, and, I think, sold on the Center's programming.

After the tour, I thought Bill and Ken might like to do something, you know, like dinner, maybe a tour of Duluth, a few drinks. Both of them liked the idea of a few drinks, so the question got to be, "Where?" Ken suggested the Saratoga Club, Duluth's rather infamous strip joint. Now how did he know about the Saratoga Club? At any rate, who was I to turn him down?

Bill had a few drinks, but basically, he was bored to death. I was far from a frequent flyer when it came to strip joints and strippers, but Ken thoroughly enjoyed himself. At one point, I leaned over to him and made a comment about one of the features on one of the girls. He leaned over to me and said, "Anything you can't get in your mouth is excess." Eventually we woke Bill up, and I brought them to their hotel.

I haven't forgotten that there were two more Mathers, Esther, Bill's wife and Kris, their teenage daughter. Esther certainly didn't have it easy having to live with Bill and Kris. I always thought that Kris was an average teenager who knew perfectly well how to play one parent off on the other. Esther tried to exert more control over Kris than did Bill, but Esther needed to choose her battles more carefully, a lesson I'm not sure she ever learned. But I guess they all survived, and survival is what it's all about, right?

The Bauer Family

And then, there was the Bauer family. I've already indicated that Peg and I sort of hit it off from our first date on New Year's Eve, 1970.

Peg was one of two children born to Louise and Larry Bauer. The older child, Larry, was married and living in Wisconsin at the time Peg and I met.

Larry always seemed to me to be somewhat distant, and then, maybe he just thought I was another wolf stalking his daughter. Me, a wolf? Yikes!

Now, Louise, on the other hand…what can I say about Louise? Louise was alive, had a terrific sense of humor, and it didn't take me long to become very fond of her.

Peg and I started seeing each other almost on a weekly basis. I thought that her coming to New Ulm and staying with me would be a little politically dangerous, given the fact that my boss, the Judge, was her uncle. That didn't stop me from driving to West St. Paul on most weekends to stay with her, however.

As time went on, Peg and I became very comfortable with each other, to the point where I began to think about marriage and a family. I'm not sure we ever spoke of marriage, but I sure as heck had myself convinced that Peg shared my feelings.

At some point, I introduced Peg to my parents, and they both (especially, my Dad) fell in love with her. So, Peg's family seemed to like me, and my family sure as heck loved her. So what the hell happened, you ask?

In 1972, I proposed to Peg. She said, "No." She wasn't ready for this marriage stuff, probably sensing that I was far from being stable in a career. She believed, and she was right, that I wasn't settled yet and ready for marriage. Given these facts of life, we quit seeing each other, but we remained friends.

More on the Kids and Their Families

I want to say a few words (probably a few thousand words) about social service systems and how they hurt people when they fail. In these social service systems I'm including schools, churches and public and private agencies.

I remember a boy about sixteen years of age. I don't remember why he was in court, but that doesn't have anything to do with why I remember him. What I do remember is that he was placed on probation, and I made arrangements to see him and his family at their home that same night.

We were talking in the family's living room. Specifically, we were talking about his school records, which I had obtained earlier in the day. His grades weren't good, but I was much more concerned about the comments that a steady and long line of teachers had made about him, including "Does not take directions, ignores instructions,"

149

etc. What I was seeing in front of me and what I was reading from the record just didn't seem to fit.

But something else puzzled me about the kid. I couldn't quite put my finger on it, but something was wrong. And then it came to me. He wasn't looking at my eyes; he was looking at my mouth. He was reading my lips.

I confronted him about it. He told me that when he had a cold or was experiencing sinus problems, he lost his hearing. He said that this had been the condition since he started school. His condition had been diagnosed when he was in kindergarten, and the condition had been reported to school authorities. No one, including the boy's parents, ever followed up on the condition. Obviously, the whole problem was forgotten, and a young man cultivated an extremely inaccurate reputation, and as a result, we were dealing with a young man who had lost all interest in school. He quit school before graduation. How many kids have I seen quit just before crossing the finish line?

David was another one of my more memorable cases. I think he'd been in Court on a petition alleging Incorrigibility.

David's family consisted of a sister close in age to David, and both parents, JoAnn and Jim. Both David's mother and his sister were very attractive physically. As I recall, JoAnn, a registered nurse, had done some professional modeling. When the two of them had their backs turned to me, I couldn't tell them apart.

The main problem in the family seemed to be the father or, specifically, the relationship between David and his father. I don't think I ever got a clear understanding of really was the problem between David and his father, but it was sad.

When kids have this kind of relationship with a parent, they sometimes work overtime at trying to get that parent's approval. This was true in David's case. As I recall, when he was in high school, he decided that he would try out for the wrestling team, believing that would please his father. He made the team but lost every match.

When the Father/Son Banquet was held, Jim amazed both David and his mother by agreeing to attend the banquet with David. After the meal, the award ceremony took place. As the athletes' names were called, father and son were to walk across the floor and accept their award. When David's name was called, his father refused to accompany him to the front of the room.

I've been in touch with David over the past 37 years, and I still can't imagine the emotional scarring that took place as a result of that banquet. David was a good kid, and he's a good man.

I wouldn't want you to believe that I liked all the kids and parents I ever worked with. There was one family that drove me absolutely crazy. There were several boys in the family, just about all of whom were being supervised through the court, and this gang of brats was led by their mother, Ma Barker (or so I referred to her.) Her boys were all pretty good-sized kids, and they used their size to intimidate other kids in town. And God help anyone in town who managed to get an upper hand on any of Ma's kids!

She was known to put her boys in the family van, drive up and down the streets of town until they found the boys who had offended her sons, let them bolt from the van, wail on the kids, and then jump back in the van and take off. I know it's hard to believe, but true.

I once stopped at the house to see her and the kids as I had at least two of them on probation. They weren't home, and the van was gone. As I was walking from the door of the house to my car, which was parked in the driveway, the van suddenly squealed around the corner and into the driveway, stopping a few feet from my shaking frame.

When I found out they had been out beating on some local kids, and with mother's help, of course, I decided to bring one of them back into court on a charge of Violation of Probation. It was my intention to recommend to the Court that it commit this kid to the Youth Conservation Commission, and that he do a little time in one of their correctional spas for delinquents. I also thought it would be good to give this kid a little time away from mom.

When I talked to Bill, he let me know that he wasn't inclined toward committing this kid, but I was determined to push the issue. When I refused to back off, Bill conveniently created some reason for me to be out of town on the day of the hearing. It, therefore, had to be postponed indefinitely.

My response to Bill's little trick was to dictate a letter, which I addressed to the Dishonorable Judge of Reprobate Court. I also signed it, Pontius Pilate. My young secretary, Sharon, was shocked and refused to type it. She agreed only after I assured her the whole thing was a joke.

I never did get this kid into court, and Bill never did explain why he was so unwilling to hear this case. And I don't know whatever happened to those kids, but the next time I saw the family name, it was on a nameplate and sitting on a desk in a nursing home. Now, doesn't that just figure?

Judge Kenneth Bull and Sibley County

My first six months with Ken Bull were a test of nerves and patience. It seemed like nothing I did satisfied the man. But I discovered that in time, we both learned to trust one another, and that trust level grew to be all but complete. That isn't to say that we understood each other completely, but we trusted each other.

A case in point: One of my tougher Sibley County cases was a young man by the name of Mike. Mike and his parents lived on a farm between the cities of Winthrop and Gibbon. Mike's parents were beautiful people, and simple people, but they didn't have a clue as to how to handle a rebellious teenage son. Mike apparently got bored with his parents' and my pressure to conform to the rules and the law, so he absconded from home, and thereby, the Court's supervision. The usual paperwork was done so that Mike could be picked up on sight.

One blistering cold winter night, something after midnight, Mike called. He told me that he was home, and he was ready to turn himself in to me, and only me. I told him that he had taken at least one wrong turn on his way home, and that he should have turned himself in at the Sheriff's office. He insisted that if I wanted him, I'd have to drive the twenty-five miles to the family farm to get him. I took one more "shot across the bow" and warned him that he'd better be there when I got there. He assured me that he'd be there waiting for me.

I piled in my car and drove the very cold twenty-five miles to the farm. When Mike's parents came to the door, I knew immediately that Mike had had a change of mind. We sat and had a few cups of coffee together, and I jumped in the car and drove toward home.

I fumed all the way home. Suddenly I noticed a vehicle driving next to me, a Highway Patrol vehicle. The temperature in my car got a lot hotter as I pulled over. A very irritated looking Patrolman, Brad Ferris, walked up to my window and scanned the inside of my car and me. He asked me if I knew how fast I was going. I told him I was going 60 miles per hour. He said that was right, I was speeding. Of course, what he didn't tell me was that he was speaking of the daytime speed limit. (For you younger readers, there was a time when daytime and night time speed limits were different.) He also kept looking at me as if to be asking, "Don't I know you?" He didn't ask, and I didn't tell him why he knew me.

He did ask me to join him in his squad car, which, of course, I was very happy to do. I love freezing cold weather! After running a check on my license number, he apparently thought better of writing me a speeding ticket, and instead, he wrote me a warning ticket. Then he said, "Good night," and I got in my car and started down the highway again.

A few seconds after starting out, I realized I left one of my gloves on the back seat of his squad. I had been smoking a cigarette when I got stopped and had one glove on and one off. I didn't put the one back on when I was invited into the squad car. For some reason, I took the second glove off in the squad car. Eventually I got home, climbed into a nice, warm bed, and began to dream about how tall a tree I was going to hang Mike from when I caught up to him.

The next night, Bill and I were occupying our usual chairs at Ebert's Chalet when the door flew open, and there was one very red-faced Brad Ferris, with a look on his face that read, "Now I know who you are!" I motioned for him to approach the counter, which he did very quickly, and I asked him if he'd found a glove in the back seat of his car the previous night. He said he'd check right away, and practically flew out of the restaurant. He reappeared a minute later, telling me that he couldn't find a glove. I thanked him for looking, and he went to join other officers for coffee. His face was still red.

A few nights later, I ran into Brad, and he asked me why I hadn't told him who I was the night he stopped me on the highway. I asked him if knowing who I was would have made a difference as to whether or not he wrote me a ticket. Before he answered, I told him that I hoped it wouldn't have. I think he knew what I was saying.

Anyway, back to Mike. Eventually I received another middle of the night phone call from a Colonel Sanders (yeah, that's what I said) who was calling from Leesville, Louisiana. He told me that he had just picked Mike up and put him on the phone. I asked him what the hell he was doing in Louisiana. He said that he had planned to run to California. I suggested that he might have taken a wrong turn at Kansas City, and that he should have paid more attention to geography when he was in school, which was rarely!

He started to complain about the way he was being treated by Col. Sanders. He related that he had kicked the Colonel and that his response was to hit him with his nightstick! Mike told me that he informed the Colonel that he couldn't do that because he was a juvenile. When I asked him what the Colonel's response was, he said he was told, "Not in this goddamned state, you aren't."

"And then, he hit me again," Mike said.

I asked him when he was going to sign the extradition papers so he could come home. He told me that his attorney told him not to sign the papers. I told him to put the attorney on the phone. His name was Preston Penny. When I asked him why he wouldn't let the kid sign the papers, he said it was because I didn't like him. I told him he was damned right about that, and that I didn't much like him either. Apparently he got fed up with my abuse, because he hung up on me.

The next day, I asked the Sheriff if he happened to have any felony charges that he might have forgotten to charge Mike with in the past. Lo and behold, he had one! He sent it to Louisiana and, a short time later, I received a very nasty phone call from Preston Penny. He demanded that I make the arrangements for getting Mike out of Louisiana. Of course, I jumped right on it. Yeah, right.

While Mike was on his way back to Minnesota, I made arrangements for him to make the necessary appearance in Ken Bull's court. At the time, I was still living in New Ulm, so when the Sheriff went to Louisiana to pick him up, he brought him back to New Ulm. I would transport him the twenty-five miles between New Ulm and Sibley County.

I'd always sensed something that wasn't right about Mike. I had the feeling that he was capable of a lot more than most kids I'd worked with. For that reason, and because of his history of running, I decided that my safety, and maybe his too, suggested that I transport him in handcuffs.

When I brought him into the courtroom in handcuffs, Ken had a canary! After taking a tongue-lashing for a few minutes, I suggested a recess. When we got in chambers, I told him that neither he nor

Sibley County was paying my life or car insurance, and that if I thought a kid was dangerous, he'd ride in my car any way I wanted him to. That meant handcuffs, legs shackled, a gag in his mouth or naked! He was mad, but so was I, and we kind of had this unspoken agreement that we could get mad at each other and let it be known. I don't remember the disposition of the case, but Mike continued under my supervision.

Sometime after this hearing, Mike wound up in the Ottertail County Jail. He had a gun smuggled to him through a broken window of the jail and broke out at gunpoint. He stole a car from a local doctor, also at gunpoint, and got himself involved in a high- speed chase with law enforcement. After being cornered, and with pistol in hand, he bolted from the car, and as he did so, I believe he hit the steering wheel, turning the gun toward himself and shooting himself in the abdomen.

I heard about the incident on the radio on a Thursday morning as I was heading to Court in Sibley County. I wondered if Ken had been listening to the news.

When I walked into the office, Ken was standing at the counter looking at the paper over the top of his glasses. I didn't say a word. He looked at me, frowned, and said, "I don't want to hear about it!"

I just smiled.

And Then There Was Henderson

When a person works and lives in a smaller community, they not only get to know the people, they get to know the town, its values, its history and, in some cases, its secrets. Henderson seemed like a very old town, almost isolated, and they didn't seem to like change. They even seemed to be suspicious of people wearing business suits. Statistically, about half the population of the world has never made or received a phone call. In those days, I would have sworn that some of those people lived in Henderson. Henderson truly had some of the scariest people and attitudes I'd ever run into.

For example, in the early 1970s, Northern States Power Company was putting up power lines in and around Henderson. A lot of the farmers in the area opposed the power line project, fearing the effects of the lines on their farm animals, especially their milking cows.

The opposition got fierce and violent. NSP workers were

sometimes shot at, and equipment was torched, including large road graders. NSP hired people at $8.00 per hour, a very good hourly wage in those days, to sit in the weeds and guard the equipment, armed only with a police radio. They also were shot at occasionally.

I was tempted to do a little moonlighting, as $8.00 per hour was a lot more than I was making at the time. But Ken nixed the idea and forbid me to go into Henderson, as it appeared that some of those being shot at had been wearing business suits like I did. It was a good thing that he nixed the idea, because I found out later that the guards' radios didn't always work because Henderson was located in a valley. Eventually, the power lines went up and the residents were forced to accept it, whether they liked it or not.

Barney

Henderson's Chief of Police was Barney. Barney was a joke, where being any kind of law enforcement officer was concerned, and he was also an alcoholic. On one occasion, a young deputy sheriff by the name of Willis Decko and I decided we were going to raid the park in Henderson. We knew that the local kids liked to do their partying in the park, including the use of alcohol, right under the not-too-watchful eye of the Chief. We decided to include him in on the bust in order to give him a little credibility.

The plan was for Willis and me to sneak into the park in a cruiser with all lights off and then to turn the headlights, flashers and siren on. We knew this would result in the kids' flying down the hill toward the street, where Barney would grab one or two of them for us.

Willis and I managed to sneak into the park, and we managed to surprise the kids with the lights and siren. And the kids ran down the hill, but when Willis and I got to the edge of the hill and looked down at Barney's squad car, he was sitting in the driver's seat sipping on a pint bottle of hooch. The kids were laughing and running around the car, climbing over the car, and to add insult to injury, some of them were crawling through the back seat of the squad. So much for Barney.

Henderson and the Minnesota Twins

I had two brothers from Henderson on probation. I don't

remember anything about them except that both were in their early teens, and the family seemed to be very poor. During their time under my supervision, they could talk of little else but the Minnesota Twins. They'd never been to a game, and they talked as if they'd never get to a game.

I decided it would be fun to take them to a Twins game. I got the okey-dokey from the parents and then told Ken Bull, just in case he had any particular reason why I shouldn't, or couldn't, do such a thing. He didn't object, but he did think I was nuts.

On the day of the game, and all the way to Municipal Stadium, the boys just stared out the windows at the skyscrapers of the big city. When we got to the stadium, the boys were so preoccupied with the stadium itself that I'm not sure either of them ever saw a pitch, to say nothing about the fact that the Twins actually won the game. And, of course, they sampled several of the stadium's menu items.

I don't know whatever happened to those boys, but I picture them as still living in Henderson. If so, I hope they're making time for the Twins. If not, maybe they turned into professional ball players!

Patrick – Here and Gone

One morning, I found myself sitting in Judge Bull's chambers discussing a case we were about to hear in Court. The phone rang, and Ken picked it up. He handed me the phone, telling me that it was long distance from Duluth. Of course, my first thought was that someone in the family was sick, had an accident, or had died.

I took the phone and discovered it was my old teenage nightmare, Patrick (Pissquick.) He asked me what I was doing the following weekend. I told him I wasn't doing anything. He said, "Good! Then get your ass up here for my wedding."

I asked him how pregnant she was.

He said, "About six months."

I told him I'd be there.

As I sat in the church witnessing the ceremony, I was reminded of Mich's telling me that this kind of event was what was really going to make the kid business worthwhile, like those rare occasions that I would be invited to a wedding of one of my kids, or the baptism of one of my kids babies, or being asked to be the Godparent to one of my kids babies. I was beginning to realize what he meant.

After the wedding, we retired to the Tracey group home (Tom and Donna's) and Patrick and I found ourselves sitting alone at the kitchen table. It had been a couple of years since we had last seen each other, but Roy and Marla had told me that he had enlisted in the Army and was stationed in Germany.

Pat thanked me for my help and support during the time he was on parole, and I told him that I was very proud of him.

At some point, the new wife walked in the kitchen and said, "Patrick, it's time to go." He got up and got her coat. I remember telling her that she'd been much more successful at getting him to mind than I'd been.

Pat and I shook hands, hugged each other, and they were gone. A few weeks after the wedding, I got a phone call from Donna Tracey, who told me that Patrick had been killed on the autobahn in Germany. I think he was about 20 years old. At last word, Pat's son was living in Florida.

Kevin's Story

Memories aren't always memories because of the force of time. I met Kevin as a result of an Incorrigibility petition initiated by his parents. Sitting in the Sibley County Juvenile Courtroom with Kevin and his parents was not the way I would have chosen to spend a Friday afternoon. Kevin had the kind of attitude that made me want to slap the crap out of him. He had the disposition of a king cobra, and he certainly wouldn't have won the Mr. Congeniality Award.

The net result of the hearing was that Kevin was adjudicated to be a delinquent child and was placed on probation. After the hearing, I escorted him and his parents to my office where I prepared a formal Probation Agreement, specifying the rules of his probation period.

As curfews seemed to be one of his bigger problems, according to his parents, I paid special attention to setting a curfew. I finally sent them home, and my week had come to an end—or so I thought.

That same night, Kevin called me to ask for an extension on his curfew for that night. I usually didn't do this until the kid proved to me that he was willing to cooperate with the curfew I gave them. I said, "No" and warned him that if he were seen out after his 9:00 pm curfew, law enforcement had been ordered to pick him up and lock him up. As I hung up the phone, I wondered how long it would take him to decide to ignore my warning.

At about 9:15 pm, fifteen minutes after his curfew, I received a phone call from the sheriff, Maynard Hahn, who told me that Kevin had been involved in a car accident and had been killed. He'd been drinking. He'd been speeding down a dirt road in the local cemetery and hit a tree. The driver's door popped open, and Kevin was propelled, head first, into a gravestone. The car's engine popped out and was found to be resting on his chest when the accident was discovered.

At Kevin's funeral, the minister's comments were directed at his classmates. But instead of taking an empathetic tone, he sounded frustrated and even angry. He made the statement that the unfortunate thing about the whole incident was that within a few weeks, most of the kids in the church would forget Kevin's death and go right back to the drinking and the drugs. I wanted to stand up a applaud him. I find it a little odd that I think of this kid as often as I do, given the fact that I knew him for less than a day.

The Star of the Team

Jim was one of only a few of my Sibley County cases who was a ward of the Minnesota Department of Corrections. After his release from one of the department's juvenile institutions, he returned to his hometown of Winthrop, and I re-enrolled him in the local high school.

Jim had an interest in trying out for the school's football team. I certainly had no objections to a kid getting involved in school athletics, so I encouraged him to try out for the team.

He didn't have much trouble making the team, and during the course of the season, he became one of the team's stars. I enjoyed watching him progress as an excellent player because I was hoping to use him to help me free myself from a little political vice I found myself in.

During the football season, someone had told me that the Gaylord High School football team, the town where my office was located, had beaten the Winthrop High School team, the town I lived in now 20 months in a row. During the course of the season, the talk intensified about the big game between these two archrivals, and the question got to be one of which team I was going to be cheering for. Even Ken Bull asked me.

As I was a public figure, everyone from the grocery store owner to the Judge wanted to know which side of the field I was going to be sitting on the night of the big game. I had walked the line until the night of the game, which was played in Gaylord.

On the night of the big game, the ticket-taker asked me which side of the field I was going to sit on, the winners or the losers. I told him I was going to sit on the winners' side, the Winthrop side. As I sat there, I wondered if even Ken Bull would have something to say about which side of the field I was sitting on. The residents of these two towns took their high school football very seriously.

I spotted Jim and his teammates passing the ball to each other a few minutes before the start of the game. I motioned to him, and he walked over to me. I asked him how he was feeling. He said he was feeling great. I asked him how he liked being out of the institution. With kind of a queer look on his face, he said, "Great." I asked him if he wanted to stay out of the institution. "Of course," he said, still with the look on is face.

"Then you'd better win," I said.

He was shocked. "You'd take me back if we don't win?"

I just smiled.

From the beginning kickoff, Jim played like a man on a mission. The Gaylord team was literally dragged around the field all night long. I don't remember the final score, but Winthrop won the game handily. As I walked off the field, Jim ran up to me, still with that concerned look on his face. He asked me if I would have really returned him to the institution had Winthrop lost the game. I told him we'd never know as Winthrop won the game. I wonder what the YCC would have thought if I'd brought a kid back for losing a football game?

A year or two later, Jim decided he wanted to get married. By this time, thank God, he was no longer on parole. At the time, I had a police radio in my car, as I had gotten tired of getting home at night, only to be called somewhere I'd just been by a sheriff's department or police department. I could check with law enforcement on my way home.

Anyway, one morning, I was driving from Gaylord going west on Highway 19 toward Winthrop. I was hearing more than the normal volume of chatter on the police radio. I turned up the radio a little and discovered that the chatter involved Jim.

Apparently he hadn't been able to get any time off to enjoy a honeymoon with his new wife. He got married on Saturday and had to work on Monday. The chatter on the radio had to do with the Sheriff's Department arresting a young man caught running south on Highway 15, right outside of Winthrop, dressed only in his under shorts, and they were on backwards. Talk about a little suspicious!

Later, I stopped at the Sheriff's Office and got the scuttlebutt. As the story went, Jim had decided to go home for lunch and surprise his new bride. He walked in the house and found her in bed with his best friend. Jim pulled the guy out of his bed, threw him on the floor, and grabbed a shotgun. He shoved the shotgun in his friend's mouth, but thought better of it. The kid got up, grabbed his Fruit of the Looms, and started running and putting on his shorts both at the same time! He didn't stop running until deputies stopped him on the highway.

A Few Words about Community Celebrations

I think most small communities express their community personalities with some kind of annual celebration. New Ulm had Polka Days. Even though the celebration was only a few days in length, and was the brainchild of a relatively small city of slightly over 13,000 people, it was no small or insignificant event. The population swelled to some 50,000 during Polka Days, and visitors came from as far away as Europe.

I'm not into crowds or a lot of noise, so taking in these events wasn't in the cards for me. Instead, Polka Days always meant long workdays. The Police Department always expected that I would occupy the front passenger seat of a squad car well into the wee hours of the night.

The interesting thing about these local celebrations was the attitude of the local residents. For example, shortly before my first Polka Days experience, I began getting office visits from some of my juvenile caseload who informed me that it was legal for them to drink alcoholic beverages during Polka Days. I had a hard time believing that they would actually try and sell that bull.

I always told them that legal or not, if they were caught drinking, they'd wind up sobering up in a jail cell. During the four annual celebrations I experienced, the Police Department and/or I caught seven kids, all on the same night, and all girls. I remember no other problems during Polka Days.

The City of Henderson had its Sauerkraut Days. During one such celebration, two local teenage boys decided to lend a little more excitement to celebration by streaking. Remember streaking?

The main street in Henderson was highway 19. As you entered the town from the west, you found yourself driving down a hill. The two boys involved planned to disrobe in some bushes and streak right down the center of Highway 19.

But teenagers are known for being at least a little unreliable. They disrobed in the bushes, but on the agreed on signal, one of them got up and started running, but the other chickened out and not only didn't run with his friend but he ran in the other direction, taking his friend's clothes with him.

Of course, the first kid was caught and shuffled off to the Sheriff's Office. Sheriff Hahn called me and then the boy's father. I got to the office shortly after the boy's father. Dad was very busy ripping his kid a new one, if you know what I mean. Maynard asked me what I thought he should do by way of charges. I told him that judging from the sound of the father's voice, the kid wasn't going to live to get home anyway. Maynard decided to turn the kid over to his father and file no charges. Incidentally, there was a picture on the front page of the local paper, several days later, showing the "bare facts" of the incident.

Joel and the Great White Shark

I've already mentioned Deputy Sheriff Willis Decko. Willis and I raided the park in Henderson—remember—with the help of Barney, the Chief of Police? Well, I also recruited Willis and his wife, Mary, to be foster parents for a 14-year old case of mine by the name of Joel. Unfortunately, a week or so after placement, Willis had to put in his two weeks with the Guards. I was a little concerned about his being gone that long so shortly after Joel's placement, but it couldn't be helped. I told Joel that sometime during the two weeks, I'd take him out for a pizza and movie.

Thanksgiving fell during this two-week period, so naturally I went home to spend the holiday with my family. During Thanksgiving dinner, my brother, Jack, was talking about a movie he'd seen recently that actually made him sick. He went into great detail in his description of scenes in the movie, and he warned everyone to refrain from seeing it. The movie, by the way, was *Jaws*. I didn't pay a lot of attention to my brother, as this was not my kind of movie anyway.

In all too short a time, the long weekend ended, and it was back to work on Monday morning. Shortly before closing the office for the day, my phone rang. It was Joel. He reminded me of my promise to take him out for a pizza and movie. I decided to get it over with, and I thought a Monday might be a good night to do it. Then I made the mistake of asking him what movie he'd like to see.

"I wanna see Jaws!"

"Damn," I thought. I should have guessed, but I was, as they say, "Screwed, glued and tattooed." You'd think a probation officer would have more authority over a 14-year old probationer, wouldn't you?

I picked Joel up at home, and we headed to Mankato and a pizza joint I knew of located very close to the university campus. We inhaled the pizza and headed for the theater. Naturally, when we got into the theater, Joel wanted to sit in the front row so he didn't miss anything. I didn't argue with him as I felt I would be more successful in missing some things I was sure I didn't want to see if I sat in the front row.

Joel got through the first half of the movie without tossing his cookies, although I didn't fare as well. He seemed to take great joy in watching me cover my eyes periodically. He was acting like a real big shot.

Sometime during the movie, the action slows for a while. The shark hunters are out in a boat hunting the Great White. They've been on the water for several days, the weather is hot, and the crew is getting a little off guard.

During one of the scenes, one of the crewmembers is seen throwing bait into the water. I noticed that the man's head is at the very bottom of the screen, and it's relatively obvious that something is going to fill the screen at any moment. Suddenly, the shark leaps out of the water and scares the ba-jeebers out of Joel, and most of the audience, for that matter. That kid jumped so high out of his seat that I had to peel him off the ceiling of the theater, I swear. I laughed so hard I almost wet my pants! That movie must have given Joel, Willis, and Mary something to laugh about when Willis got home. A little more help God sent when it was needed.

Like Father, Like Son?

One day, I received a petition concerning a young man who was being charged with Possession of a Controlled Substance, specifically, marijuana. The boy was a tall, blond, handsome kid with an IQ of 162. His school records indicated a kid who couldn't pass a hands on course in Sex Education. There was a picture of this kid beside the word "stubborn" in Webster's Dictionary. It didn't take me long to figure out where he got it.

The young man's father was as tough as a Marine sergeant. Well, actually, he was a Marine sergeant. I think he thought the best way to raise children was the Marine way! The kid's way of dealing with his father was to passively resist his father's every wish. If dad expected "A's," the boy would give him "F's." If you want to upset dad, get caught smoking marijuana. You get the point!

For some time, my client branded me as "The Enemy." He anticipated that I was going to come down solidly on his father's side on at least most issues. The fact of the matter was that I didn't even like dad. I really felt sorry for both the kid and his mother.

One evening, I did a family session in their home and, sometime during the session, I asked dad if he loved his wife. He almost yelled, "Of course I love my damned wife," or something close to that. At the end of the session, I played the tape back for him, and he almost didn't believe it was he who was making the statement. Although I hoped that session had done something for him, it hadn't.

The other major problem I had with this family was that the boy always forced me to deal with his behavior. I put a lot of pressure on him where school was concerned. I was concerned about the fact that he seemed like he was willing to continue in a self-destruct mode just to get dad's attention.

I made two things very clear to this kid from the start. First, if he wasn't in school for any other reason than sickness (and even then, he'd better be pretty near death), he'd spend the weekend in jail. Secondly, he was to quit his part in the problem with his father. That problem was keeping the heat turned up in the house and making the whole family uncomfortable.

To some extent, he made some effort in resolving the second problem, but that still left a hardheaded Marine running the home. The first problem took a little time and effort, but in time, he walked in my office and proceeded to teach me a lesson. In order to apply as much pressure on him as possible, I arranged to monitor all of his grades, practically on a daily basis. I also arranged with the Principal to be able to approve electives the kid might want to take.

One day, he showed up in my office to show me his class schedule for the next grade period. He asked me, "What would you do if I told you I was going to turn over a new leaf?"

I told him I'd probably "tear off his leg and beat him with it." He asked me why.

I told him that, if he could do that now, he could have done it six months earlier and saved both of us a lot of grief!

Then he said, "It took me that long to figure out you were a friend."

I had always told kids that I didn't think that our relationship necessitated our being enemies, as long as we both respected each other's legal position of probationer and probation officer.

The boy handed me his new program for the new grade period. On it were Advanced Algebra and Trigonometry. I realized the Principal must have approved the program already. I asked him if he really expected me to sign the program. He said, "Yes," and I smiled and signed it. He got straight "A's" that grade period. I don't remember his having anymore school problems from that point to graduation. Gee, come to think of it, I'm glad he didn't try to get me to approve a lab class in Sex Education.

Even though the boy apparently decided to quit the self-destructive stuff, I think he continued to have problems with his father. On Christmas Eve night, I happened to be riding around in a squad car as I often did, and we got a radio message to stop by New Ulm Ford where a Christmas party was being held. The partygoers invited us for coffee.

When we arrived, the first person I saw was a very drunk Marine of my acquaintance. He came over to me and proceeded to say, "I don't understand why my son will do anything you ask him to do, but he won't do what I tell him to do." I told him he might start by asking him to do something. You can always tell and yell if he refuses. He just turned and walked away from me.

Just A Few Thoughts

At this point, I'd like to take a short break and say a few things about the power of words. Most of us are never going to be rich, at least, not as measured by the thickness of our wallets. But we all have the power to say things that can comfort a child, a parent, grandparent, elderly person, etc. Words can also crush people. When you receive comments like, "thank you," or "you're my best friend," or "I love you," please don't forget them. They should mean something very special. Conversely, don't speak in words you don't mean. If you do, the worth of your words is de-valued, or cheapened.

The Beginning of the End

I always enjoyed working with clients, their families, the courts, judges, schools and public and private agencies. But I've come to the realization that God doesn't like people to get too comfortable in any situation.

I've already mentioned the kinds of troubles I was having with my supervisor, Paul Wagner. I felt like to some degree I was threatening him. For example, when I mentioned starting a big brothers-type program in New Ulm, his comment was, "It won't work. I tried it. New Ulm is too conservative for that type of program." So, should I have forgotten the idea?

And then, there was the change-over of the courts from Probate/Juvenile to County Courts. I was wishing that Bill would tell Paul to lay off, but I knew that his doing that would only make things worse. I also knew that Bill wasn't assertive enough (or at least I decided he wasn't) to do that without getting angry about it.

And then, there was Judge Bull's invitation to be his first Court

Services Director. Given the statutory mandates, Court Services personnel could find themselves involved in several new arenas as dictated by the County Court. As it turned out, Judge Bull did not expand my role and responsibilities, possibly because those responsibilities had traditionally been handled by the Social Services Department, and maybe he was happy with their service. I don't really know. What I do know is that in time, I became bored. I simply didn't have enough to do.

To add to my problems, the State Legislature went on what I considered to be a "stupid spree." For example, it passed a law lowering the legal drinking age from 21 to 18 years of age.

The first night the law was in effect, I found myself riding around in a squad car. During the middle part of the evening, we got a call to a local bar. One of my Youthful Offenders, age 18-21, was drunk and had been maced by the bartender.

When we got to the location, we found the kid wincing in pain on the sidewalk outside the bar. As the officer, Mike Hemauer, got out of the car, I warned him to stay away from the kid's arms. He bent over the kid and told him we were getting some cold water in order to wash out his eyes. As he did so, the kid's fist came up and hit Mike in the jaw so hard that I thought I saw his neck snap! With that, I bolted from the car, and the fight was on.

We called for backup, and eventually we succeeded in getting him into the cage in the back seat of the squad. We got him to the station, and five officers and I wrestled him into the station. We finally got him into a cell and called a doctor. The doctor gave him a sedative, and then Mike and I got back out on the street.

After an hour or so, we went back to the station to get the kid and take him to the local lock-up ward of Loretto Hospital. We got him into the hospital locked ward with no trouble. We had him in bed and were getting him undressed. In the room were three police officers, one nurse, and me. We four were going to hold him down while the nurse removed his engineer boots.

As she walked toward his feet, I told her to be careful. Just as I did, his foot came up and hit her squarely in the nose, knocking her to the ground and out cold. One of the officers managed to get his legs under control, and I was lying across his knees. The other two officers managed to get his hands secured while the third managed to secure his feet. The nurse survived, albeit with a broken nose and two black eyes.

A check of his clothing resulted in our finding marijuana and pills in the pockets. A day or two later, he was lodged in the local jail and charged with multiple offenses. As a result of his activities on that night, he was returned to prison. I wonder if he enjoyed his night on the town?

Another law that had been passed by Minnesota's bunch of elected legislative idiots was the Morrissey-Brewer Act. The thrust of this piece of legislative buffoonery was that an alleged parole violator had the right to an on-site hearing. That meant that if an alleged violation occurred in Seattle, a parolee could demand an on-site hearing in Seattle. If that happened, the parole agent was responsible for finding a site for the hearing, coordinating travel arrangements for those involved, find a date for the hearing that fit the schedules of the State Public Defender's Office, the Attorney General's Office if the parole agent wanted representation, etc.

I believe I had one of the first cases to be affected by this law. His name was Daniel. He was a parolee out of the prison in St. Cloud. He had been married and had a child. He was under a Court Order to pay Child Support, and as I recall, an Order for Protection was also in effect.

I secured employment for Daniel before his release from prison. It didn't take long for him to start missing work, fail to make support payments, and to have contact with his ex-wife. One night, law enforcement notified me that Daniel had been out drinking and was driving toward his ex-wife's residence. I ordered him to be picked up and lodged in jail. It took a roadblock to accomplish the purpose.

The next day, I called my State Department of Corrections Supervisor, told him the situation, and requested a hearing be convened with a DOC Hearing Officer, which was another resultant creation of the Morrissey-Brewer Act. His reaction was to tell me that he didn't think I had enough for a violation. I was furious. I told him that the only way this guy was going to get released was after a hearing or after he drove to the jail and released the kid himself.

A hearing was arranged and took place before a DOC Hearing Officer, one Morrie Heilig. The net result of the hearing was that Daniel admitted to all charges including several I hadn't accused him of. By way of consequences, Heilig added two or three more rules to the list that Daniel had already proven he was unwilling to keep.

Daniel was released, but within a few weeks, he'd taken off with two juvenile females and transported them across state lines. He waived extradition back to Minnesota, was convicted of several felonies in District Court, and was sentenced to ten years.

A few weeks after this sentencing, Morrie Heilig made the statement to me that I had finally gotten what I wanted for Daniel. I asked him what he thought that was. He said, "You finally got him back in prison."

I shook my head and told him that, "What I was trying to get was a preventive return to prison, not another ten year sentence."

A third bit of legislative stupidity was the Status Offender Bill. This bill, to put it simply, said that any act committed by a juvenile that would not be considered a crime if committed by an adult could not result in the juvenile's detention. Specifically, that meant Incorrigibility, Truancy and being a runaway. It was, and is, my feeling that in some cases, a juvenile cannot be reached until it can be proven to him that his body can be controlled.

At a regional staff meeting, I asked one of the authors of this bill how to handle the case of a thirteen-year-old who gets caught three hundred miles from home. Where do authorities secure him until someone from home can arrange to pick him up? He said, "You'll think of something." I remember telling him that not all Minnesota counties had a facility to handle this kind of eventuality. He looked at me and smiled.

So you see, in my opinion, State law was heading in a direction that was in no one's best interest, including correctional clients. I was angry, depressed, and probably worst of all, I felt professionally impotent.

I began to consider my options. A friend of mine who was the Court Services Director in another county, called me in Gaylord and told me that he was leaving his position, and he had suggested to his judge that I would be a good replacement.

For several months, he kept on calling. I kept putting him off, thinking that this would only be a lateral transfer doomed to have the same problems and frustrations as did my present position. But I couldn't figure out what to do, so I concluded that supervising what was promised to be a far more active caseload was an acceptable second choice. So an interview between the Judge and I was arranged. I informed my State Supervisor of the interview. His response was, "You won't like it." When I asked him what he meant, he repeated, "You won't like it!"

Another County, Another Interview

I told Ken Bull about the interview just before he left town for a judge's conference. He said he'd be anxious to hear my reaction to the interview when he got back.

On the appointed interview date, I found myself to be far more nervous than I would be in just about any other similar circumstance. Bill Weber's telling me, "You won't like it" really bothered me. Why he wouldn't tell me why he felt that way bothered me even more. Regardless, I had the feeling that something was about to change, and I was encouraged by that thought.

I arrived in the County Seat and managed to locate the Law Enforcement Center, the building housing the Sheriff's Department, Jail, Court Services, and Social Services Departments. I was greeted by the Court Services secretary, Beulah, who offered me a much needed cup of coffee. We had a pleasant conversation about the county and some of its more interesting characters when, suddenly, there appeared one Judge John Henry.

After introducing ourselves, the Judge and I retired to the Court Services Director's Office, which adjoined the secretary's office and the Sheriff's Office. We closed both doors. The Judge invited me to take a chair. He wheeled the Court Service Director's chair over to me and took a seat.

I don't remember much about the specifics of the interview, but I do remember his saying that, "In this county, I'm the Judge, and you're the Court Services Director. I don't do your job, and you don't do mine. If you need something, you let me know, and you'll get it, OK?"

I was getting a pretty good feeling about this guy. I was surprised by his age, though. He was sixty-nine years old. As we continued to talk, the door from the Sheriff's Office blew open and the sheriff charged in, grabbed the back of the chair that the Judge was sitting in, turned it and gave it a shove toward the opposite wall. The chair, complete with Judge, banged against the wall. I looked at him for a reaction. None! He just sat there with a smile on his face.

The sheriff looked at me and said, "Don't look like much of a probation officer to me!"

I looked at him and said, "You'll find me to be more than you can handle." With that, he smiled, got up, and left.

The Judge didn't attempt to explain the sheriff's behavior. We just continued our conversation and, within a short time, he offered me the Court Service Director's position. I accepted. We didn't settle on a starting date. We decided that could be done after I broke the news to Judge Bull.

I made the trip back to Gaylord, wondering whether or not I was making the right decision. I wasn't looking forward to telling Ken, but he knew I wanted more to do or to work in a more metropolitan county. In any event, the decision had been made, and once again, I was looking at separating from friends and planning for a new adventure in a new county. I still wasn't sure, though, that this change was going to bring enough satisfaction to arrest my growing dissatisfaction with the direction of correctional legislation. I guess only time would tell.

Over the next few weeks, I tried to see my Sibley County clients for the last time and prepare them for the transition to another Court Services officer. I also spent the time saying goodbye to friends, including Ken Bull.

The Last Stop

During the weeks after this last interview, it was decided that my starting date in my new position would be Oct. 1, 1975. I moved to town and into a dumpy hotel room until I could find an apartment. Didn't I do this once before? I'm having déjà vu!

On the morning of October 1, 1975, I was again greeted by my secretary, Beulah, and a cup of coffee. I invited her to sit down and teach me what I was going to need to know. I told her that Bill Weber told me that I wasn't going to like it, and asked her if she knew what that might have meant. Before she could answer, the door between my office and the Sheriff's Office flew open, and the sheriff flew in and plopped his ass on my desk. It was obvious that he was trying to

171

impress as well as intimidate me. He succeeded at neither. When he was satisfied that he'd accomplished his purpose, he got up and left.

Beulah told me that he was one of the characters I'd have to deal with, and it wouldn't always be easy. He had an overpowering personality, a lot of political power, and he subscribed to the philosophy that the end justifies the means. She warned me to always be on my guard.

She also told me that the sheriff and the county attorney worked very closely together. In time, I learned just how close that could be. Together, they made a formidable team, and together, they usually managed to pressure Judge John into doing things their way.

Beulah went on to describe others that I would find myself having to deal with on a regular basis. These included school officials, police chiefs, and of course, Judge John himself.

It was widely known that John had a major problem with alcohol, widely known by everyone but him and me. In the year or so that I worked for him, I don't ever remember him not showing up at work and on time. It always seemed, though, that he was well on his way to being drunk within fifteen minutes of the time the courthouse closed.

Armed with this information, I set about reading case files in order to get myself prepared for dealing with them and their families. One of the things I noticed from canvassing the file cabinet was that I was going to have to deal with a lot more adolescent females than I was used to.

On the days that followed, I made it a point to meet the county's city police officials. On the Police Department, the individual I was to work most closely with and become close friends with, was one Sgt. Edwards.

It didn't take long for me to "draw a bead" on Ed. One day, I walked into my office and found a note on my desk. It was from Ed. The note said that he had arrested a young man I'll refer to as NIBS. The note said that NIBS was in a cell, and he wanted me to see him ASAP. It was about suppertime, so I thought I'd go back and see him before I went home. When I told the jail deputy that I was there to see NIBS, he told me that he wasn't there. When I asked him where he was, I was told that Ed took him home for supper. That sure proved that I was dealing with a hard core cop!

Another ally I was to meet was Dale, the School Social Worker at the local Middle School. Dale and I were soon dubbed "Starsky and Hutch," who were two young TV detectives of the 70's, by local teenagers. As a matter of fact, the police called me one night to tell me that some unknown kids had actually climbed to the top of the city's water tower and had spray-painted "Starsky and Hutch" on it.

Dale was young and relatively new to his job. We grew to like each other a lot, and we developed an excellent working relationship.

On one occasion, he accompanied me to the State Training School at Red Wing, so he could see the facility and familiarize himself with the institution's program. He would also get a chance to meet some institution staff and some of my older cases.

We got to the institution and checked in at the Superintendent's office, which was a ritual for me. Then we proceeded to one of the cottages to check on one of my cases. I purposely neglected to inform the kid that I was coming.

The cottages were shaped like a "T." When we walked in, there was no one around except for a young staff member at the desk. From down one of the wings of the cottage, we could hear a group of kids who were yelling, and another kid who was cussing and swearing. Dale and I walked down the hallway very quietly, until we got to the room that was the scene of the action.

One boy was ringed by ten or so other boys, and they were yelling back and forth. The boy in the center of the ring was my boy. Dale and I stood there for a while listening to the kid call me every name in the book, and some that weren't, and threatening every part of my anatomy.

Dale was turning red with anger. I stood there smiling. No one had noticed we were in the room, so I tapped one of the boys on the shoulder. He turned, noticing us, and the ring of kids parted like the Red Sea. My boy, Mike, was on his knees with his head in his hands. Suddenly, he looked up and saw me staring at him. His eyes were saying, "Damn, I'm in a lotta trouble." His mouth was saying, "Holy shit!"

I grabbed Dale by the arm and sort of pushed him out the door. When we got out in the hallway, I said, "C'mon, let's get out of here!" Dale was shocked, wanting to know why I wanted to leave rather than stay and pound the kid into a dry hole! I suggested to him that it would

173

be a far more meaningful punishment to allow him to stew in his own gravy for a while, wondering how I was going to make him pay.

I think I got the first phone call from the boy before we got home. I must have gotten a dozen more over a period of the next week, none of which I chose to answer. Beulah got quite good at telling Mike that, "He can't answer right now" or some variation on that theme. At some point, I took one of his calls, Mike apologized, and that ended the problem.

I've already suggested that the sheriff thought quite a bit of himself. He bragged quite a bit about how he could manipulate people, including Judge John.

One morning, he flew in my office brandishing a legal document. He pointed at it and asked, "Do you know what this is?" It was a Commitment Order concerning an inebriate. I told him that I knew what it was.

He placed it on my desk and signed it with the Judge's name. I looked at it and told him that John was going to know it wasn't his signature. He asked me how he would know. I told him, "I'll never tell you. I'd like to see your ass in your own jail!"

The next morning, I received an almost panicky phone call from the Judge who asked me to come to his office right away. When I walked in his chambers, he looked at me and said, "I think I'm losing my mind. I don't remember this guy, and I don't remember signing this Commitment Order."

I said, "John, that's because you didn't sign it."

"Who did?"

"Take a guess," I said.

"Which one was it," he asked, "Frick or Frack?" He was referring to the sheriff and another county official.

I told him that the sheriff signed it in my office, on my desk and with me looking on. He took no action.

John was far from just about anyone's definition of a strong judge. It made me angry to see him manipulated because I really grew to love the man.

We developed a ritual. John had a habit of going to a local restaurant, at 9:00 p.m. every night, Monday through Thursday nights. He ordered a hamburger, short order of fries, and coffee, each and every night. The order never changed. I joined him most of those

174

evenings.

In time, I found out that, every night John went to the restaurant, one of the Police Department squad cars would hide behind the restaurant until he left, and then follow him home so that they could make sure he didn't accidentally drive into the lake. When I was with him and they saw my car, they would leave, knowing that I would follow him home. I have no idea if he ever knew about these escorts. If he did, he never mentioned them to me.

As the time passed, I found myself spending more time riding around in squad cars during evening hours. After all, I was still a happy bachelor.

One of the officers I spent a lot of time riding around with was Officer Steve. Steve was a big man and had a mouth and ego to match. He sometimes had problems in his dealings with juveniles, and my caseload in particular. I'll mention Steve again a little later.

Another officer I spent a lot of time with was Officer Brian. Brian and Sgt. Ed are probably best described as Officer Steve's polar opposites, and it was typically reflected in their handling of, and relationship with, my caseload.

One day, I found myself in court with Sgt. Ed's 14-year old supper guest, NIBS. As I recall, the charge involved his being picked up for driving his father's pick-up. He was taking a load of garden goods to the local farmers market. The interesting thing about this particular incident was that after NIBS pled guilty to the charge, his father told me that he told his son to take the trip to the farmers market.

NIBS was to become one of those kids that I thoroughly enjoyed working with. It soon became obvious that there were a whole lot of things going on in this family. NIBS used to like to spend his evenings standing on downtown street corners with or without friends. Under most circumstances, when a squad car rolled by, the kids would wave. When Steve was on duty, NIBS would give him "the finger." Steve, of course, would hassle NIBS.

Eventually, NIBS came in to complain to me. I suggested that if he was ready to mend his relationship with Officer Steve, it might be easier than he might think. I suggested that he go back and stand on those street corners. When he saw Officer Steve go by, I suggested he wave, only wave with all five fingers instead of just one. I told him that it might take a while for Steve to believe what he was seeing, but in time, he'd come around.

A few days later, NIBS walked in the office and told me that he'd done what I suggested. He said that after a few trips around the block and getting "five-fingered waves," Steve stopped the car, opened the door, and told him to get in. Of course NIBS thought he was in trouble again. Instead, the two of them rode around in the squad car for a while, and got to know each other.

NIBS had been adopted by his parents. He had, I believe, both a younger brother and sister. I don't know what the trouble was with regard to NIBS and his parents. It seemed to me that they simply didn't know how to communicate with him, nor did it seem like they were consistent with him. And what does his father's telling him to take some things to a farmer's market in his pick-up when he wasn't old enough to drive suggest to you? I'll leave NIBS for now, but I'll come back to him.

The sheriff, as I've already indicted, had an ego the size of the Pacific. One Saturday morning, that ego got him in a lot of trouble.

As you might recall, during the 70s, America found itself invaded by a religious group, or sect, referred to as the Moonies. The group was accused of brainwashing some members. Opposition groups snatched members of the group and deprogrammed them.

One day, the parents of a Moonies member, a legal adult, walked into the Sheriff's Department and wanted to talk to the sheriff. They told him of their daughter's situation and asked if there was anything he could do to help them get her back. Of course, he was more than willing.

The parents told the sheriff that the Moonie group, including their daughter, was going to be at a motel in Rochester for a Moonie service on the following day, Sunday. The sheriff got to the motel before the Moonie group. When the Moonies showed up and began getting out of their cars, the sheriff and his accomplices jumped out of their car, grabbed the girl, threw her in their car, and sped off. What they hadn't counted on was one of the Moonies getting the license plate number and calling it in to the Rochester Police Department and Olmstead County Sheriff.

A young Olmstead County deputy sheriff spotted the other sheriff's car and gave chase, and was finally able to stop the car. He ordered all of the occupants out of the car at gunpoint and demanded identification from the occupants. The sheriff produced his official ID. The young deputy, of course, was shocked and bewildered. He radioed to his sheriff that he was holding a county sheriff at gunpoint and asked for instructions. He was told to bring them all in. This description of events was related to me by a member of the Sheriff's Department.

In the ensuing weeks and months, there was talk of criminal charges being brought against the sheriff and others. To my knowledge, that never happened.

The End of a Local Icon

One Saturday morning, the Sheriff's Department was about to deliver a Mental Illness Commitment Order to a local farmer. The Department's chief deputy was preparing to deliver the Order and take the farmer into custody.

The sheriff, who was home, overheard radio chatter concerning the deputy's leaving the office to go to the farm. He had problems with this farmer in the past. The farmer had told him that if the sheriff ever had any business with him, he'd better send the chief deputy to handle it. The farmer told the sheriff if he came out to the farm himself, he would kill him. The sheriff ordered the chief deputy to stop at his home and pick him up. The deputy stopped by the house and picked his boss up as ordered. The sheriff wasn't even wearing his uniform.

When the two law officers arrived at the farm, the sheriff told the deputy to stay in the car. The sheriff got out of the squad car, went up to the door, and knocked. The door opened, a shotgun appeared, and a blast from the shotgun followed. The blast hit the sheriff and killed him. The deputy pointed his gun at the door, ordered the farmer to drop the shotgun, and come out. He did so with no trouble and walked out to the squad. This is the story as told to me by the chief deputy. For the next few weeks, the farmer occupied a cell in the jail, and over and over again, I would hear him say, "I killed the devil. I killed the devil!"

"At the Pleasure of the Court"

State law at that time required judges to retire by the end of the term in which they reached their seventieth birthday. I knew the rule, and I knew that Judge John was getting up there in age, but it never occurred to me to talk about his age and retirement plans at my interview. Now, in 1976, I was looking at losing Judge John and having to face, for the first time, being re-appointed by a new judge. The front runner became one G. T. Lawrence.

Before I deal with the appointment of the new judge, I'd like to mention some things that are, shall we say, more pleasant. Specifically, I'd like to talk about what a Court Services Officer did with his free time.

In those days, my average weekday started at about 7:00 a.m. and ended at about midnight. Evening hours were usually spent making home visits throughout the county or riding around in a squad car. Was it all necessary? No, but it usually made things easier in the end.

On weekends, my best friend, Marty, usually came down to spend the weekend with me, or I would travel to the Cities and spend the weekend with him. We spent the time talking, playing cards, hanging around favorite restaurants, and barhopping.

Brenda and Farrah

The great difference between living in a metropolitan community and a rural community can be described in one word: politics. All public officials liked to occasionally get away from the community's scrutiny.

At the time, Marty had two cats, one named Brenda and the other, Farrah. I'm not a big lover of cats, but these two were a lot of fun. So when I was spending a weekend in Minneapolis, these two cats were the cause of a lot of laughing on my part.

My friend, Dale, used to call me up just about every Sunday evening when he was sure I'd be home after a weekend in Minneapolis. He would ask all sorts of questions about what I did all weekend.

One Sunday night, he called and began asking his usual questions. I told him that Marty and I had spent the weekend with two pussycats, one black and named Brenda, and the other white and named Farrah. At this point Dale started getting all sorts of excited. He asked me what we'd done over the weekend. I told him that on Saturday morning, I woke up and Brenda was curled up and sleeping between my legs, which was true. I also told him that Farrah took a shower with me, (although more accurately, she fell off the edge of the tub while I was taking a shower.) I'll leave it to your imagination just what he might have been conjuring up in his mind.

Anyway, the next morning, I walked in my office, grabbed a cup of coffee, and sat down to talk to Beulah for a few minutes. She asked me how my weekend had been. I told her it had been fun. She asked how Brenda and Farrah were. I asked her what was up. She said that my friend Dale was telling everyone about my black and white girlfriends. I told Beulah that under normal circumstances, I might appreciate that rumor, but in this case, Brenda and Farrah were just what I'd been calling them. Pussycats!

She started to laugh. I never heard anything more about "Larry's girlfriends." You can imagine what kind of trouble that might have caused me.

My Friend, Max

The County had a contractual agreement with a mental health center in a nearby city to provide mental health services. One Max Wells, ACSW, furnished those services to my county.

The County furnished Max with a bare bones office on the third floor of the courthouse. Anyone over fifteen years of age had a hard time climbing all the steps. In time, my office was moved from the Security Building to the Courthouse Annex that was located right behind the courthouse. As Beulah's position was only part-time, I offered Max her office for his weekly Tuesday visits. This offered both him and his clients a little privacy and their own small parking area.

Over the months, Max and I got to be very close. We talked a lot about each other's work, counseling philosophies, etc. More on Max a little later

A Change at the Helm

As I mentioned, John was about to turn 70 years of age, and that meant he would be forced by law to retire. Of course, this fueled speculation as to who would succeed him.

As I understood the process, the local Bar Association would make a recommendation to the Governor, or furnish him with a list of possible candidates, and the Governor would appoint one as the next County Court Judge.

My assessment of the process was this. The local Bar Association met, probably at a bar someplace, and developed a list of possible candidates. My feeling was that the top candidate for the position was the local attorney who either couldn't make it as a practicing attorney, had an ego the size of an elephant's rear end, or the attorney who could most easily be manipulated in the courtroom.

In this case, the choice was one G. T. Lawrence. This was the local Bar's recommendation, and he became the Governor's appointee. He was also, of course, my new boss.

The Honorable Judge Lawrence

How do I describe Judge Lawrence? Well, first of all, he was a recovering alcoholic. I think I would have liked him better and had more respect for him if he had remained a drunk.

It's also important for you to understand that in those days, Court Services Officers served "at the pleasure of the Court." They weren't protected by a union, for example. That also meant that a lot of us survived because we knew how to brown-nose with our Judges, our bosses, when the opportunity presented itself.

We never had a formal conversation about Judge Lawrence's desire to appoint someone else to my position, but he made his feelings quite clear to me by his actions. May I present the following examples as cases in point.

He once told me that he felt that any juvenile's appearance in his courtroom had its core reason based on alcohol or drug use, and that's what he wanted me to indicate via my recommendations during delinquency hearings. I told him that I could do that when there was evidence to support it, but I couldn't say it without evidence supporting it. Obviously, I wasn't smart enough to kiss butt in this situation

As I was anticipating additional duties to become part of the job, I spoke to him about the possibility of adding another person to the Court Services Department. At the time, I was carrying a probation/parole caseload of one hundred ten clients. He told me that I could go to the County Board of Commissioners about it, and that it

180

would be fine with him if I could get their approval. He had the legal authority, by the way, to appoint one with or without board approval. I went to the board, made my request, and was practically laughed out of the room.

A few months later, he called me to his office and told me that he was going to hire a second person to add to the Court Services Department. I asked him if he had anyone particular in mind. He said, "Yes," but, when I asked him who it was, he told me that it was a secret. Eventually, I was to find out that his choice was one of the sons of a former sheriff.

At some point, the Principal of the Middle School and I both became frustrated by my young client, NIBS's, failure to cooperate on the issue of school attendance. The only recourse I thought I had was to bring him back to Court and see if we could be frightened into cooperating.

The hearing date was set for one very cold morning. The Judge, Middle School Principal, and I were in Chambers. NIBS and his father were waiting out in the courtroom. His Honor seemed to be in particularly good humor, which scared me. He had even given the Principal one of his long, green cigars to smoke.

Suddenly, the Judge realized it was time to go into Court. He got up and went to his coat closet to put on his judicial robes. After doing so, he looked in a mirror and saw himself in his robes with a huge cigar protruding from his lips. Then he saw his black, felt, Russian-looking hat and put that on his head. He bent over in a Groucho Marx pose, hands behind his back, and cigar bobbing up and down in his mouth.

I was thinking, "Oh, my God! He's actually going to go out into the courtroom behaving like a buffoon!" The Principal lined up behind Groucho, and I lined up behind the Principal. We walked in the courtroom, Groucho leading the way. He sort of skipped up the two steps to the elevated platform and plopped his butt in his chair, which promptly rolled to the other side of the wooden platform and down the two steps on the other side. I ran around to the other side of the bench and saw Groucho, still sitting on his chair, which was on its back, cigar still in his mouth, and pointing straight up toward the ceiling. Don't believe it? Well, I didn't either, but it's absolutely true! Obviously, that hearing wasn't very effective in dealing with NIBS's truancy problem.

One day, in a small city located just to the south of town, the police chief was standing on a street corner talking to some people. A man was making nasty remarks and yelling obscenities at the chief, who had his back turned to the man. He was doing his best to ignore the jerk.

Finally the guy disappeared, but a little while later, he reappeared with a rifle. Initially unobserved, the chief and the others continued their conversation. The man began to aim the rifle at the chief's back. Someone finally saw the man lining the rifle up, using a mail box to rest the rifle on, and alerted the chief. The chief turned, ran across the street and tackled the guy after he managed to pull the trigger. Luckily, the rifle jammed. Naturally, the man was charged and appeared in Court before Judge Groucho.

In Court, the Judge chided the chief, telling him that it was obvious that he hadn't done a lot of positive public relations work in his own city. The guy either pled guilty to the charge or was found guilty. His Honor then decided to do some creative sentencing. He sentenced the man to ride in the squad car with the chief for a number of hours, apparently so they would get to know one another. The chief was so mad that he resigned.

A Short but Wonderful Diversion

In the midst of turmoil, God tends to understand when enough is too much, and He sends a little pleasant diversion. In my case, and at about this time, that short, pleasant diversion came in the form of a phone call from my mother.

She told me that she had just been reading the local Duluth newspaper, and the feature article was about Henry Engler, my hospital physical therapist of almost twenty years before. The headline read, "Local Physical Therapist To Receive Key To The City For 52 Years Of Service." She started to read the article to me.

During the course of the interview, Henry was asked if there was one patient he remembered above any other. He began telling a story about a ten year old who was paralyzed, and who the doctors were saying, was not apt to walk again. Without going into more detail, it seemed like Henry was talking about me. Mother asked me if

I was okay with her calling Henry's boss and asking exactly who he was talking about. I told her to go ahead. She did so, and a short time later, she called and told me that indeed it was me he had been talking about. The boss told mother that they were hoping that the article would find me, because they wanted me to be Henry's big surprise. Of course, I told mother to call Henry's boss back and tell her I wouldn't miss it for the world.

On party day, my family and I walked into a huge party room, where I first saw several television cameras and a hundred people taking pictures. I looked for Henry, and when I spotted him, his back was turned to me. I approached him from behind, and a television cameraman who was filming Henry while he opened a gift, nodded at him and then at me. Henry turned, saw me, and hollered my name in his broken English. We hugged each other while the TV camera lights blinded us.

After a short on-camera interview with the two of us, Henry and I found a quiet corner where we could have a private conversation. The first question he asked me was why he hadn't heard from me in all the years since my hospitalization. The fact of the matter was that this little boy had stopped to see him a few times since my release from the hospital in 1958, but unfortunately, memories are short.

When he asked the question though, I answered him with one of my own. I asked him why he thought I would think he would remember me after all the clients, young and old, whom he'd treated over fifty two years. In other words, why would I think myself so special that he would remember me?

On the other hand, he was the only physical therapist I'd ever known, with the exception of Mr. Shabatura, at Kate Barnes. I would never have forgotten Henry, but I certainly never expected him to remember me.

Henry and I saw each other on quite a regular basis over the next few years. He passed away a few years shy, I believe, of his ninetieth birthday. Please, never fail to realize the impact you can have on another person.

Finally! A Little Therapy!

Now, back to the real world. As you might suspect, working in

183

this atmosphere with Judge Lawrence didn't do a whole lot for my happiness level or my sense of job satisfaction. As a matter of fact, I was beginning to suffer some physical symptoms of the kind that don't allow you to get too far away from a bathroom, which really caused me some concern. Apparently people I worked with were beginning to worry also.

One afternoon, my office door blew open and Sgt. Ed and Officer Steve came in. Each grabbed me under one arm, lifted me out of my chair, and carried me out to Steve's brand new truck, which had a new boat and trailer hooked up to it. They kind of pushed me into the truck, started the engine, and headed out of town. I asked them where the hell we were going? They told me we were headed for Green Lake in Spicer, Minnesota. The next day was opening day of Minnesota's fishing season.

It was a beautiful day, especially in Spicer. We set up a campsite and were on the lake shortly before midnight. We caught nothing, but the moon sure was beautiful. What a lousy time to be with two guys!

The next morning was sunny and warm. We got out on the lake along with about a million other people. After several hours and few bites, I reeled in, in favor of sunning myself. Over a period of an hour or so, the sky became darker and darker, and as it did so, more and more people were seen heading for shore. I asked Steve if he didn't think we should head for shore too. It was beginning to look like Dracula was flying overhead. He assured me there was no problem. I climbed off the front of the boat in favor of a rainproof roof over my head. And then, it started; rain, wind, lightning, hail, and waves the height of which I'd never seen before.

I looked at Ed who was sitting behind me. He looked frozen. He asked me, "How many feet of water are we sitting on?" I looked at the depth finder that was at my feet. It was reading ninety feet. By the way, did I mention that Ed couldn't swim? Then Steve turned to me and said, "Hey, Lar, stick your head out there and see if you can find the shore." I told him to stick his own head out there, that he was the one that got us in to this mess.

Finally we got to shore. After securing the boat, we went over to the camp store. We stood in front of the counter and waited for a clerk. From behind a curtain appeared an elderly lady who appeared to be about four feet tall. She looked at the three of us and asked, "Where have you three been?"

Steve, who was well over six feet tall, answered, "Fishing!"

She answered, "That was stupid!"

We walked out to our campsite and put up two tents, one for Steve, and one for Ed and me. Ed was still in shock. I don't think he'd spoken a word since he asked me how many feet of water we were sitting on. After we put up the tents, Ed produced two bottles of Windsor Canadian. We opened both bottles and began to drink empty both of them. While we were doing that, we were talking about how we should kill Steve. Roasting him over a campfire was suggested. Waiting until he was asleep and setting his tent on fire was also suggested. After Ed and I had drank most of our bottles, we went to sleep.

The trip home the following day was kind of quiet. We made it home, tired and hot and not just a little sunburned. I would say that the net result of the whole weekend was that Ed was mad at Steve, I was still mad at Steve, I was still experiencing physical symptoms, and Groucho Marx was still on the bench. And then, some real help came my way.

A Rescue Plan

One Tuesday morning, Max walked into my office and asked if I had a few minutes to talk. He said he thought he had an idea that I might be interested in.

He said that he'd had a good deal of time to listen through the wall between Beulah's and my office to the way I dealt with and counseled my clients. He said that whether or not I realized it, I was an Adlerian psychologist philosophically. I told him that I'd studied Adlerian psychology, but I'd never identified myself with a particular school of thought.

He went on to say that I had made it pretty plain that I was unhappy with my job. He told me that he was also unhappy with his job, and we'd talked about that before. He asked me if I'd be interested in going into the private counseling business with him. I was shocked and excited.

He said that if I was interested, I'd have to get the required credentials. This meant attending and graduating from the Alfred Adler

Institute of Minnesota, located in Minneapolis. I had no idea how I was going to attend classes in the Twin Cities and earn a living at the same time, but I told Max I would contact the Institute, get a class schedule, and see if I could put a program together that would allow for both.

I went to the county manager to make sure the county wasn't going to call it a conflict of interest. He gave me the green light. I also went to the Judge, hoping that he would see this as a means of getting my resignation a short time down the road. I was pretty sure he didn't want to simply fire me, as I did have my supporters in the community, and in particular, with law enforcement. He told me that it was alright with him if it was alright with the county manager.

I contacted the Adler Institute, got a class schedule, and arranged to attend an orientation meeting for new students. In looking over the class schedule and plotting it out on a calendar, I discovered that I could complete all of the requirements in nine months. All of the classes took place from 6:00 pm to 10:00 pm or on weekends.

I made an interesting discovery at the orientation meeting. This class was comprised of eighteen students. Of the eighteen, there were, I believe, three Ph.D. level psychologists, six Masters level psychologists, one Court Services Officer, one nun (Sister Emily) and one psychiatrist who was dying of cancer. I remember the instructor, Ethelyn Cohn, asking each of us why we were there. Almost to a student, we were all looking for a counseling philosophy that made sense. After getting home that night, shortly before midnight, I remember asking myself if this was going to be worth the effort. It was going to mean a lot of hours in classes, driving, working and studying, but I decided that it was my best chance to move to a full-time position doing what I liked doing best, and that was helping people feel better.

The next morning, I called Max and made my commitment to him. Then I called the Institute and signed up for my first class.

I have to mention a few of these classes. The first was the Sexuality class. Now this class was a weekend class. These weekend classes ran from 6:00 pm to 10:00 pm on Friday night and from 8:00 am to 6:00 pm on Saturday and Sunday. These 24 hours fulfilled the hours requirement to grant graduate credit.

The Sexuality instructor was Ethelyn Cohn, a professional Sex Therapist. One of the first things she did was to pair us up for the weekend. I was paired with, guess who, Sister Emily! Now, make no mistake, Emily was a few years younger than me, and was very attractive, even wearing a habit!

After pairing us up, Ethelyn played George Carlin's, "The Seven Dirtiest Words." Those words were, "shit, piss, fuck, cunt, mother-fucker, cock-sucker and tits." Emily turned a different color every time each of those words was spoken. It would have been very painful for me to watch had it not been so funny.

After Carlin's piece, Ethelyn played two tapes showing her clients having sex! This was tough enough on Emily, but the second film featured some of her gay clients having sex. I wasn't expecting Emily to last the night, and if she did, I wondered if she'd be back in the morning.

She was back in the morning and again on Sunday morning. On Sunday afternoon, we had to give each other a sensual massage of the hand. We were furnished a hand cream to make it easier and more sensual. By the end of the day on Sunday, Emily and I had become friends, and I could make humorous sexual remarks without fear of offending her. I offered to let her see my motel room before we took off for home, but she didn't have the time. I never saw her again.

Cecil Blaisdel taught Communications. This class was also a weekend class. On Friday night, he went into great detail about communicating and getting things said that were necessary to be said. As he was speaking, I was thinking about my Dad and me, and I asked myself if we didn't need to talk about some things having to do with my career choices that I knew he wasn't comfortable with.

On Saturday morning, the entire class showed up on time, but Cecil walked in a little late. He looked distracted. He began his lecture, which, first of all, none of us could hear, and secondly, none of us could understand. Some of us looked at each other, wondering who was going to say something. Finally, someone did. He regained his composure and told us that when he got home Friday night, after our class, his wife told him that his father had passed away. He told us that he and his father had some things that they should have talked about but never did, and now it was too late. It took me about another five years to have that conversation with my Dad, but we did come to an understanding.

Somehow, I managed to hang in there for nine months and qualify to receive my certificate in Psychotherapy and Counseling.

Before graduation day, we had to choose two instructors and go through a final interview. I chose Bob Barthelow and Tom Wright. During the nine months we students spent in classrooms with these instructors, we got pretty close. The classes were taught in their offices or conference rooms at local motels. There was no Adlerian school building at that time. Ours was only the second graduating class. Partly, I think, because of this de-centralized method of schooling and because of our small numbers, we got to know things about each other that we may not have wanted to share.

In my case, I must have made it clear to my instructors, at least, just how rough a life I'd had, how much I hated my doctors (after all, they lied to me, remember?) etc.

At this interview, Barthelow and Wright went on and on about my anger. They talked between themselves, but in front of me, and joked about how funny it seemed that I could be that angry, and they bet the people I was mad at didn't even know it. I found myself getting mad just listening to them, but then it hit me that they were exactly right. I must have given them some sign of acknowledgement, a smile, shaking my head, something, because then they looked at me and I at them.

I told them they were right. I was a captive of my own anger, and the people I was mad at didn't even know of my anger toward them. But they were going to. That anger had been eating away at me for about twenty years. I made a promise to Bob Barthelow and Tom Wright that night. I would see the people I needed to see and get my life and attitude on a positive road. I saw those individuals several weeks later, unloaded on them and reclaimed my life.

I've said this a thousand times. The experience at the Adler Institute was probably the single most mind-altering, life-changing experience of my life. I don't think a day goes by that I don't thank those instructors for what they did for me.

Developing a Plan

It was now June, 1978. Max and I had a lot of fun talking about starting a practice in his hometown. He had friends, family and clients there. I had friends and acquaintances in nearby cities.

By this time, the Judge had hired my replacement, and he

seemed to be just fine if I never showed up at the office. I was very well aware of the fact that I was the Court Services Director in title only. Beulah and I always stayed in touch about my court caseload, especially NIBS, with whom I stayed in close contact.

One day, Max called and said that he thought he'd found us some office space. He wanted me to drive over to see it. I didn't need to be asked twice.

When I got to town and met Max, he took me to a mortuary. Not a good sign, I was thinking. I was introduced to a veterinarian who had purchased the building to open a clinic and lease office space. He talked to us about his plans for building offices around the building, and of course, asked us what we thought we were going to need. By the time the meeting came to an end, the doctor told us that he would do some thinking and planning and would get back to us.

The three of us got back together about a week later. The doctor said he would build the offices with built-in desks, coat closets, and book shelves so that Max and I could save something on buying office furniture. He also said he would put dimmers on the light switches.

We asked him what his requirements would be in terms of rent and of a lease. He told us that he would require that we sign an annual lease and asked us how we felt about a monthly rental cost of $100.00. Max and I looked at each other, and it took us about ten seconds to accept his offer. A little further conversation resulted in a deadline for having the offices constructed and ready. That date was set at Sept. 1, 1978.

The next day, I had a meeting with Judge Groucho and I told him of my plans. With much glee, I handed him a Letter of Resignation effective September 1, 1978. He could hardly contain himself. He was so happy that he offered me an extra week's paid vacation, so my resignation turned out to be September 8, 1978. What a generous, considerate, s.o.b. he was!

A Very Mixed Bag

I spent most of the next six weeks saying goodbye to caseload, friends, and others I'd worked with. The friends I would naturally stay in touch with, and even the Judge said he'd refer some court cases to

189

me for counseling. I sure wasn't going to hold my breath waiting for that to happen, although the new Court Services Director said he'd make referrals, and I believed him.

For a while, I kept my apartment, but I knew I was going to have to give it up soon. I began to consider ways of reducing expenses until I could build a practice, and there was nothing certain about that.

Living with the Emperor

One of the ways I considered as a means to cut expenses was to look for one of those "elderly gentleman wants live-in caregiver" things you sometimes see in the newspaper. So I decided to keep my eye on the local newspaper for such an advertisement.

Surprisingly, I spotted one within a few weeks. The contact number was within a short distance from the office. Arrangements were made for the elderly gentleman's two daughters and two sons-in-law to come to my office for an interview.

I found my interviewers to be very friendly people. The conversation was casual and informative in both directions. At the end, they offered me the job. The ladies' father lived in a city located seven miles from my office.

The terms of the deal included room and board and a small salary. The house, they said, was large enough for the two of us, and I would have my own bedroom. At such a time as I wanted some time off, all I needed to do was to give one of the daughters notice, and they would stand in for me.

As they all stood to leave, one of the daughters, Shirley, said, "You should probably know Dad's name."

I made some comment like, "That would be nice."

She looked at me and said, "His name is Napoleon Bonaparte." I didn't laugh, but I'm sure a smile must have come to my face. She explained that as a newborn, her father was left on the steps of an orphanage in a nearby town. He was found wrapped in newspaper and placed in a cardboard box. He was raised at the orphanage and was named Napoleon Bonaparte, for some reason, by its staff.

We set a date to meet at Napoleon's home. I believe the meeting was set for the following Saturday morning.. I had no problems finding the house. It was a very old home with a detached garage. The front door opened into a large living room, and my large bedroom was located off the living room. The dining room joined the living room, and the kitchen, bathroom and "Poly's" bedroom were all located off the dining room. The rear entrance was in the kitchen.

Napoleon, himself, was eighty-six years young, between 5' and 5'2" in height and had a great smile which was accentuated by a single tooth in the upper part of his mouth. He was unsteady on his feet.

He was also a town icon. He'd been a custodian at the local high school, which was about a block from the house. But his first job, and first love, was the railroad. He thoroughly loved giving lectures on how to lay track straight.

My first railroading lecture, of course, came that same evening after everyone had gone home. During that lecture, the doorbell rang. Poly got up and walked toward the dark kitchen. I turned my attention to the program on the TV. Suddenly, I realized that I wasn't hearing anything coming from the kitchen. I turned my head toward the kitchen but heard nothing, and the lights were still off. I was thinking, "Damn, I lost the man on my first day on the job!" I bolted from my chair, ran to the kitchen, and turned on the light. In the open doorway stood Napoleon and 86-year-old Mrs. Hanson, who lived across the street. Poly was planting a warm wet one on her lips! I excused myself and returned to my chair in the living room.

After that, a ritual developed every time I left the house. Poly would see me to the back door, and I would look at him and say, "Now you keep that thing in your pants!" He would start to laugh, and inevitably, lose his balance. I would then grab him at the shoulders, bend down, and kiss him on his bald head. He loved being told to "Keep it in your pants." What a wonderful little old man!

A Reminder of the University Days

I got in the habit of continuing to look at the local paper's Employment Opportunities section just in case I might find another opportunity to reduce my expenses or make some money. I should say that Max and I had decided to charge counseling clients $25.00 dollars per session whether thirty minutes long or three hours long. The going hourly rate at the time was $75.00 dollars per hour. It was our feeling that we wanted average people for clients, and that meant they had to be able to afford the help.

One day, I spotted an ad seeking a part-time instructor in Psychology at the University of Minnesota Agricultural College, located some ten miles from home. I noted the desired qualifications. The salary was $800.00 per month, not bad for the number of hours involved. I submitted a resume' and received a phone call to set up an interview.

On interview day, I went to the University, found the Professor's office, and knocked on the door. When I was told to come in, he had his back turned to me. When he turned, he looked at me and said, "You don't remember me, do you?"

I said, "No, I don't think so."

He said, "UMD, 1970, Psychology Department?"

Still didn't ring any bells. Then, he added, "Dr. DeYoung?"

Still nothing.

Then he said, "I'm the guy that brought you the petition asking for the dismissal of Dr. DeYoung, and you refused to sign it."

Oops!

Well, we sat down and had the interview. As a matter of fact, I thought it went quite well. The interview ended, he wished me luck, and I headed for the door. As I reached the door, I turned to the Professor and said, "By the way, I still think you and your friends were wrong about that petition."

A few weeks later, I got a phone call from him, telling me that I had not gotten the job. He wanted me to know that he had advocated for me, but the majority wanted someone with teaching experience. It truly, truly, is a very small world.

As Luck Would Have It

One of the things that newly unemployed people tend to think about is their health, or, more specifically, health insurance. I was quite aware of the fact that I would have no health insurance after September 8, 1978, the effective date of my resignation as Court Services Director. That concerned me greatly!

Maybe I should not have assumed that I'd have need of medical services just because I had no insurance. Maybe the question should have been how much need I'd have for medical care and not if I'd need it.

On the morning of Oct. 11, 1978, I awakened with what I was sure were the symptoms of a bladder infection. The pain was intense, and I found myself to have a temperature slightly above 102 degrees. I was miserable, and I knew I was going to feel worse unless I did something.

I called Max and asked him if he knew a local doctor who could handle me as a patient. He recommended one Dr. John Henry. I called his office and managed to speak to him directly. I told him my symptoms, and he told me to get to the office as soon as possible, and to bring a specimen.

When I got to the office, I was escorted to an examination room. The doctor came in and introduced himself. He asked for the specimen. He took the bottle, glanced at it, turned and walked out of the room.

In a short time, the doctor returned, took some medical history and wrote a prescription. He told me that I should start feeling better about eight hours after taking the first dose. After making another appointment, I left, anxious to get to the pharmacy and get that first dose of medication into me.

If I hadn't felt so rotten, I might have remembered that I'd always felt that medications usually didn't work for me as doctors told me they would, and this one turned out to be no exception. I didn't sleep all night, the burning continued, and the fever rose past 103 degrees. Even though I felt rotten, I went to the office every morning. I couldn't forget that I needed to continue to see the few clients I had, and I needed to beat the bushes for new clients. Maybe it was a good thing that I kept myself busy. I think it helped keep my mind off the pain and discomfort. Over the course of the next two and a half months, I had to make frequent trips to Dr. Henry's office so that he could fondle my prostate. I finally started to feel better during the Christmas holidays.

Shortly after the first of the year, 1980, my car decided to have an argument with the rear end of a semi in a dense fog. The box, which was the only part I could see, had only one small light on it. When I hit the right rear corner of the box, I hit my head and cut it badly enough to warrant stitches.

When the ambulance got me to the local hospital, staff cleaned me up in preparation for the sewing job. Suddenly, there was Dr. Henry with needle and thread in hand. As he began stitching me up, he asked me if I remembered our first meeting. I asked him how he thought I could possibly forget feeling that rotten. He asked if I remembered his taking the specimen bottle from me and walking out of the examination room.

I said, "Yes, I remember. Why?"

He told me that when he took the bottle from me and looked at it, he got sick and left the room in order to throw up. He said it looked more like Jello!

Yup! Sounds like something I could do to a doctor!

Let me say a little more about Max. As I mentioned, Max and I spent a lot of time together while he was covering my county for the mental health center. Another bond that kept us close was the mutual dislike that we had for the Judge and his dislike for us. In my case, as mentioned before, the Judge had no use for me because I did not have a background in alcoholism, and I was not willing to blame every client's criminal/delinquent behavior on alcohol and/or drugs. In Max's case, the Judge disliked him because he was a drinker. At the time, I was also known to drink alcoholic beverages, and Max and I didn't bother trying to hide the fact that we sometimes had a drink after work.

The county hired an Alcohol/Drug Counselor who was a close friend of "His Honor" Gee, wasn't that a coincidence!

One day, this moron actually sneaked into Max's office at the mental health center, and broke into a locked desk drawer, apparently looking for booze. That was the first time the guy broke into Max's desk. The second time, he found a pair of bull castrators. I wonder if the man ever got that message!

One of my private practice clients was my Juvenile Court client, NIBS. NIBS was always calling on the phone and finding his way to my office to talk, share a cup of coffee, to get some encouragement, and lastly, a hug. I believe his parents were threatened by my presence in NIBS's life, because I could count on a visit from father very shortly after every visit from his son.

As soon as it was possible, NIBS enlisted in the United States Army. He was sent to Fort Leonard Wood, Missouri, to complete his basic training. One afternoon, I took a break from the office and walked across the street to my favorite local diner for a cup of coffee.

As I sat there looking across the street toward the office, I saw our volunteer secretary running across the street toward the diner. She burst through the door and told me that NIBS was on the phone, and he was very upset. I bolted from my stool and ran across the street to the office.

I grabbed the phone. Yes, NIBS was very upset and crying. When he calmed down, he told me that three of his young friends had just jumped from the third floor roof of one of the dorm buildings and had been killed. We talked on the phone more often after that for a while, but eventually, things settled down.

Another one of my clients was a young man about 21 or 22 years of age. I don't remember his stated problem, but I do remember our first meeting. I remember asking him about his biological family. He told me that his parents had been killed in an automobile accident when he was very young. He was then taken in by an aunt and uncle whom he loved very much. They also were killed in a fiery car crash. He was then placed with a foster family and also learned to love them. They, as I recall, were both killed in a home fire. As I listened to these stories of loss, I began to imagine that he was going to speculate that his problems derived from these terrible losses, and that he would blame God, for example. When I asked him what he felt about these losses of loved ones, he said, and I'll never forget it, "Shit happens."

It didn't take long for me to realize that the type of counseling that I didn't particularly like was marriage counseling, because after all, what the hell did I know about marriage from a practical standpoint? Now, Max, on the other hand, specialized in marriage counseling. I was always tempted to refer marriage cases, but I couldn't afford to.

The first question I asked any potential marriage counseling case was always, "How many counselors have you seen before me?" If the answer was more than one or two, I always considered the possibility that the couple's main goal might be to defeat the therapist rather than save the marriage. As I've already said, though, I couldn't afford not to take on all comers.

One such couple was referred by a friend of mine. At the time of their first appointment, I remember the young husband's telling me that the problem was that his wife found out that he had been carrying on affairs with other women. Specifically, this couple was from a small town located very close to my new home. The husband worked every day, and the wife was a housekeeper. One of the wife's daily rituals was to meet half a dozen lady friends at a small diner every morning.

One morning during a conversation among these seven ladies, someone said something that hinted that she had something going with my client's husband. That lady's comment led to more conversation among these women, and by the time it was all over, it was determined that the poor, poor, male half of my counseling clients had an affair going with all six of the other ladies who sat at that table at the diner every morning. The marriage counseling turned into divorce counseling for the rest of the session.

One day, I received a phone call from a man in the Twin Cities who wanted to set up an appointment as soon as possible. On the evening of the appointment, a really pathetic sight walked in the office. The man probably weighed in the area of 250 to 300 pounds. He had a pudgy face that looked incapable of growing a beard.

His stated problem was the relationship between him and his wife. He spoke of a wife who would call him at work and tell him that she was with another man, and what a fantastic lover he was. Or she'd leave the house and not come home all night, and then return in the morning and describe her sexual encounter of the night. What became apparent over time was that my client reacted to his wife's behavior by doing things like getting a tattoo, buying and wearing a pair of leather pants, and wearing engineer boots. That behavior seemed to get more and more bizarre by the week. I eventually began to be concerned about the possibility of his becoming so angry that he might physically hurt her. I decided to try and pop her bubble.

One night, I told my client that I'd really like to meet his wife, and I asked him to tell her that I'd be calling her. I hoped she would be eager to meet me.

A short time after this meeting, I made the call to my client's wife. As I had hoped, she was eager to come to the office to see me.

On the evening of her appointment, she showed up at the office without her husband, as requested. She was also dressed seductively, as I'd expected.

My plan was to let her do what she seemed to do best, seduce men, and in this case, to seduce me. It didn't take long for her to start bragging about herself and her abilities. After letting her go on for a while, I decided to make my play.

I told her that I really envied her boyfriends. She asked me why. I told her I envied them because being in bed with her would give me the opportunity to tell her what a lousy lay she'd been.

She got mad, grabbed her coat, and stormed out of the office. What she didn't know was that I had tape recorded the session, just in case. And, yes, I do realize my little stunt was a professional "no-no," but it felt so good to say.

I saw my client several more times and centered those sessions on self-esteem issues. We also covered the subject of divorce. I have no idea how, or if, these two resolved their issues.

I had another client who was suffering from intense pain in her neck and shoulders. The pain had been going on for a long period of time. She was about seventy years of age, was married, and had several children. I asked her if she'd been to a doctor, and she answered in the affirmative. After listening to her describe her pain in great detail for a while, I told her to look at my face. When she did, I asked her, "Who the hell are you mad at?" I hardly had the last word out of my mouth when she named her husband and a couple of her sons, complete with descriptive adjectives.

After a few minutes of venom-spewing directed at those members of her family, she suddenly stopped talking and began rolling her head and moving her shoulders back and forth and up and down. She told me that the pain was gone. I suggested to her that anger tends to lodge in the neck and shoulders, and that if she experiences the same symptoms in the future, she should ask herself who she might be mad at. That was the first and last time I ever saw this woman.

I want to mention one more "non-client" client. I never met her, and she would not tell me her name. She would only talk to me over the phone.

The first time she called, she was crying and told me that her husband had a long history of physical abuse aimed at her, and recently, her 16-year old son had begun to follow in his father's footsteps. The abuse took the forms of slapping and kicking. I asked her what she was doing about it. She said that she was trying to get her husband and son to go to a Christian counselor, but they were refusing. After a few more questions, she must have felt threatened and hung up on me.

A few days later, she called again. After several minutes and several questions, I told her that I wanted her to tell me what her payoff was for continuing to tolerate the abuse. Of course, she denied knowing what I was talking about.

I told her that I wanted to know what she was getting, e.g., what was the reward for allowing them to abuse her. After a few seconds of silence, she said it was what she would receive from the family will.

After thanking her for telling the truth, I asked her if she had thought of the possibility that she might not live to benefit by the will.

To make a longer story shorter, over the next few phone calls, we developed a plan for her that involved her exiting the house without telling anyone where she was, renting an apartment, and finding a job in order for her to experience some independence. She expressed some fear of doing this because she'd never been on her own or even had a job. She did agree to carry out the plan. The last time I heard from her, she had moved to another town, got a job at a manufacturing plant, and was living on her own. She was uncomfortable living alone, but she also told me that she was hanging in there. I never heard from her again.

Another Change in the Wind

You might be assuming that the building of a counseling practice was going pretty well for me. Let's just say that it wasn't going as well as I thought it might, and as the time rolled around to sign the lease for another year, I began giving serious consideration to pulling up stakes and moving back to Duluth. I hadn't a clue what the heck I was going to do to earn a living, but I could probably convince my folks to let me move in with them for a while, and spend what money I had renting on office and trying to build another practice. Over the years, I'd also invested in two lake lots in Northwestern Wisconsin and found them to give me a lot of peace while working for Judge Groucho. I used to spend weekends on this property, always taking an ax with me to release my frustrations. I arranged to transfer title to these lots to my folks and use what cash I had for other expenses.

I contacted Mich, who by this time had quit Corrections after nineteen years, and was managing an office building in downtown

Duluth. He told me that he would rent an office to me on a month to month basis for the same $100/mo. I was currently paying. So the Duluth side of the plan looked like it might work. But what about Max and the private practice? What about Napoleon? I decided that I needed a counselor.

One morning, I walked into Max's office and asked him if he had some time to counsel a friend. We sat with a cup of coffee, and I kind of laid it out to him. I told him that I was really excited about the possibility of moving back to Duluth. I told him that I wasn't exactly sure why, except for the fact that I wasn't happy where I was. I also told him that I was concerned about getting myself into a position of remaining in Owatonna solely because of the practice. After more conversation, Max looked at me and said, "If you want to move back to Duluth half as much as I'd like to move back to southwest Nebraska (his birthplace) then do it!"

The next problem was telling Napoleon and his family. That concerned me even more than closing my practice and leaving Max. What would the family do with him? Would they have to put him in some kind of home? Would he even understand why I was leaving?

I made arrangements to meet with the family first. I remember its being a very hard meeting for me. I felt guilty. I felt like I was about to abandon an old man whom I'd grown to love. But as the family reminded me, I had to get about the business of getting happy myself. I knew they were right, so we went to the house to tell Poly.

When we told him, he cried and hugged me. When he calmed down, though, he told me that he understood my wanting to go home. Now I felt free to plan to return home.

Going Home Again

In the next few weeks, I arranged for my return to Duluth, met with clients for the last time, and said Goodbye to friends, especially, Max. I spent a lot of time with Napoleon and assured him that I would try and see him periodically. I'm not sure he believed me, but he behaved as if he did. I also made sure that I saw all my friends all over Southern Minnesota. And now I was ready to go home

I was nervous about moving back into my parents' home. I don't think they were worried about it, but I was. I wasn't sure what I

199

was going to do for work, but I knew I was going to start working on it the very first morning.

On my first full day at home, I went downtown to see Mich. I can't tell you how good it felt to see my old friend. We had lunch together, and then he showed me the office he had in mind for me. It was large and had several pillars. Mich even threw an old scratched up metal desk in with the deal. I also made the arrangements to get some business cards printed and a telephone installed. Not bad for the first day back in town, huh?

As I was back to living in the house I grew up in, it didn't take long for me to remember that there was a restaurant about a quarter mile down the road. I purposely got in the habit of walking to this restaurant every night at around 8:00 pm. Depending on whom I might find sitting at the counter, I might sit there for a few hours or better. Of course, in time, a small group congregated at that restaurant counter every night.

One of the people I got to know at that restaurant counter was Dennis. Dennis could be found at the counter every night, Monday through Saturday evenings. Dennis was a professional cleaning contractor. He had contracts to clean four businesses each night.

In time, I made it known to Dennis that I was available to help, if he ever needed it. Eventually, and for some reason, he told me he'd like my help.

On my first night, our first stop was a Shakey's Pizza restaurant. I did the sweeping of the carpeted floor in order to pick up all the paper cups, plates, napkins, etc. Then, I had to vacuum the carpeted floors while Dennis was washing the kitchen floor. Anyway, you get the idea.

From there, we rode down the highway a mile or two to the Highland Supper Club. We walked in the kitchen and found all of the burners were on, flames shooting a foot above each burner. The several rats we saw were big enough to throw saddles on. Anyway, we had to throw all the empty booze bottles away, wash the bar, sweep and wash the kitchen floor and vacuum the carpeted floors.

Next stop was the Saratoga Club, Duluth's infamous "strip joint." When we got there, Dennis introduced me to the owner, Jim. While we were talking, Jim mentioned that the plumbing was held together by bubble gum.

When Dennis and I got to work, I started to wipe down the bar, sinks, etc. Guess what? The plumbing actually was held together by bubble gum! This joint was a first class dive. You can imagine what cleaning the toilets was like. The worst part of cleaning the Saratoga was that it was located in the middle of nowhere, but only yards from the shores of Lake Superior. During a storm, the sound of trillions of gallons of water crashing on the rocks was absolutely deafening.

Oh, yeah, did I mention that the work hours were from 1:00 a.m. to whatever time these businesses opened? Anyway, our last stop for the night was a plasma donor business.

Now, I've got to describe this place to you. In the lobby was a huge chart containing the names of the plasma donors. Seems all right, huh? The second thing I noticed was a plaque containing the name of the Medical Director. It was the man who had been my pediatrician. In doing the math, I figured that he was well over retirement age.

Then I started to read the names of the donor members. I couldn't believe my eyes when I saw the names of former probationers and parolees of mine who were drug users. I realize that miracles can happen, but what the hell was going on here?

Then we walked into a huge room where the action took place. The room was wall to wall with tables with thin mattresses on them. Donors would, of course, lie on the tables and the procedure would begin.

Dennis got ready to wash the floors, and he asked me to empty the trash baskets located at the foot of each bed. He also told me to be careful. These small baskets contained used needles with plastic tubing still attached. The tubing and/or needles were simply dropped into the baskets, and blood could be seen dripping from the tubing onto the floor. Occasionally, I would spot a sheet with blood on it. I wondered how long it would take someone to stick himself with one of these needles and find himself with a case of hepatitis, a venereal disease, or AIDS. At least some of those who frequented this facility were doing it for the money, and I knew some of them, as I said. I wouldn't have trusted anyone who came in here and said they were healthy.

For reasons I don't remember, there came a time that Dennis asked me if I'd like to take over the contract at The Club Saratoga. Yeah, me, with my college degrees and Adlerian Psychology credentials and my experience, I could now add being the chief janitor in a strip joint to my resume! What was wrong with this picture? I don't think Dennis liked the way I vacuumed or something. Actually, I think he got another more lucrative contract and needed to give something up.

I still needed to eat until I got re-established, so I jumped at the chance to take the contract as it was worth $600.00 per month. Of course, we talked to the owner about it, and he approved the plan.

I didn't have any problem with the work or the hours, but I never quite became comfortable with the location. The building was a real dump and located where no one would hear you if you yelled. Jim was also a drinker and was known to leave the door unlocked when he left for the day. The light panel was located on the far side of the building from the door, which meant that I had to walk through the bar in the dark in order to turn on the lights. To add to the problem, Jim told me that he made sure that he had $25.00 in each cash register in the hope that any thief would take the money and leave the inventory alone. By the way, he always kept those cash register drawers open for everyone to see.

I do have to thank this job for one first in my life. One night, I walked into the joint a little before closing. One of the girls was doing her thing. When she saw me, she shouted, "Larry, you got a card in the mail!"

As you can imagine, I was just a little shocked, especially since every drunk in the place turned and looked at me. I went up to the bar, and Jim handed me the postcard. It came from Berlin, Germany and was signed by Cleopatra. Now how many guys can say they ever received any mail from Cleopatra? In case you haven't guessed, Cleopatra was a stripper who had performed at the club. She was on tour in Europe. Yes, she really was that good.

The Curse of Age

A short time after I moved back to Duluth, I found out that Napoleon's daughters had put him in a boarding home very close to daughter Shirley's home. Nursing homes wouldn't accept him because he wasn't in need of that much care.

I never saw Napoleon again after I left his home, and I don't think he lived very long after moving into the boarding home. I was told that one very cold, winter morning, he walked through the house in his bathrobe. As he went through the kitchen and headed toward the rear door, he was seen with his arms extended in front of his body and saying, "I'm coming, Ruth! I'm coming!" He walked out of the house and was later found frozen to death. He often spoke about how much he missed his wife. I never liked the idea of his having to move into a boarding home, so I've always been glad he didn't languish long before he could join Ruth again.

Donna and the Baby

I had gotten into the habit of spending a few hours before going to work each night, sitting at the counter at my favorite restaurant, talking with friends and drinking coffee. One night the door opened, and a lady carrying a baby in a carrier came in and sat down on the stool directly on my left. She looked like she'd just seen a ghost. I waited a minute before I said anything to her, but finally, I couldn't take it anymore. I introduced myself and asked her if there was anything I could do. She told me that she was a student at a local vocational school, had finished an evening class and had picked up her son at the babysitter's place. She decided to stop for a cup of coffee on her way home and was stopped at a traffic light just a block from the restaurant. A car pulled up beside her, and the occupant in the other car's passenger seat rolled down the window and pointed a pistol at her.

We engaged in conversation until I had to go to work. At that point, I walked her and the baby, age two, out to her car. We also agreed to meet at the restaurant the following night.

The Beginning of Something New

Donna and I met several more times at the restaurant, and then I was invited to her apartment. We did a lot of talking about our backgrounds, present circumstances, and our plans for the future. Over the ensuing weeks, we became quite comfortable with each other, and I was really beginning to enjoy the baby, Lloyd.

Donna had been married. Her husband, Jim, developed terminal cancer during the time she was pregnant with Lloyd. As I recall, the doctors had told them that if Jim chose to fight the cancer, he

203

might survive until the birth of the child. He chose to fight, and lived to see his son born. He passed away several days later.

Lloyd was born with eye problems that required several surgeries. Donna was making payments on those medical bills and also trying to earn a degree in Quantity Cooking and Baking.

There came a time when we decided that we were comfortable enough with each other that we should get an apartment together. Between the two of us, we weren't making much of an income, but we were able to find an apartment we could afford. I was also anxious to get out of Mom and Dad's hair.

Within a few months of our renting this apartment, things started to take a turn for the worse. I had managed to acquire a few private clients, but I couldn't devote the time to building the practice, so I closed my doors. Where the club was concerned, Jim began to leave the doors unlocked, and I became more concerned about entering the building every night. Also, my working hours were Donna and Lloyd's sleeping hours and vice versa. I was getting a little depressed and worried about the future.

My Old Friend, John

One day, I received a letter from Judge John, who told me that he had been diagnosed with cancer and was going to have his voice box removed. I wrote a few letters during the weeks following the surgery, and John's letters to me didn't sound very encouraging.

I made a decision to drive down to his home to see him. I got a couple of friends to tackle the Saratoga for me, and I made the trip, but afraid of what I might see.

When I got to the house, John answered the door. He gave me a hug, and we took seats opposite each other in the living room. He told me that he didn't want to use the device such cancer victims typically used to amplify the voice.

We had fun talking about all the good times we had meeting at the restaurant, at night, and what a great personal and working relationship we had. We even joked about the two of us storming the courthouse and throwing the Judge out of office. Suddenly, I looked at John and saw tears in his eyes. I asked him what was wrong. He looked at me, pointed his forefinger toward me then at himself, clasped his hands, and then raised his arms in the victory sign. And then we both cried. A while later, I took my leave and promised to keep in touch.

Several months later, I received another letter from John, this time from the local hospital. He indicated that the cancer was back, and the outlook wasn't good. I decided to go see him in the hospital. We talked about plans for the future, both mine and his. When our visit ended and we said our goodbyes, we again agreed to stay in touch. I'm very sure that neither of us believed we'd ever see each other again. As I walked out of the room and down the hall, I could hear him crying. I'll never get that sound out of my head. A few weeks after this visit, I received a call from John's son, who reported that his father had died. He said that he could never understand why his father and I were so close, but he knew we were. I told him that it really didn't matter why. We just were.

Light at the End of the Tunnel

One night, just before taking off for the Saratoga, I was reading the Want Ads in the local paper. I noticed an ad for Group Home Parents. I remember looking at Donna over my cup of coffee and asking her how she thought she'd like being a group home parent. She said she always wanted to work at home. So we decided that when I got home in the morning, we'd make a phone call.

It was a rather short night, and I'm not sure how good a job of cleaning I did. I was preoccupied by the prospects of becoming a group home parent, and I was excited about the possibility.

When I got home from work, I made the phone call. The agency was a Native American placement agency. They were looking for a couple with experience in the "kid business." I gave them my verbal resume' and Donna told the secretary that she had a vocational school degree in Quantity Cooking and Baking. They seemed interested in us, and we became very interested in them. They said they'd send us the paperwork and arrange an interview. The agency, by the way, was the American Indian Fellowship Association, or AIFA.

We received and completed the paperwork, collected recommendations, and were scheduled for an interview. That interview went well, and within a very few weeks, we were offered the position.

Larry Bauer-Scandin

That was followed by my resignation from my executive position at the Saratoga, and Donna, Lloyd, and I were ready to embark on a new career. This was gonna be fun!

The Facility

The agency brass took us to the house that was to be home for us, and hopefully, up to ten, teenage male delinquents. The home was located on Arrowhead Road in a very nice section of Duluth.

It was also the most beautiful home I'd ever seen. It was a split-level, with a large living room, dining room and kitchen on the top level. There was also a bathroom and three bedrooms on the top floor. The lower level had three bedrooms and a fourth that functioned as an office. It also had one full bathroom. The lower level also had an entrance into the two-car attached garage.

What really struck me about the home was its furnishings. The dining room table was huge and, obviously, expensive. It was made of oak and had ten or twelve captains' chairs lining its perimeter. The color television was large. The furniture was well-built and expensive. Even the beds and bedding looked, and I'm sure were, expensive.

Flies in the Ointment

The physical plant looked great, but as usual, there were flies in the ointment. Part of the agreement with the agency involved free room and board and groceries that were to be delivered. All expenses incurred by the household were to be paid by the agency.

Our first delivery of food consisted of three frozen walleye and five boxes of Pop Tarts (all strawberry). I bought our groceries before any kids were placed, and without doing any complaining, but after Bill was placed, and we still got no groceries, I did complain. Here, we compromised. I did the actual shopping, and the agency paid for it.

We had yet another problem. In time, we became aware of the fact that we really were dealing with two Native American groups that didn't get along with each other. At times, those disagreements almost broke out into open warfare.

For example, the agency had neglected to tell us that it had not hired a garbage service. I called the office about it, but nothing was

206

done. I asked for a meeting at the house after several months and several placements. It was a very hot summer day. Members of each group walked in the house and promptly took seats on opposite sides of the living room. I started talking about problems Donna and I were having with running the house, including getting rid of the garbage. I even brought them out to the garage and showed them over one hundred 33-gallon garbage bags filled with garbage. I really wanted them to get close to it so they could smell it. The end result was that they gave us permission to hire any garbage service we wanted. I think that chore was accomplished before the meeting was over.

This experiment in trouble lasted for nine months. The agency then decided to terminate the program citing the fact that Donna and I weren't married as the reason for a lack of placements. According to several social workers though, word had gotten out about the in-fighting between the two Native American groups. Placing agencies also had to pay a daily administrative fee for each child which sometimes became an issue for some smaller placing agencies.

Before leaving the AIFA experience though, I have to mention one of the placements, Bill. Billy was one of those tall, blond, blue-eyed, loud, always in a good mood type kids that, frankly, I had to work at being mad at. I only remember three things about his background. First, he liked to drink; secondly, he didn't like going to school, and thirdly, he was a ski bum.

As much as I loved that kid, the Juvenile Court Judge, Jerry Martin, didn't. I was in Court with him once, and the Judge was so mad at Bill that he told me that, if I ever even suspected that he had been drinking, I was to take him to Detox.

One winter night, all the kids were in bed except for Bill. It was after curfew, and he wasn't home yet. Donna and I were pretty sure that either Bill wouldn't show up at all, knowing that he'd be grounded, or he'd show up drunk and knowing that I'd have to take him downtown to the Detox Center.

When we heard the door open on the landing, we were relieved to know the prodigal son had returned.. But when Donna and I heard a very loud, "Hi, I'm home!" I had a feeling.

I went over to the top of the steps and looked down. Bill was trying to walk up the steps still wearing his skis. I went down to the landing, and somehow, we managed to get them, and him, up the steps to the living room. He looked at Donna and me and said something like, "I guess I'll go to bed." He walked into his main floor bedroom, and we heard the door shut. In a few minutes, we heard his door open, and he appeared in the entryway to the living room. He stood there with a goofy look on his face and said, "Good night." Then he turned, walked straight into a wall and collapsed on the floor. I looked at Donna and asked her if she thought he was drunk. She just shook her head.

I helped him get off the floor, and I informed him that I was going to take him to Detox, as per the Judge's order. He didn't argue, but he also wasn't very helpful when it came to getting him dressed for the trip. He even insisted that he should be allowed to wear his skis.

As we hit the road, it was very cold outside, and Bill began to get his wits about him. As we got close to the Detox Center, he turned to me and said, "You know you'll never get me there, don't you?"

I looked at him, smiled and said, "Yeah, I know, but it's a nice night for a drive."

Now, think about this. You're taking a drunken teenager to Detox. Of course, he doesn't want to go, and you know it. The kid isn't wearing any cuffs or other means of restraint. When you park the car, how the hell are you going to get out of the car and around to the passenger side before the kid bolts?

Of course, he did just that. I barely managed to stop the car in front of Detox when Bill bolted from the car. He didn't run right away. He just stood there on the sidewalk. When I got out of the car, I looked at him across the hood of the car. He smiled at me and I smiled at him. I told him to take care of himself and stay in touch. Then he started to walk up the avenue. I got back in the car and drove home. Donna was smiling when I walked in the house. She was pretty sure I'd never get him to Detox either.

In the morning, I called Judge Martin and told him the story of the previous night. He was just a little bit angry. I think Bill managed to stay on the run for a couple of weeks before being picked up. We went back to Court, and Judge Martin ordered him back to my house under House Arrest. I think he put him back in my house because he wasn't sure anyone else would be willing to put up with him. I think he also knew that I liked the kid.

As I've mentioned, the agency experience lasted some nine

months. Bill and the other kids were all dispensed to other homes. The last thing I heard of him was on a local radio commercial he made at a recreation area in Duluth called Park Point. That was Bill!

Foster Care, Phase Two

During the application process for going to work for AIFA, Donna, Lloyd and I met one Larry Modean, a Social Worker for St. Louis County. We met him because AIFA held their foster care placement license through St. Louis County.

When it became clear that the AIFA experiment was going to fail, Larry approached us about the possibility of our going to work for St. Louis County Social Services directly. The licensing procedure was relatively easy. The problem was one of housing.

We decided to start with a license for one teenage boy. When we left AIFA's home, we moved into a rented home in the Woodland neighborhood, of Duluth. It was a rather small house, even though it had three bedrooms and a finished basement. It was also rented to us on an option to buy basis.

Our first, and as it would turn out, only placement at this house was Greg. He was also our first chance to deal with a child with a Developmental Disability of retardation, as it used to be called. Greg was probably 6' tall and weighed perhaps 180-190 pounds. Donna and I were also specifically asked to keep an eye on his weight and his eating. We found out that the eating problem was a bit more than a standard eating problem. We caught Greg eating frozen cookie dough, for example. As a matter of fact, we discovered that in order to keep Greg out of the garbage can, we had to sprinkle the contents with cigarette ashes or some other repugnant substance.

Welcome Homes and the Girls

As you might suspect, our finances were strained again. We were no longer getting free room and board, and we only had the one placement for which we were getting support. I began to think again about another job outside the house. I decided to keep my eye on the local Want Ads again.

It didn't take long for me to spot an ad wanting a Director for an

209

adolescent group home for delinquent females. I made the phone call and was scheduled for an interview. The appointment took place in Duluth, but the facility was actually in a small town located about twenty miles from Duluth.

The interview was scheduled for the morning, and it was a good thing it was, because the interview lasted twelve hours. I was also asked to come back the following day, and by the time the interview, including supper, was over, it lasted another twelve hours. By the end of Interview, Part 2, I'd been offered the job. Actually, it dawned on me that the interviews took a total of twenty-four hours because they couldn't find anyone to take the job.

My interviewer was the Executive Director of the facility and others located in the Twin Cities. She was also a very good friend of the owner. That became one very big problem.

The agency's house was very adequate for ten girls. The girls were mostly imports from the Twin Cities. It took me a while to figure out who and what some of these kids were.

Now, it didn't take long for me to figure out that this agency, group home, and locked shelter were not the most welcome child placement agencies in town. The juvenile officer in the city's police department was a friend of mine from our college days. Within a day or two of my starting day at the home, this friend asked if I could stop in at the PD. When I did, he went into great detail about the department's attitude about the group home, its owner, and the Executive Director who was my boss. Both the owner and the ED drove Mercedes automobiles, and people, including police officers on patrol, frequently saw the two cars parked in the parking lots of local motels in the middle of the night. That didn't exactly suggest church services were taking place, if you know what I mean.

The next thing my friend said was that my girls were, in many cases, prostitutes that Twin Cities child care agencies wanted to get away from the metro area and their pimps. What usually happened was that the placement of one of these girls was usually followed by unfamiliar cars being seen in town and hanging around the group home.

As my friend spoke, I became more and more concerned about having accepted this job. The last thing he said to me was that if I stayed with this agency, he and I would wind up being enemies. I left the Police Department hoping that I could keep that from happening.

One of my duties at the house was to do a nightly group session with the girls. After doing one or two such group sessions with my boss present, I quit doing them When my boss asked me why I wasn't doing the groups, I told her that I would, as soon as she left me alone with the girls. It was beginning to feel that the boss didn't want to give up the mother role.

Occasionally, the owner of the agency would show up at the house and disrupt the entire schedule. One night while he was at the house, the phone rang. It was the director of one of the agency's Twin Cities homes. He told me that he'd like to send one of his girls up to me. I told him to send me the girl's file, I'd look it over, make my decision, and let him know. His response was, "What?"

The owner had been standing by my desk listening to the conversation. He motioned to get my attention, and when I put the other guy on hold, he told me that it would mean another bed filled. That, of course, was a hint that I was to get back on the line and accept the placement.

Another problem I had with my bosses was over a decision I made to send my girls to AA meetings, in Duluth rather than have them attend the local meetings. I was picking up on conversations among some of the girls that people were drinking at the AA meetings, and my friend in the Police Department told me that they'd had similar reports. My bosses, of course, reminded me that sending the kids to Duluth wasn't very good PR, as if they knew what positive public relations was!

After about nine months in our home in Woodland, the owner notified us that he had a buyer for the house, but he wanted to give us first option at buying it. Donna and I talked about it at some length. We had room for one more foster placement, which would add to our income, but I wasn't counting on my surviving the girls' home, or the agency surviving the community.

We talked it over with Larry Modean, our social worker, and he suggested that we think about the possibility of getting licensed for ten boys. He suggested we think about foster care as a business, a full time business. After more discussion, we decided to go for it, but we needed a house, a very large house.

Larry Bauer-Scandin

The Search for Another Home

Donna and I found a realtor who impressed us with her interest in helping us find a house for the specific purpose of housing ten teenage boys, Donna, Lloyd and me. We looked at several homes before finding one located in the Lakeside area of Duluth. As a matter of fact, it was located right across the street from the shore of Lake Superior, the "low rent" side of London Road.

The house had four floors. The basement floor was one huge room containing a fireplace, laundry room, a small workshop and a very small bathroom, located off the workshop. The main floor had a small office, a bathroom, large living room and dining room and a kitchen. The third floor had a bathroom and four bedrooms, all large enough for at least two kids. The top floor was unfinished, but contained two rooms. The floor was all framed in, but the sheetrock had been removed.

Now, it was time to find a bank that would loan us the money to buy the house. Thanks to the realtor, such a bank was found. It was a hard sell, because of the potential variations in our monthly income, but the deal was finally sealed and a move-in date was set. Donna, Lloyd, Greg and I were ready to move into our new home. Before I go any further, I want to mention that every year, I took a break from the kids and the family and returned to Southern Minnesota to see old friends.

The Importance of People

On a trip to Southern Minnesota, I stopped in to see my old friend, Sgt. Ed. I asked him if he knew how I could contact my old local juvenile case, NIBS. He told me that he had heard that he was attending the University of Minnesota, Mankato. I was shocked. If you recall, the reason I brought NIBS back to court to appear before Judge Groucho Marx was his unwillingness to stay in school.

Mankato was the direction I was heading, so I decided that I'd try and find the kid. I stopped at the Happy Chef Restaurant and called the University's Registrar's Office. I asked where I might find NIBS. I was told that "She's living in the girl's dorm."

"The girl's dorm?" I asked. "Could I have her number?"

She gave me the phone number, and I made the call. The phone was answered by a young lady. I asked her if MF was there. She said, "Yes. Can I tell him who's calling?" I told her to tell him that his probation officer wanted to talk to him.

I heard her put the phone down, and then someone picked it up. A soft voice said, "Hello. Who is this?"

I answered, loudly "This is your probation officer! What the hell are you doing living in the girls' dorm?"

A much stronger voice came back with, "This isn't my probation officer, but it used to be!" We both started to laugh. MF had one of those first names that most people wouldn't recognize as unmistakably male or female. I asked him if he might be available to meet me at the Happy Chef. He said he could be there in a few minutes.

I hadn't seen him for quite a while and, given the relationship I'd had with his father, I never tried writing to him at home. I was excited about seeing him again. I had a lot of questions for him.

Suddenly, the door opened, and there he was. We hugged each other and took seats at the counter. The conversation started on a light note, but he got more serious with time. At one point, he said, "Every year, I get three cards on my birthday, one from my grandma and grandpa, one from my girlfriend, and one from my ex-probation officer."

Apparently he didn't receive cards from his parents. I told him that it was always nice to get that kind of affirmation from parents, but people can do without it if they have to. After about an hour, we both needed to get on our way. We walked out to the parking lot together, hugged each other one last time, and went our separate ways.

A few weeks later, I got a phone call from Ed, now Sheriff Ed, who told me that NIBS had hanged himself in the county jail after having been arrested on drug charges. He left a letter addressed to young people, urging them to stay away from drugs and alcohol. He was 21 years old. His birthday was January 19.

Identical Twin Brats

One day, Larry Modean and a social worker came to the house and asked Donna and me if we thought we would be interested in taking on a set of identical twins. Actually, Larry told us that he would advise against taking both of them, because they were a handful, and had not done well at other foster homes. They liked to fight with each other.

Donna and I didn't discuss it very long. We were anxious to increase the size of our family, and neither of us thought it was a good idea to split family members up. After a little more discussion, it was decided to try the two boys out together.

Todd and Kelly's mother died at child birth, and dad's reaction was to turn to alcohol. He also blamed the boys for the death of his wife. This was probably the main battle we were going to be stuck with for the duration of the time they were to be with us. They missed their mother and fought hard to develop a positive relationship with their father, but he had a long record of rejecting the kids emotionally, even when they were very, very young.

On Memorial Day, the boys were going to visit their mother's grave with their father. At the last minute, dad couldn't go, or he didn't want to take them. I forgot the reason. Donna and I decided that they should go to the cemetery and visit their mother's grave. Donna took Todd and Kelly, and I stayed home with the other boys. I was on edge the entire time they were gone.

Finally, Donna's car pulled into the driveway, and everyone got out looking like there hadn't been any problem. The boys went in the house, and Donna and I stayed outside to talk. I asked her how things had gone. She said that when they got to the grave site, both boys started to cry and then started to kick dirt at the grave, asking their mother why she had left them.

As I recall, Todd and Kelly had a few older brothers and sisters, and an aunt who was close to them. Other than that, they only seemed to have each other. And when they were close, they were really close, but when they were mad at each other, they could really get it on. These two kids also found themselves having problems with other kids quite often, because they tended to be less mature than other kids their age.

At one point, Donna and I decided that we couldn't keep Kelly, because he wasn't getting along with anyone in the house, including Todd. In time, Todd had the same problem, and we had him removed. In the ensuing months, there would be several times when one or the other of the brothers would be removed from the house, and we would take the other one back.

I think that there were times when these boys felt like they were too close, and I think they unwittingly, created a problem between the two of them that would get one or the other removed. And then, there were times when they felt like there was too much distance between them, and they would create another problem between themselves and the kids, or maybe between themselves and Donna or me.

One of the things I was learning was that in most cases, I had it easier than Donna. Most of the kids that we were to have over the next fourteen years had mothers, but for one reason or another, had no involved father. Kids often didn't know what to do with feelings of anger at mother and affection for Donna. It was much easier for them to feel close to me as a father, because to do so did not cause of any guilt. Todd and Kelly probably had more conflict with this issue than most of the other boys.

Todd and Kelly were sixteen years of age. One afternoon, the kids began to arrive home from school. Todd and Lloyd and the others all raided the refrigerator as usual, and then dispersed all over the house. After a while, I noticed that the main floor of the house was very quiet. I walked from the kitchen through the dining room and into the living room. When I got to the living room, I could hear faint laughter coming from upstairs. I sneaked upstairs and decided that I was hearing laughter coming from the bathroom. It was Lloyd, age 5 or 6, and Todd, age 16. I panicked! I could hear them splashing in the water, and of course, my mind saw them naked and God knows what.

I have to explain the layout of the bathroom in question. When you opened the door, you found yourself directly behind the wall containing the shower mechanism, plumbing, etc. Therefore, I could hide behind that wall and hear anything being said in the entire bathroom. In this case, all I could hear was the stamping of feet in shallow water. I walked out from behind the wall and saw Lloyd and Todd, both with clothes on, but very wet, and having a ball stomping in about two inches of water. I told them it was time to get out, dry off, and change clothes and to make sure the bathroom was cleaned up, picked up and dry

The Story of Robbie, My Best Friend

Robbie came to us one early and snowy afternoon. I'm not sure about the reason for his placement, but Robbie was developmentally disabled, and I remember that dad had a difficult time accepting that fact.

I took an instant liking to this kid. He had a toothy grin the size of the Pacific and the whitest teeth I've ever seen. For a few minutes after his social worker left, he sat with me at the kitchen table and just let himself be mesmerized by the falling snow.

I asked him if he liked snow. "Oh, yeah," he assured me. Then I asked him if he liked to shovel snow. Again he answered, "Yes." I asked him if he'd like to shovel a path from the alley to the back door so the kids could take their boots off in the back porch.

He got up, got into his coat, and grabbed the shovel. He went out on the back porch, put on his boots, and disappeared out the door. After watching him for a few minutes, I decided to get about my chores.

After about an hour of non-stop phone calls, etc, it struck me that I hadn't seen or heard from Robbie. I thought I'd better check on him. When I got to the kitchen window, I saw a sight I'm sure I'll never see again. Robbie had shoveled the entire back yard...the ENTIRE back yard! You could have landed a plane in my back yard. He was so proud, and I took the opportunity to lavish praise on him and gave him my first hug.

Taking a Chance

When Robbie had been with us long enough for us to get to know something about his abilities, we decided to allow him the opportunity to hop on a city bus and go downtown all by himself. We gave him a role of quarters and pinned our address and phone number on his jacket. He'd taken the bus from the house to school, so he knew where to catch the buses and where passengers were dropped off. We sent him out the door with his usual smile on his face, and Donna and I looked at each other and crossed our fingers.

Several hours later, there was a knock on the door. When I answered it, who do you think I found standing in front of me? It was

Robbie's social worker, who told me she just found herself in the neighborhood. I invited her in. What the hell choice did I have?

Of course, she asked to see Robbie. When I told her he wasn't home, she asked where he was. When I told her we let him go downtown on a city bus, she almost had a stroke. She started to lecture us about Robbie's limitations, etc., etc., etc. As the lecture was going on, the back door opened, and there was Robbie, happier than a pig in a mud bath. After satisfying herself that Robbie was fine, hadn't been robbed, raped, or whatever, she took her leave, and Donna and I got another chance to hug this kid and congratulate him on his accomplishment. Robbie, if you're out there, son, I hope you're still riding the bus!

Dealing With the Facts of Life

As a general means of dealing with the fact that our charges were teenage boys, I left not too subtle hints on each new boy's bed that I realized they were boys. I left a bottle of hand cream and a box of Kleenex on each new boy's bed. And I never had anyone ask me what they were for either.

Humor aside, sexuality was a very important issue for my boys, as it is for all boys. We were aware that we were going to get kids who were gay, straight, gay and behaving as if they were straight, and straight and behaving as if they were gay. As a matter of fact, as I think about the 31 total placements we had in Duluth, about twenty percent fit the non-straight categories.

It's my belief that a gay youngster simply discovers that he/she is gay, just like a straight kid discovers that he/she is attracted to members of the opposite sex. We can all choose the way we behave, but why do we make it so difficult for gay teens to accept their sexuality? In the 42 years I've been working with young people, I've lost 13 to suicide and AIDS. American society is much more accepting of the gay culture now than it used to be, but I think it's still very hard to be a gay teenager in America.

One of the things that foster parents, and especially group home parents, are expected to be is suspicious. Robbie was usually the first of our kids to get home from school in the afternoon. One day, he stormed in the back door with the usual smile on his face. Without saying a word, he ran upstairs and slammed his bedroom door shut. My first thought was that he was sneaking something upstairs that he didn't want me to see. I followed him up the steps quietly, and pressed my ear to his door. What I heard was a young man bouncing on his own bed and, obviously, enjoying taking things into his own hands. This became a daily ritual for him.

One summer, I decided to take the kids on a week's vacation to a resort my family used to inhabit every summer when I was a kid. This lake resort had at least two things going for it. First, it had an excellent swimming beach. Secondly, it was full of decent sized pan fish.

On the first morning, Robbie was awake before the roosters, grabbed his fishing rod and was out on the dock, fishing in maybe two feet of water. I walked outside to watch this wonderful kid having the time of his life.

Suddenly, he pulled his line out of the water, all the while screaming at me that he'd caught a fish. Of course, I told him to bring it to me so I could see it. And, of course, he asked me if he could keep it. Under normal circumstances, I would have encouraged him throw it back, as it was every centimeter of three or four inches long. It couldn't have weighed more than a few ounces. But Robbie told me that it was his first fish. That fact changed everything. I took the appropriate photographs, and the thought even d my mind that I should look into the possibility of having it mounted or something. That never happened, but I still have the photographs.

Robbie and Paul Bunyan

On our way home, the family stopped in Brainerd to see Paul Bunyan Park. When we got through the gate, I sent Robbie and the other kids off to explore. I found the person who was responsible for Paul's tendency to suddenly starting to talk to specific people in the crowd. I was sure Robbie would appreciate the huge statue's specifically talking to him. When the enormous statue welcomed Robbie to the park, asked him several questions about where he was from, what grade he was in, etc, he was absolutely shocked and excited beyond belief. Some of the other kids were behaving as if they were shocked also, but doing it was for Robbie's sake especially.

Witnessing all of this bordered on being too much for me. I told myself that he'd probably never do this again, and I wanted to find another first for him. The second "first" came in the form of a helicopter ride being offered at the park. He didn't hesitate. I asked him if he wanted to tour the City of Brainerd from a helicopter, and he was excited beyond description. Robbie had a very exciting day, and my day was just as happy.

Jason

Jason's basic problem was that he didn't get along with his stepfather. His mother struck me as either the type of woman who wasn't strong enough to take on her husband, or simply wasn't willing to do so. Either way, I would have found it hard to believe that she could honestly side with stepdad all of the time, and that made me feel sorry for her.

Jason was kind of a funny kid. He had long, brown hair, was slightly on the pudgy side, had a slight limp, as I recall, and he was forever dressing in camouflage jeans and t-shirts. I don't think this kid ever considered being anything else than a soldier when he grew up. And a soldier is exactly what he became when he grew up.

I few years after Jason left our house, I found out that he had fought his way through the system, psychologists, etc., and found himself to be a proud member of the 101st Airborne. One day, he called and asked if I could pick him up at the Twin Cities International Airport. I went to the airport and looked for him on the sidewalk outside the massive building. Suddenly I saw a young man dressed in dress a military uniform and proudly wearing a red beret. I knew it had to be my son Jason. I honked the horn, he looked at me, and walked over to the car. I was almost crying as we hugged each other. He seemed a foot taller and looked like he'd managed to shed about thirty pounds of baby fat and replace it with muscle.

He stayed with us for a few days before heading to Duluth to wipe his shiny boots on his stepfather's chest.

Yeah, I know. You're asking yourself how the heck I got to the Cities and why did we leave Duluth? All I can tell you is stay tuned.

Jason stayed with us for a few days, and during that time, I don't think he ever took that beret off, not even in the shower. We

Larry Bauer-Scandin

haven't been out of touch since, about twenty years.

Jason is currently earning a living as a chef. He is out of the military after having met what he thought was to be the woman of his dreams. It wasn't to be. The resultant problem is that he became the parent of a son that he's not involved with. For that, I'm tremendously sorry.

Junior

About ninety-nine percent of our placements over fourteen years were teenagers. Periodically though, we accepted a child a little younger than a teen. One such placement was Junior. Junior was eleven or twelve years old and was living with his mother. His father was around but was not living with mother. Junior also had one brother.

As I recall, the reason for Junior's placement involved mother and her boyfriend who were both fond of their alcohol and drugs, and, at times, Junior would leave the house at night to find his mother. When he would find them in one bar or another, they would sometimes sell the boy for sexual services.

Soon after his arrival, I began to learn what we'd actually accepted as a placement. Junior would frequently wake me up, during the night and complain about some pain in some part of his small body. Frequently, it was a leg cramp, headache, toothache, stomach ache, etc. He'd walk in my bedroom and wake me up. That, I was to learn, quickly, was to be my signal to pick him, carry him downstairs, sit in my rocking chair, and rock him to sleep. Then I'd carry him back upstairs and put him in his bed.

I'm not exactly sure where Junior went when Donna, Lloyd, and I left Duluth, but I looked for him for about fifteen years. I never found him in phone books, and the only address I had was that of his mother. I wasn't even sure she would give it to him. He finally found me in 2006. Sometimes, one gets lucky when opening a box! Junior is now thirty-four years old, and we're very much in touch with each other again.

My Native Americans

I don't know about anyone else, but I was always told that Native American kids would be found to be very quiet. Well, as I recall, I had three Native American kids, and none of them were quiet. One of them even had curly blond hair and blue eyes.

But my favorite was Ray. Ray was sixteen, average height and weight, and long black hair. He had a beautiful smile that always made me think he was hiding something. But quiet? I don't think so!

One winter night, Ray sneaked out of the house. I don't remember if I'd grounded him or if he had just sneaked out after curfew. I couldn't quite figure out how he got out of the house until I went upstairs to do a bed check and found him to be sound asleep. Now I was trying to figure out how he got back in without my being aware of it.

I decided I was too tired to wake Ray up and try and squeeze an answer to my big question. I thought I'd let it go until morning.

As I checked the second floor bathroom to make sure everyone had turned off the water and left it in halfway decent shape, I noticed the light coming into the bathroom window. It was a street light coming from the alley behind the house. As I took a glance out the window, I noticed footprints leading off the roof covering the steps outside the back porch. Problem solved. Now I knew how he got out, but how the hell did he get back in?

The next morning, I confronted Ray about his sneaking out of, and back into, the house. From the look on his face, he could hardly wait to tell me. He had climbed back onto the roof and walked backwards into the bathroom window, using the same tracks he made on his way out. I had a hell of a time keeping a straight face. What a kid.

Some years after we sold the house and moved to the Cities, I got a letter from Ray from an address in Oklahoma, Wyoming, or somewhere down in that area. I think I tried writing a letter and sending it to that address, but I got no answer.

So, Ray, if you're out there and you happen to run across this book, I want you to know that I'd love to know where you are and how you're doing. I'm in the St. Paul phone book.

Larry Bauer-Scandin

A Few Things I Learned On My Way
To Becoming a Dad

I'd like to mention a few lessons I learned that I'll never forget. One was an amazing learning experience and the other, one of those warm happenings that make you feel good and warm inside.

One of those events involved Todd, one of my identical twin brothers. One night, Todd pulled some stunt that really made me mad. I called him into the office and shut the door. Then I began my lecture. During the most heated part of the lecture, I told him that I was so angry with him that "I could take you over my knee and tan your ass! Do you think that would help you grow up?"

And without the usual smart look on his face, or a smart crack coming from his mouth, he looked at me and said, "It might."

It was a few days before Christmas, and I was trying to figure out what to get the kids for Christmas gifts. I didn't have a lot of money to spend, so I drove to Target and just started looking around. I walked past a table piled high with blankets. I stood there for a minute wondering if anyone would appreciate a blanket for Christmas. As I continued to look around, I found nothing I was more interested in. I loaded a dozen blankets into my basket and headed for the checkout counter.

When I got home, Donna and I headed for the basement, and with a little luck, we managed to get the blankets wrapped without any of the kids seeing them. We carried them upstairs and placed them under the Christmas tree.

On Christmas Eve night, all the kids were anxious to get their gifts. As they were being passed out, I wondered about their reactions to the gifts. Much to my surprise, as they were opened, all of the kids wrapped the blankets around their shoulders. After everything had been opened, each boy sat in front of the TV, watching "A Christmas Carol" wrapped in his blanket. It was truly a sight to behold. I'll never forget looking at the backs of eight or ten kids, wrapped in cheap blankets, and all looking like they'd just won the lottery. One of those boys recently told me that he still had that blanket.

Billy

Like so many of the other kids who came to live with me, I don't remember why I met Bill. He was a very bright, articulate, and handsome kid of about sixteen years of age.

To the best of my memory, Bill was an only child. Mother was divorced from the biological father, and Billy and dad had nothing to do with each other with the exception of one thing, his last name. He had lived most of his life with a stepfather with whom he seemed to get along pretty well. For a reason I've forgotten, the problem resulting in his placement was the relationship between him and his mother. Mother grew to not like me too well, as she as well as a lot of other parents, tended to believe that I was in foster care for the money.

And, as long as I'm on the subject, let me speak to the issue of foster care back in those days. I'll return to Bill a little later.

The Foster Care System

I don't know what the foster care system's standards were for foster parents. It seemed to me like each agency decided what they needed each applicant to do, e.g., provide a very structured program, or a very family-centered program, etc.

Those of us who dealt with teen delinquents were, potentially, at least, paid best. For example, a placement that came to me with a history of violent behavior or illegal sexual behavior or emotional problems would typically warrant the most reimbursement to the foster parent(s). In those days, that top pay, as I recall, was $1019 per month. If a parent had ten placements in that difficulty range, they appeared to be getting extremely well paid. What the public didn't know, though, was that if a placement came to me with a driver's license, my insurance premium went up. There were designated amounts that had to go toward clothing, etc., and if someone destroyed something in the house, its replacement was not covered by the department. It was very possible that a placement could cost more in a month than the agency was paying.

During the roughly six years we were in Duluth, we foster/group home parents experienced several traumatic days every year. Each and every year, the county published its budget in the local

223

paper. Naturally, that published list of expenditures included monies spent on foster care, so if the budget read that I had received $100,000 from the county, readers, I believe, tended to look at it as a salary. For several days, some of us would receive anonymous and threatening phone calls. With a little work, we discovered that those making the calls were social workers who were making some of the placements. They simply didn't understand the financial side of foster care. Once the department educated them in Finances 101, everything was fine.

All of this reminds me of another indirect contact with a former client. During one of the five and a half years we were foster parents in Duluth, I was elected president of the county's Foster Parent Association. Sounds impressive, right? Well, I was elected while taking a washroom break at a meeting of the county's foster parents, and wasn't there to defend myself.

After my election, or "railroading," as I called it, we started talking about how we could stop the threats and misconceptions. We decided that it all had to start with my meeting with the agency brass. Everyone who'd been around for a while warned me that I'd never get past Marge.

I asked who the hell Marge was, and learned that she was the Commissioners' secretary. I told the members that the Commissioners had to authorize the financial education of their social workers, so we had to get past Marge. They agreed but still warned me that I wouldn't get past Marge.

I decided that I wouldn't call and try and make an appointment. I'd simply walk in the office and try and get an appointment made by talking directly with Marge.

I walked into the office and took a chair. Marge was fifteen feet away, sitting behind her desk, her right side facing me. She continued to bang away at her typewriter (remember them?) and showed no sign that she even knew I was in the room. I was feeling like I was beginning to understand what the other foster parents had been telling me.

My eyes scanned her desk, and I was startled when I looked at her name plate. Just as I stared at the name plate, I heard her say, "I'll bet you don't even remember me, do you?"

I smiled and said, "Oh, yes I do. Your name is Marge, your husband's name is Dave, and your son's name is Mike. He'd be about

224

29 years old. And you both make great coffee!"

The infamous Marge was the mother of the kid who walked away from the institution because he was afraid to come home to all the girls. She told me that Mike was happily married and a salesman. She said he spent more time in planes flying coast to coast, than he does on the ground.

By the time I left the office, I had my appointment with the brass. Marge also told me that if I ever needed anything from the Commissioners, all I had to do was contact her, and she would, as Larry the Cable Guy says, "get 'er done."

The Dangerous One

One day, we were asked to take a young man that I had some serious reservations about. I don't remember anything about his background. I do remember that his social worker caused me as much concern as did the kid.

The first night, Donna assigned the kid, whose name I've forgotten, to do dishes. We wanted to find out how he did his chores under supervision. It didn't take long to find out. I could hear him yelling at Donna. Soon he walked into the living room with blood dripping from his wrists.

At first I panicked, but then I saw that he'd cut himself on the top of his wrists. He was standing over me, bleeding into my lap. I told him that he'd better start praying that the blood came out of my pants. He walked back to the kitchen, wiping his bleeding wrists across the dining room walls as he went.

Somehow we all made it through the rest of the evening and through the night. But I knew when I went to bed that I was going to call the social worker in the morning and have the kid removed. I was damned sure the kid was mentally ill, if not downright dangerous.

I did call the social worker early the next morning. I told him I wanted the kid out of my house within an hour. He argued with me, telling me that I had promised to keep the boy. I told him that I'd keep him until he came to pick him up, and that had better not be long.

The boy was removed, and eventually was placed in another group home belonging to a friend of mine. A year or so after leaving this home, he was in a downtown Duluth alley. Someone walking the

Larry Bauer-Scandin

street passed the alley and was grabbed by this kid, who stabbed the man in the chest, killing him. He was sent to the Minnesota Security Hospital at St. Peter. At last word, he was still there.

The Doctor's Son

Mike was the son of a local mental health professional. I believe that the relationship between Mike and his father was the reason for his placement with us. I also remember that Mike was a quiet kid and never caused us any serious trouble.

He wasn't with us for a long time before he was returned to the family home. I also know that it didn't last for long.

One night, I was at my favorite Perkins Restaurant picking up some of my coffee-drinking kids. While I was at the cash register paying for my coffee, I spotted a man at the door that I recognized as a local gay pimp known for recruiting young boys in Leif Erickson Park, right across the street from the restaurant. As I moved around the area of the cash register, I looked down a row of booths and saw Mike coming toward me and picking up bits of food off plates that had not yet been picked up by bus persons. I walked up to him and asked, "Mike, what the hell are you doing?" I asked him if he was involved with the pimp, and he admitted that he was. I asked him why, and he said, "Because I'm cold and hungry, and don't have a home. What would you do?" Then, I proceeded to do nothing. Today, I would have taken him home with me. Whatever happened to you, Mike?

And Here Comes John

One of my favorite kids of all time was John. As usual, I don't remember the reason for his placement. I know that there was no father in his life, but his mother, Mary, was a nice lady and I grew very fond of her. She was also the kind that was very willing to work with you and not against you.

John was the sort of kid who always seemed to be up to something. If something was going on in the house, you could bet that John was either a part of it, or he knew about it. But John was a fun kid to have around. Back to John in a bit.

226

Woofer

When I met Russ, aka Woofer, he was a resident of a juvenile drug treatment program called 2001, which was located in the West End community of Duluth. I attended his graduation ceremony, and I was able to come to the conclusion that he was a very popular resident in the program. All the residents gave him a farewell hug before he left, and they all signed a farewell card. As he and each resident said goodbye, Russ would answer with "woof, woof" and that, obviously, is how he got his nickname of Woofer.

We walked out to my car, and I opened the trunk. We easily engaged in conversation, and he seemed to be very excited about starting a new adventure in my house. As we were throwing his gear into the trunk, I asked him if he was concerned about his ability to stay away from drugs. He had no doubt that he could stay clean. I asked him what he thought he'd do if he fell off the wagon.

He answered, "I won't."

That concerned me greatly.

My first impressions of Russ were very positive. He seemed to like the other kids, and they seemed to like him. He and John seemed to get particularly close. He also seemed to take Robbie under his wing. In time, it became apparent that Russ was going to be a leader in the house.

The first thing we had to deal with was getting Russ into school. Our residential location dictated that he be enrolled in Duluth East High School. He didn't fight it, but he was concerned about being in a school full of wealthy, upper class kids. He tried it for a while, and then asked if he might transfer to Duluth Denfeld High School, located on the west end of town. I wanted him to invest in a school situation, so I agreed, with reservations.

Before I go on, I want to describe Woofer's family situation. His father lived in Superior, Wisconsin. He was a drinker, and that took its toll on the relationship between dad and his son. Russ's mom and dad were divorced. She and her husband were living in Duluth. Another fact that affected the relationship between Russ and his mother was that she was a Jehovah's Witness. Over the course of the time that Russ lived with me, I came to feel that one of his problems was that, to him, he was either all good or all bad, depending on his behavior

227

decisions. Everything was either black or white to him. He couldn't admit to any gray in his life. I'll elaborate on this a little later. Russ also had a 16-year-old brother, Mike, who was living with his father in Superior.

Russ's behavior and performance, as measured by the usual yardsticks, was just fine during most of the time he lived with us. He was, however, still a kid. On Christmas Eve, 1985, the whole family seemed excited about having supper at home with both sets of foster grandparents, opening gifts afterward, etc. Unfortunately, the group of kids we had at the time couldn't go home for the holiday, so we had quite a house full.

During the afternoon, John and Russ asked if they could go out. About that time of the day, Donna and I considered it a treat to get rid of a few kids for a while so we could get ready for the big Christmas meal, so I told them to go. They flew out the back door and disappeared. A few hours later, they flew in the back door, and without saying a word, they ran upstairs. Because I was so busy, I didn't think much of it.

Supper came and went, and I think everyone enjoyed it. We all retired to the living room and opened presents. After some chatting and a few cups of coffee, the adults began to don their coats and go home. In another hour or so, the kids began to get tired and go to bed. Pretty soon, Russ and John, both of whom had been unusually quiet all evening, also went upstairs. Even Donna had gone to bed. Only Ruth, Donna's mother, and I were still up having a last cup of coffee at the dining room table.

When we were done, Ruth went to bed, and I found myself sitting alone on the living room sofa. I always tried to be the last to go to bed so I knew everyone was home and safe. On this occasion, I was also taking the opportunity to reflect on how happy I was to be acting as the stand-in father for these kids. I don't think I could have been any happier than I was at that moment.

As I was sitting there, deep in thought, John and Russ came down the steps and took seats beside me on the couch. They just kind of sat there and smiled. Finally, it dawned on me. These guys were waiting for me to go to bed. Now what were they up to, I was thinking.

I looked at the two of them and asked them what the hell they were up to. John denied being up to anything. Russ, on the other hand, turned red. As John started to run off at the mouth and Russ continued to stare into his lap, it finally struck me that they were waiting for me to go to bed. Then I remembered their being out of the house that afternoon, coming in and running upstairs. I looked at Woofer and told him to go upstairs and get whatever it was they didn't want me to see. They both got up, but I grabbed John by the belt and pulled him back down on the couch.

Russ went upstairs and came down with a VCR movie, an XXX movie called "Debbie Does Dallas," as a matter of fact. I could hardly keep from laughing. With my best irritated look on my face, I told both boys to go to bed. "We'll talk about it in the morning," I said. "Now, go to bed." I'll bet Russ didn't sleep all night.

In the morning, I did set the two boys down and did some butt-chewing. John attempted to take a "What's the big deal?" attitude, but I cut him off. Russ apologized and promised he'd never do such a thing again.

I told both of them to get that movie back to the store and get their asses home. I'd think about how long they'd be grounded while they were gone. Without another word, they got up and left.

A while later, the phone rang, and it was John's mom. She said she wanted to tell me what a great movie the kids had! Those brats had taken the damned movie to Mary's to watch before they took it back to the store!

"Mary," I said, "What the hell are you doing?" I told her to tell the two boys to get their asses to the store and get home. I don't remember how long I grounded the boys, but we never had a repeat of the incident.

Beginning of the End

One day, Russ came to me and asked if he could attend a hockey game his school was taking part in. The game was to take place in Minneapolis as it was a tournament game. He told me that he would be going on a school bus supervised by two chaperones. I told him that I'd give him permission, provided that a check with the school confirmed what he'd told me.

The next day, I called Denfeld High School, and the office confirmed the information Russ had given me. Three buses were

229

going, each having two adult volunteer chaperones. Armed with that information, I gave the school permission to put Russ on their list of attendees. When he got home from school, I told him I'd called the school and signed him up.

On the day of the big game, I began to have second thoughts like a lot of concerned parents might have. I told Russ to behave himself and to have fun. Then he hopped on the bus and took off for school. I crossed my fingers.

Within an hour or so, I received a phone call from a hysterical female Denfeld student, who informed me that Russ had been drinking before the buses had taken off for Minneapolis. I tried to check this out with school people, but nobody could, or would, confirm the report.

It was an extremely long day. I picked Russ up at school at the appointed time. It was obvious that he'd been drinking, and he didn't deny it when I asked him. What he couldn't do is tell me why. As I found out later, a lot of the kids on all three buses had been drinking all the way to and from the game and during the game as well. I remember going to school the following day in the hope of getting some answers, but I got none that made any sense. What I really wanted to know was who the chaperones were.

I'm also sure that I would have notified Russ's St. Louis County Probation Officer of this incident, but I don't remember his reaction. What I do remember is that his probation was not violated. Maybe he simply decided to let me handle it.

The real unfortunate result of this incident wasn't that it was so serious in and of itself. The real tragedy was that, for him, this mistake made him all bad in his own eyes. His conscience was that fragile. Another thing that I'm sure didn't help was that his mother was said to tell him that he was going to go to hell. Guilt was something Russ felt very easily and very deeply. I'm very sure that this incident made him decide that he had disappointed me to the point where he could no longer live in my house. No matter how much I tried to talk to him about the incident, he couldn't seem to forgive himself.

Between this incident and the time he left my house, he contrived another behavioral problem that I believe was meant to encourage my anger, and perhaps a decision on my part to throw him out.

One night, the kids were congregated down in the basement. I was in the basement workshop. Russ was telling the others that he had run into Kelly, my twin who was not living with us at that time, that afternoon and had knocked his tooth out. The kids knew I was in the workshop, so they weren't surprised when that comment brought me out to the main room. I looked at Russ and asked him, "What did you say you did?"

I knocked Kelly's tooth out," he said.

"Why did you do that?" I asked.

"I don't like him," he answered.

"Who's going to call your probation officer, you or me?"

"I'll call him," he said. Then I went upstairs.

Russ did call his probation officer and set up an appointment to see him. I asked him if he wanted me to be there, and somewhat to my surprise, he said yes.

On appointment day, I got to the courthouse about a half hour early. Russ was going to come to the courthouse directly from school. As I sat out in the hallway, the probation officer, whom I knew well, came out to chat. He looked at me and said, "You don't really expect to see him get off that elevator, do you?"

"That's exactly what I expect."

He smiled, shook his head, and walked back into his office. I continued to keep my eyes glued on the elevator.

Finally, the elevator door opened, and there he was. He walked over to me and smiled. I asked him if he wanted me to go in with him. He said, "No."

I said, "Good luck," and he turned and walked into the office.

I'm not exactly sure what I was praying for, but I was praying. Russ was eighteen years of age, so I knew that there was a good chance that the probation officer would lock him up in the St. Louis County Jail, and possibly, charge him with Assault.

After about fifteen minutes, both of them walked out of the office toward me. Both of them were smiling. When they got to my chair, the probation officer told me that he was not going to lock Russ up, but only because of the faith I had that he would show up for that appointment. We thanked the man and walked out to the car. I hoped this might alter Russ's attitude about leaving the house and moving out on his own, but it did not.

Within a short time, Russ had managed to find an apartment in the downtown area of Duluth. He had been working at the Jolly Fisher Restaurant for quite some time, so he was able to afford it. After he left, he continued to call frequently, but he never came to the house. On a few occasions, he asked me to come to his apartment. On each occasion, I'd hoped he wanted to talk, but it never happened until November 12, 1986.

Michael's Death

On October 23, I got a phone call from Russ telling me that his 16-year old brother, Mike, had been killed in a motorcycle and semitrailer truck collision at a city intersection. Russ sounded numb and asked if we could get together. We did get together, and I asked him to come home with me. He declined. He said he'd let me know when and where the wake and funeral were to be held.

Of course, Donna and I made sure that the kids were kept informed about Mike's death, how Russ seemed to be dealing with it, and whether or not they wanted to go to the wake to view the body and offer Russ their condolences. We kept a heightened watch on all the kids so that fear or panic didn't set in.

In a day or so, Russ called and gave us the day, date, and the name of the mortuary at which the wake was to take place. He still sounded numb.

On the evening of the wake, a few of the older kids decided to go to the mortuary in advance of Donna and me, in order to lend Russ their support. When Donna and I got to the mortuary, she held my arm all the way to the door as if she was anticipating my collapsing or fainting. As we approached the door, I could see Russ's outline against the light of the open door. Suddenly, that outline was broken by John's form walking toward us, obviously crying. After getting a hug, he grabbed my other arm. I wasn't anywhere near collapsing or fainting, but I wanted to give John, especially, the feeling of supporting me in a time of need.

When we got to the steps, Russ was standing there staring straight ahead and saying nothing. He didn't even acknowledge our being there. I just took his hand and gave it a gentle squeeze. Then Donna and I went inside and approached the body. As I looked at this young man, I couldn't help but think about how his loss was affecting a lot of other people, both directly and indirectly. I'd seen other young people in this same setting, but for other reasons, but it has never and will never get any easier to accept.

Donna and I went over to the parents and offered our condolences. Mother was quite talkative, but dad didn't say a word to me. We stayed for a while, hoping that Russ would come inside and give us some indication that he was alright, but he did not. We decided to leave. When we got outside, we found Russ still surrounded by friends, most of whom we didn't know. I looked at him and said, "You know where we are." I told John and a few others of our kids to take care of Russ, but to make sure they made it home at a decent time.

Two Days in November

On the night of November 12, 1986, I was out of the house doing some shopping. Suddenly my pager went off. It was Donna. I got to a phone and called home. She told me that Russ was there and wanted to talk to me. I was ecstatic and told her I'd be there shortly.

When I got home, what I found was a very upset young man. He looked like he hadn't slept in several days, and I was pretty sure he was high. For some reason, none of the kids were home, so I quickly escorted him to the basement. That was his favorite room in the entire house, so I knew that if it was going to be possible to calm him down, that would be the place to do it. Besides, I could lock the basement door.

We talked for several hours, but much of what he said didn't make any sense to me, and he seemed unable to answer my questions. He kept saying, "He betrayed me! He betrayed me!" I had, and still have, no idea what he meant. He also complained of pain, but he wouldn't agree to let me take him to the hospital.

After rambling on for a few hours, he looked at me and asked if he could lie down on the couch, put his head in my lap, and close his eyes. He lay down on the couch and placed his head on my right leg and closed his eyes. We were silent for probably an hour. Russ fell asleep, and I sat stroking his head with my left hand and trying to figure out what to do next.

Eventually he awakened, and seemed to be much calmer. I suggested that he get ready to go to sleep. He stood up and got out of his clothes. I got a pillow and blanket for him, gave him a hug and told him I'd see him in the morning.

Donna and I got up in the morning and got the kids off to school. It was Thursday, November 13, 1986. We let Russ sleep a while longer while we had a cup of coffee and talked about last night's conversation in the basement. After filling her in, I went downstairs to invite him to go out for breakfast with us. He seemed to be in a normal mood and accepted our breakfast invitation. He asked if he could take a shower first.

He took his shower and we went out for breakfast. Everything seemed quite normal, but he kept talking about his treatment program at 2001. From the content of his conversation, it sounded like he might want to make contact with his old 2001 counselors and or friends. Sometime during breakfast, he looked at me and asked if it would be possible for me to take him to 2001 that night. Of course, I agreed, as I felt this visit might serve to bolster his spirits.

When we got home, he asked if we could go back in the basement and talk. Again, we retired to his favorite room, and we sat on his favorite bed, the couch. We spent the entire rest of the day talking, but as the time went on, he seemed to get more excited about going out to 2001. I made a call to his counselors, Darlene Slotness and Kerry Gauthier and told them the situation, and they were anxious for me to have him come out and visit.

It was probably around 7:00 pm when we arrived at 2001. Russ was greeted with many hugs and handshakes. I used that time to tell Darleen and Kerry what had been happening the previous twenty-four hours or so. Then Russ asked if he could talk to Kerry in his office. The two of them retired to Kerry's office, and I spent a few minutes talking with Darlene. Kerry and Russ spent probably fifteen minutes together and then reappeared, both smiling and hugging. After a few more hugs and handshakes, Russ and I took our leave and drove home. He seemed relaxed and satisfied during the fifteen minute trip back home.

When we got home, Russ raided the refrigerator that never closed, poured himself a glass of milk, and asked, again, if we could retire to the basement. He said good night to Donna and the kids milling about the house, and we went downstairs.

Again, we sat on the couch, Russ with his head resting on my right shoulder, and my right arm draped over his shoulders as we talked. One of the things he told me was that he had been told by Social Services that he had to check into the Lincoln Hotel in the morning, in order to establish a residence so that he could get some help. Apparently, he'd lost his job at the Jolly Fisher and was living with a friend and his mother.

He was beginning to yawn and close his eyes, so I suggested he might want to get out of his clothes and go to sleep. I intended to take his clothing upstairs so he couldn't disappear during the night.

He got out of his clothes and lay on the couch. He covered himself with the blanket and closed his eyes. I asked him how he was feeling. Without opening his eyes, he said, "Peaceful."

I said, "Good night. I'll see you in the morning." I turned off the lights and went upstairs.

By this time, all of the kids and Donna had gone to bed. Donna always went to bed several hours before me, and she always got up several hours before me, so there was very few hours of the day that one of us wasn't awake.

Finding myself alone, I went into the kitchen, poured myself a cup of coffee, sat down at the kitchen table, and stared out the window into the darkness. Sometime in the past, I'd been in the Lincoln Hotel. It was a first class dump. I sat at the table, thinking about offering to take him to the Lincoln the next morning and see how we might spruce things up if need be.

It was approaching 2:00 am, and I was getting tired. Our usual breakfast time at Perkins was 9:00 am, so that didn't leave much time for sleep, so I hit the sack hard.

I woke up at about 8:00 am and quickly got dressed. When I got downstairs, I heard the voice of my mechanic and friend, Henry. I walked in the kitchen, greeted Henry, poured myself a cup of coffee, and sat down with him, Donna, and Lloyd. After a cup of coffee or two, I took my leave to go downstairs and wake Russ.

Friday, November 14, 1986

As I walked down the steps, I heard nothing. I assumed he was still asleep. As I approached the back of the sofa, I spotted a light coming from the workshop/bathroom area to my left. As I walked toward the light, it struck me that I was still hearing nothing.

When I entered the room, I found Russ hanging from an extension cord that he'd wrapped around a ceiling pipe. Directly behind him was a padded barstool that I used when working at my work bench. There was a twisted look on his face, and his hands were formed into fists. It was clear that he had been seated on the stool and eased himself off the seat and suffocated. All of this, of course, was observed in an instant.

At the same instant, I grabbed his legs under the knees, praying that the look on his face was indicating that he was still alive. I tried to lift him while looking around for something to cut the cord with. I spotted a small saw hanging from a hook above the work bench, but I couldn't quite reach it and still hang on to Russ. I had to let him go. I grabbed the saw and cut the cord, almost in one motion.

The stiff body dropped into my arms and felt like a bundle of 2x4s. As soon as I laid him on the floor, I untied the knot in the cord. As I did so, air escaped his lungs. I checked for a heartbeat. There was none. I flew into the main part of the basement, got on the phone, and called 911. I flicked on the intercom system between the basement and the kitchen. Donna answered.

I said, "Is Lloyd dressed yet?"

She said, "Yes, why?"

I asked, "Is Henry still here?"

She said, "Yes. What's wrong?"

I said, "Listen to me, and don't ask me any questions. I want you to put Lloyd's jacket on him, and ask Henry to get him out of the house."

Within a minute or so, I heard the kitchen door shut. At least, I knew Lloyd wasn't going to have to see any of this. I knew that now that all the kids were off to school and no one was home except Donna and me, she was going to be heading down the steps to the basement. I intercepted her at the top of the steps. I told her that Russ was dead, that he had hanged himself in the workshop. I told her that I'd called 911 and they should be arriving at anytime. I asked her to stay upstairs until they arrived and direct them to the basement. I returned to the basement.

The Unsuspecting Visitor

The first to show up at the house were two police officers. Donna stood on the porch and directed the officers to the basement. A short time after the officers pulled up, my dad pulled up right behind the first squad car. He had been painting my office, and before he'd left the house the previous day, I'd told him to just come on down to the house anytime he felt like painting. No sooner had he gotten out of the car than an ambulance pulled up behind him and ran right past him on my front steps. And, finally, a second squad car appeared.

When Dad got to Donna, all she could say was, "Hanging!" He walked in the house, looked around and saw no kids and knew that Donna was on the porch. His conclusion? Larry, me, his son, had hanged myself.

He walked down the steps to the basement. When he got downstairs, he was already white. He looked to his right and saw me sitting in a chair answering a barrage of questions. As he looked at me, the EMTs pulled the gurney containing Russ's body out of the workshop and carried it up the stairs and out to the ambulance. I followed the body out to the ambulance and watched them drive off. Without saying a word, Dad got in his car and drove off. In case you were wondering, I got all this information from Dad himself during a phone conversation later that day.

All of this actually happened in a very short period of time. When I got back in the house, I called Larry Modean, our family social worker, and told him what had happened. He came right over to the house. As I recall, he called Russ's parents.

After the phone calls, Donna, Larry, and I sat down to a cup of coffee, and I filled in the gaps for both of them. It had come to me that I had missed a sign. I told myself that I should have picked up on a clue Russ had given me last night. When I asked him how he felt, and he answered "Peaceful," I was thinking I should have picked up on that as being an indication of his plan. I also thought about the fact that the Adler Institute had taught us that no one but the victim can be blamed for a suicide, but somehow, that wasn't helping.

I hadn't much of a chance to clean up, so I told Donna and Larry that I was going to go downstairs and take a shower. When I hit the bottom of the steps, I heard someone running across the living room floor and down the steps. As I stepped toward the bathroom, I glanced at the extension cord that was still dangling from the pipe. I turned to Larry, and it hit me that he thought I might be preparing to hang myself. For a second, I was angry at his apparent believing that I would hang myself, but in another second, I realized I had to appreciate his concern. I smiled at him and asked him if he intended to take a shower with me. As I went into the bathroom, he removed the cord from the pipe and took it upstairs.

As the day wore on, we had to plan how to tell the boys about Russ. We were particularly concerned about Robbie and Greg, our two developmentally disabled kids.

A Lethal Change in Policy

Some months before Russ's death, the county changed its policy to reflect the feeling that placing teenagers in foster care was not getting the desired return with regard to improved behavior generally. I'm sure that the real concern was money. Openings in foster homes were needed for younger children, so teens were given a very short time to shape up after placement.

Shortly after this policy went into effect, Duluth experienced a teen suicide. To the best of my recollection, this was the first of at least ten teen suicides in as many weeks. Shortly after Russ's death, a young man who had been in foster care with a friend of mine, grabbed a gun, sat on a rock on the shore of Lake Superior, and killed himself. I believe he was fourteen or fifteen years of age. He had heard about one of the previous suicides and was very upset.

As I mentioned, I knew that some of Russ's friends, some being former residents of my home who had left after their eighteenth birthday, were living on the street. I also knew that news of Russ's death would spread rapidly. Donna and I decided to seek some of them out and bring them home.

With the help of other foster parents, their foster kids, the Social Services and Police Departments, we sort of put out a net. As it turned out, we began to get phone calls from the kids, and I would get in my car and go pick them up. Russ's friend, John, called and was so upset he couldn't even tell me where he was. Finally, he was able to describe his surroundings sufficiently enough for me to know where he was. In all, we must have had a half dozen extra kids in the house, and we told them all that they could stay as long as they thought they needed to. In the end, one stayed for three days, and another stayed for five months.

Strange Things Happen

One of the things that I frequently did as a matter of routine, was to do bed checks. If someone was missing when I went to bed, I wanted to know about it. With the situation as it was, I was particularly concerned about the kids' state of mind. For several weeks after the funeral, I developed the emotional need for getting up two or three times during the night, and walking through the house in order to check on each kid. I would look at each boy and look to see if I could see the chest rise and fall, indicating they were breathing. I would even bend over someone to see if I could hear them breathing. And then, there were those who would be found to be experiencing nightmares. I realized what was happening to me, and a part of me wanted to laugh, but I needed to do this for me, even if not for them.

The Funeral and Burial

Eventually, Russ's mother called with the funeral arrangements and plans. She said that the entire thing was going to be limited to family members only, but she invited Donna and me to attend.

On the morning of the funeral, I was dressed to leave for the church. The phone rang, and it was Russ's mother. She said that Russ's father had decided that he would be very uncomfortable with my presence in the church, and she was calling to ask me not to attend. I was devastated, but I understood and told her so.

By way of explanation, when some kids want to tell their parents that they're upset with them, they develop very hurtful ways of sending the message. Russ was no exception. We were in Court one day, and Judge Martin asked him if his father was present. Russ said, "He's sitting right beside me." He was referring to me. His father was in the room. On another occasion, also in the courtroom, Russ spotted his father, and suddenly he put his head on my right shoulder.

He got a butt-chewing on both occasions. I never condoned any willful act or gesture that was meant to hurt a parent. I especially had a problem with being used as the instrument used to inflict the pain. My belief is that by and large, most parents do the best they can with the resources they possess. Sometimes, that just isn't much.

Dealing with the Pain

I have to tell you about some of the things that I experienced as a result of the death of this young man, who, admittedly, I grew to love. I guess everyone's experience under such circumstances would be different.

Strange as it might seem, I had registered for a training session on the topic of teen suicide. Against some peoples' advice, I decided to attend the training. I remember nothing about it except for two statements made by the trainer, a psychologist. He said that teenagers tend to think that everything is temporary, including death. Somehow, that statement seemed worth the trip to the Iron Range. He also said that the suicide of a teenager could take two to eight years to deal with emotionally, and there could be relapses after that. Twenty-three years after Russ's death, I still find many times when I can't talk or write about him without tears coming to my eyes.

For the first three nights after Russ's death, I found it next to impossible to shut my eyes. I was afraid of having my own nightmares. When I finally had to sleep, my only nightmare consisted of seeing a photograph of Russ under an inch or so of rippling water. The motion of the water distorted his face. That dream made me realize that I had nothing as a reminder of him, as if I'd ever need one.

One morning, I was lamenting that fact to Donna. She looked at me and said, "Look on your desk." I thought she was ignoring me. She said it again. "Look on your desk." I got tired of being told to look on my desk, so I went to my office to look on my desk. There, I found a picture of Russ taken for that year's school yearbook. I immediately got the idea of making copies of the pictures for the kids. I thought that maybe a picture for the kids would be helpful to them when they again hit the streets.

I went to my favorite K-Mart store with the picture in my pocket. As I approached the clerk who would take the photo from me, I found myself getting angry, and I wanted to warn him of dire consequences if anything happened to the photo. I knew it was all in my head, but even so…

Several days later, the pictures came in. I've never had a nightmare about Russ.

I was having a very hard time thinking that I couldn't go to the funeral service or cemetery. I caved in to the need to drive over to Superior and see the church. I really wanted to go in and feel his presence, but I couldn't quite do it. I never did develop the courage to walk into that church.

Some months after Russ's death, I had to attend my niece's wedding at a large church in Duluth. I remember driving into the parking lot and walking into the church. It was a beautiful spring day, and I was actually looking forward to the wedding. I walked into the church, found my family, and took a seat with them.

I do not remember a thing about the entire ceremony. Suddenly, I remember someone's tapping me on the right shoulder and realizing that the entire ceremony was over. People were trying to get out by stepping over me. I was in a state of shock. The only thing I experienced during the entire ceremony was total silence, and a kind of total, overwhelming peace. It would be several years before I could step into a church for any reason without experiencing that same peace.

David's Story

One thing I could always count on Russ for was to feel free enough to bring friends home to introduce to the "old man." In David's case, he sneaked him in the house and hid him in his room for a few days, undoubtedly because he was AWOL from his group home or his parents' home. The kids always enjoyed smuggling food to friends hidden in their closets or under their beds. In any event, Russ eventually left my house, but David never really has. And I thank God for that every day of my life.

David had been a foster son of a friend of mine, but he never managed to adjust to the program, and in particular, to his foster mother. After figuring out how to set her up, his foster dad finally tied the sidewalk to his butt and threw him out.

Getting himself thrown out of a group home didn't do much toward getting some problems solved at home, so much of the time, he was at my home. I don't think his mother and stepfather had much use for me because they thought I was getting paid to keep him, or that I was making a lot of money on foster care. Neither was true. But, over the last twenty-six years, David has become one of my sons, one that I refer to as my "Number one son." He's also a friend.

David was one of the kids we brought home after Russ's death. He was also the one who stayed with us the longest. As a matter of fact, he was with us on Thanksgiving Day, 1986.

Thanksgiving Day, 1986, was an absolutely beautiful day. Donna and Lloyd were spending the day with her family, and I was going to dinner at my sister's home. I called her that morning and asked her if she minded if I brought David with me. He was a bashful kid, but he didn't fight going with me.

We had dinner, and David and I headed for the front steps of the house for a cigarette. As we sat there talking, he noticed the basketball hoop two thirds of the way down the driveway. He walked down the driveway, picked up the basketball, and started shooting baskets.

A minute or two later, the garage door began to open, and my brother-in-law, Chet, appeared and began walking down the driveway toward David. When he saw Chet, he turned to me with a look on his face that could only be interpreted as one of panic. I wasn't sure whether to cry or laugh. And then Joe, my nephew, walked out of the garage and toward Chet and David, and then one of Chet's sons-in-law, and before he knew it, David had been engaged in a basketball game, and probably more importantly, conversation. I hope this was a defining experience for him. He was a kid who never quite knew why it was that someone would like him.

Kevin's Story

Kevin was one of our younger placements. I don't remember the placement meeting with the social worker, Becky Brunner, but Kevin's history alone would have been enough for both of us to agree to take the kid. As I recall, he had a few sisters and brothers. Mom and dad were divorced, but both were living in the vicinity of Duluth.

Kevin's mother apparently enjoyed hanging around local bars, and she was known to use both alcohol and drugs. It became common practice for Kevin to go out looking for mom when the bars closed. He usually managed to find mother and her boyfriend, and at times, would be sold for the night. This, undoubtedly, was one of the reasons for his placement with us.

Kevin was never a behavior problem for us, but he was one that had to be monitored and nurtured. Somewhat surprisingly, Kevin enjoyed being hugged. My experience with sexually abused kids had been exactly the opposite.

One of the surprises that this kid brought with him involved our wood burning insert that we put into the fireplace, located in the living room of the house. When I would do my frequent bed checks, I would frequently find Kevin missing from his bed. At first, my finding him missing from his bed made me panic. I would run downstairs and find him sitting in front of the raging fireplace and just a few inches from it. I would always find him sitting Indian-style, chin resting in his hands.

One morning, I found him sleeping in front of the fireplace. As I approached him, his chin forced his hands open, and his forehead struck the hot door of the insert. He had a very rude awakening. That was the last time the stove was ever used.

Another thing that often became a common event where Kevin was concerned, was his waking me during the night and complaining about having some sort of pain. He might complain of a leg ache, toothache, headache, tummy ache, etc. I soon learned that he was being awakened by nightmares. After experimenting with several remedies, I discovered that the sure cure was to carry him downstairs, sit in my rocking chair, and rock him to sleep. This rarely took long. Then, I would carry him back upstairs and put him back to bed where he would sleep for the rest of the night.

Christmas, a Time for Reflection

As Christmas, 1986, approached, I was still depressed and the thought of celebrating definitely was not something I was looking forward to. But I knew that, for the kids' sake, I had to get my shit together.

On Christmas Eve, while Donna busied herself cooking the day's dinner, I took a break. There was too much noise. I felt hemmed in. I got in the car and drove to Perkins and an atmosphere that was always friendly.

I took a seat by a window, ordered a cup of coffee, and stared at the soft snow falling on the cars in the parking lot. As I sipped my coffee, I started questioning myself, as I'd done many times, as to whether Russ had planned to commit suicide when he came home on November 12th, or whether the idea came to him after his arrival. And the worst part about it was that I was never going to have an answer to that question.

Suddenly, I turned and found a familiar young man standing in front of me. It was Tony, my Little Brother from my university days. It had been fifteen years since we'd seen each other last. We shook hands, and I asked him to sit down. We talked about his family, and he mentioned that he had a daughter. He had successfully battled an alcohol problem and was, for the most part, happy. He thanked me for being there for him fifteen years earlier, and I assured him that it had been my pleasure. We wished each other well and parted company.

I paid for my coffee and headed for my car. A gentle snow was still falling, but things somehow felt a lot brighter. I was telling myself that God had, again, sent me some help when I really needed it. Christmas might be nice after all.

Reflecting on a Rough Year

Over the years, I've gotten in the habit of spending a lot of time reflecting on the gains and losses of the year, rather than anticipating the upcoming year. It may be a little clinical depression and/or the realization that I'm not getting any younger. But 1986 was particularly traumatic, and the question of whether or not Russ had his suicide planned when he came home was still haunting me.

One cold Sunday night, shortly after the first of the year, 1987, Jason, my wannabe solder, called from his home in Superior and asked if I could come over for a talk. He said that he had something to tell me that might help. I wasn't feeling like going out at all to say nothing of driving to Superior for a conversation with Jason, but he assured me that I would feel better after we talked.

I agreed to pick him up. All the way to Superior, I was trying to figure out what the heck he could possibly tell me that would make me feel better. When he got in the car, I couldn't keep myself from telling him that I wasn't feeling much like talking. He told me that that was okay, that he was the one that wanted to do the talking, and he wanted me to do the listening. He also told me that what he had to say wouldn't take long.

He asked, "Do you remember all the nights you sent us to bed and then heard us all whispering? You'd yell upstairs and tell us to 'shut up and get to sleep?'"

I'm sure I was smiling when I told him, "Of course I do."

He said, "Well, on a lot of those occasions, we were all talking about death and dying. What I want to tell you is that Russ always said that when he died, he was going to die with you in your house."

I didn't know what to say. All I could think about was that God had sent me more help that I needed desperately. Jason had helped me put things in perspective. I asked myself if I'd be happier had I received a phone call telling me that Russ had hanged himself at the Lincoln Hotel. Somehow, this information quashed a lot of the depression I was living with up to that time, and it had come from a most unexpected source.

I'm sure I had tears in my eyes as I looked at the smile on Jason's face. It was fun to come to the realization that there was a lot more to this kid than his fatigues. We hugged each other, and I headed for home. It was the brightest evening I'd experienced in quite a few weeks.

Back to Reality

The reality of things was that we still had kids to take care of, but they seemed to be fewer and fewer because of the attitude downtown concerning the placement of teenagers. Donna and I had to take a serious look at some options. One of those options was to make a jump from kids to adults. A second possibility was to specialize in a different type of kid, younger, maybe.

One morning, I was reading the newspaper and there was a Want Ad for group home parents. The number to respond to was a St. Paul, Minnesota, number. I mentioned it to Donna and asked her if she thought I should call. We'd talked about staying with teens, changing to younger kids, or perhaps getting out of the business altogether. I knew that Donna wanted to sell the house because she didn't know if I could continue to live in the house that Russ died in. So we decided to make the call.

I found myself speaking to a young social worker by the name of Debbie. I remember her asking me if I had any experience. I told her I had a little. She asked about Donna. I told her that she had a degree in Quantity Cooking and Baking. Her response was, "Oh, goodie!" A date and time was quickly set for her to come to Duluth to interview us. It was now a month or so into the new year of 1987.

The interview was held, and it didn't take long for the agency's brass to call us and offer us the job. Somewhat reluctantly, we accepted the position, even though neither of us was particularly excited about leaving our hometown, families and friends. And then, of course, there was the problem of having to explain to the few kids we had left why we had to go. I was especially concerned about Robbie, who had been with us for about three years.

Saying Goodbye

When I told Robbie about our move to the Cities, he was very upset. We tried to paint a positive face on his going home, but he didn't seem to buy it. I think we both knew that nothing had changed at home.

One day, I sent him out to my old and almost falling down garage and asked him to clean it up, organize it, you know, pick it up and hang things up. After an hour or so, I went out to the garage to check on him. He found places to hang absolutely everything. Even the bicycles were hanging on hooks on the walls.

When I walked in the garage, he was staring at the floor. I thought something was wrong and asked him what was on his mind. He looked up at me and said, "It's the floor. We need to wash it." The floor was comprised of pieces of concrete no larger than dice! That was my Robbie.

I did take the opportunity to talk to him about going home. I asked him if he was worried about mom or dad, leaving his foster brothers, etc. He said, "No, that's not what's bothering me."

Then, what is bothering you?" I asked.

"When I go home," he said, "I'm going to lose my best friend."

Moving Day Again

We decided that we would move to St. Paul on April 1, 1987.

246

We were moving into the agency's home located at 834 Marshall Avenue. We would be taking teenagers from all over the State of Minnesota. On the surface, that made me feel like we'd have enough placements to keep us going. I didn't know about the extra $17/day per kid that each placing agency had to pay, which eventually would spell trouble for both the agency and us.

Agency staff and brass didn't tell us that the house we were to occupy would be located in a heavily minority neighborhood. Now, we didn't much give a damn, but some of our placements did, and most of them knew nothing about the neighborhood before their arrival.

On one corner of our block, there was an after-hours bar. That meant that there were a lot of drunks walking the street in front of our house. On the other end of the block was a house of ill repute, if you know what I mean. Nine-year-old Lloyd was even approached by one of the ladies. How did I find out? He came to me one afternoon, and told me that one of the ladies asked him if he'd like some hair pie!

We did seem to get what would at least be considered an average number of placements. The house always looked full, because within a very short time after our move to our new home, several of our Duluth kids moved to St. Paul, and of course, needed somewhere to live. Among those kids were David, Billy, David's best friend, Scott, and John.

Mike's Story

I only want to mention one kid who was placed in this home's program. Mike came from a very wealthy family. He was a great kid to have around and absolutely no trouble. The problem was the relationship between him and his father.

From the moment this kid entered the house, he was in a great mood and behaved like he was living in Disneyland. He adjusted to the rules, the variety of kids, new parenting methods, everything, almost immediately.

One evening after supper, I went out in the living room, sat in my rocking chair, turned on the TV, and started to watch the news. Mike got up from the dining room table after eating a hot dish, charged into the living room, and sort of flopped on the couch.

My chair was in a corner of the room and behind the couch. I sat there looking at the back of Mike's head, hands folded behind his neck. I wondered how a kid from the land of porterhouse steaks could be so comfortable in the land of tuna casseroles. I was so curious, I decided to ask him.

"Mike," I said, "Can I ask you a question?"

He immediately sat up, looked at me, and said, "Sure. What is it?"

"How does a kid from the land of porterhouse steaks get so comfortable, and seem so happy, in the land of tuna casseroles?"

With a kind of indignant look on his face, he looked at me and said, "It's not hard when someone gives a damn." I nodded my head, and he resumed his position on the couch.

The Passing of My Old Friend, Max

Not long after the family moved to St. Paul, I found out that my old friend and counseling partner, Max, was going to be entering the Veteran's Hospital at Fort Snelling. I don't remember what Max's medical problem was, but I knew he was a heavy smoker and had a very heavy smoker's cough for as long as I'd known him. I'm sure that, at the very least, he was suffering from emphysema.

Of course, I took the time to visit him at the hospital. During the first several visits, he was able to speak clearly, but within a few weeks, his voice weakened, and I was getting fearful for his life. At some point, and without talking about it directly, he and I and his wife, Margaret knew instinctively that Max wasn't going to make it.

Eventually, he lost his ability to speak at all, and we improvised ways of communicating. First, he would write on a pad of paper. Then, we graduated to a chalk board, and finally, when he could no longer write at all, we struggled to communicate by my trying to read his lips. Much of the time, he was too weak to concentrate on his lip movements, and whatever he was saying went without my being able to understand him.

On the occasion of my last visit with my old friend, his eyes were shut and I was holding his hand. Suddenly he opened his eyes and looked at me. His grip tightened on my hand, and tears came to his eyes. His lips began to move, and I stared at them, wanting to make sure I could understand what he wanted to say. He looked up at me and said clearly with his lips, "I love you, my friend." I looked at him and said, "I love you, too, my friend." He smiled and shut his eyes.

Margaret called me the next day to tell me that Max had passed away. A few days later, we laid him to rest in a cemetery in the little town of Dundas, Minnesota.

It's a Very Small World

One very hot Sunday afternoon during the summer of 1987, the kids and I were watching a baseball game on TV and trying to get cool in a house with no air conditioning. Suddenly the doorbell rang. I opened the door, and standing in front of me was one Dr. Floyd Westendorp, my friend and cribbage partner from my hospital days.

I was so astonished, I could hardly speak. The first thing I could force from my mouth was, "What are you doing here?"

He looked at me with a somewhat surprised look on his face and said, "Haven't I always told you that I'd never come to town without looking you up?" I felt like I was that little boy again back in 1958.

After I recovered from the shock of seeing him, I asked him why he was in town. He said he was in town because one of his sons was going to donate a kidney to his best friend, and he wanted to be here for the surgery. I hadn't seen Floyd's kids for years, but I sure never had a doubt that he and Clare had done a great job of raising them and instilling a sense of values in them. In a few minutes, we shook hands and hugged each other, and he was gone. This unexpected visit made my day a whole lot nicer.

Another Program Failure

During the summer months of 1987, more and more social workers were calling me and telling me that their counties were becoming very reluctant to place teenagers in foster homes, given the additional $17/day additional administration fee that my agency was charging. Where did we hear that before?

One day in August, the agency brass, without warning, showed up at the house and told us that they were closing down the program.

They said that it was because Donna and I weren't married. While we were discussing all of this, the phone rang. It was our Duluth realtor who told me that she had just sold our Duluth home. Now, was that timely, or was that timely! The agency left us no alternative but to look for a home that we couldn't afford because we didn't have a down payment because we hadn't sold our house (puff, puff, puff!) The house and program would be closed effective December 1, 1987.

After some vitriolic comments from yours truly, comments suggesting that the failure of the program was the administrative fee they were charging, rather than Donna's and my marital status, they all got in their cars and drove off. I got a phone book, selected a realtor, and made a phone call. An agent was at the house within a few hours.

After an hour or so of looking at an MLS book, the agent suddenly remembered another home he said might be just the one we were looking for. It was located by the Minnesota State Fairgrounds. It had four and a half bathrooms and nine bedrooms! He made a few phone calls, and we all piled in his car and went to see the house.

As promised, the house, located at 1438 Asbury St., St. Paul, was the biggest thing I'd ever seen and was certainly large enough to qualify for a 10-kid foster care license, and four or five others to boot. We worked with a loan company, and after a lot of paperwork and prayers and a down payment we were able to make because of the sale of our house in Duluth, the sale was finally completed. As one or two of our kids had been placed by the Ramsey County Corrections Department, we had been invited to be licensed by Ramsey County. Everything was accomplished by November, and we and the family moved in on December 1, 1987.

Our New Home

The house was quite old. A previous owner had added an addition to the rear of the house. The addition added two very large bedrooms to the second floor. It, therefore, had four bedrooms, two of which had their own bathrooms.

The main floor had a front, closed in porch. The door from this porch entered a large living room which joined a large dining room. The large kitchen was located off the dining room. Off one side of the dining room were a full bath and two bedrooms. At the rear of the house was a large room I used for an office, and off this room was the rear entryway and a half bathroom. Ninety-nine percent of the human traffic entered through this rear door, which allowed me to spend much of my time in the office and still monitor who was coming in and going out of the house.

The basement had a huge bedroom with a fireplace and had its own exit to the back yard. Attached to this room was a smaller bedroom. Both of these rooms exited into the storage/furnace room. Off this storage room was another full bathroom.

Yet Another Adventure Begins

Our Ramsey County boss was one Mike Stephens. Mike was a supervisor in one of the Ramsey County Corrections satellite offices. I really, really liked this guy.

Mike was one of those extraordinary guys who felt that he lost something when he became a supervisor; his caseload! The occasion of our meeting involved his need to place two of them.

He called one morning and said he'd like to place two of his kids in my home. He told me they were good kids, and we'd like them. I told Mike that I was anxious to meet another dinosaur. He asked what I meant. I told him that I wasn't used to talking to probation officers who were willing to admit that they actually liked a kid on their caseload. I also told him I was anxious to meet a supervisor who was hiding his caseload from his boss.

Later that afternoon, Mike walked in the house with Corey and Jason. The three of them took seats at the dining room table, Mike seated between the two kids. As they sat there, I couldn't help but notice that Mike kept his arm draped over the shoulders of the kids on either side of him. I told myself that I was really going to like this guy. If you haven't guessed yet, we took both boys.

I don't remember much about Jason, except that I liked him. He was a very active kid and always on the move. He was also my usual first suspect when something was going on in the house. He wasn't dangerous or mean, but he was always up to something.

Larry Bauer-Scandin

Eventually he got to Donna, and we had to have him removed from the house. Cory, on the other hand, was a different story.

The Story of Cory Michael

As I recall, Cory had been residing at another group home before coming to mine. He had been removed from his mother's home. Mike's father was living but was not active with his placement. By the way, Mike's name was Cory Michael, but Mike Stephens always called him Mike, so we did also.

I can't explain the relationship between Mike and his mother, but I can say that it wasn't good. For example, sometime after he moved in with us, Donna, Mike, and I talked about the possibility of Mike's attending the Hubert H. Humphrey Job Corp Center, located just across the street from the house. He was interested in the Center's welding program. We were interested in the welding program and the fact that they would require him earn his GED first.

One of the things that Job Corp required of applicants who were minors was a letter from a parent requesting acceptance into the program. I made such a request of Mike's mother. She refused, giving no reason. When I got off the phone, Donna and I started talking about what to do. We were really convinced that Job Corp was the way to go, where Mike was concerned. We decided not to tell either Mike Stephens or Mike about the call to Mike's mom and her answer. What we did do was to forge a letter and sign mom's name to it. A week or so after sending off the letter, we were notified that Mike had been accepted.

By the way, the Job Corp program had other benefits they offered to their students. Each got a cash allowance and a monthly clothing allowance, all of this in addition to room and board. Several other residents of my house eventually, entered the Job Corp program. I should also say that Mike finished the program and graduated.

And Then, There was Kenny

If ever I had a kid who was born with his diapers on fire, it was Ken. This kid was tall, had long brown hair, was far too handsome

252

and was loud, very loud! Most of the time, he was an itch I couldn't quite reach, but I sure liked that kid.

While Ken was with me, we had occasion to go back to court on a minor offense I can hardly recall. The Judge was probably not the one Ken would have chosen, had he a choice. He was placed under house arrest for a month. I left the courtroom concerned about how we were going to enforce the house arrest without going crazy ourselves.

Within about three days, Ken had me on the edge of murder. The other kids, to say nothing of Donna and me, were ready to hurt him badly.

Before that happened, though, I decided to call the Judge. He started to laugh when he found out who was on the phone. I asked him exactly who he had sentenced in Court a few days earlier. He told me to do anything I thought would make him uncomfortable for a while. I thanked him for saving my sanity. I really don't remember what I did, but I definitely ungrounded him.

One Father's Day morning, I was awakened to the sound of Ken and Donna yelling at each other upstairs. These situations were always hard for me because I didn't want to be seen as rescuing"her every time she had a confrontation with a kid. On the other hand, I didn't want her to think I was being unsupportive. I listened to the confrontation from the bottom of the steps. I decided that things appeared to be getting a little too hot, so I climbed the steps and followed the yelling to the dining room.

Donna was standing at the short side of the table, and Ken was standing directly across the table from me. He looked at me when I walked through the door, and I looked at him. I told him to quiet down. He immediately turned to me and started to cuss and swear at me. He was threatening every part of my body as well as my life. In the middle of all of his, "You f—king son of a bitch! You asshole!" he said, "And by the way, happy Father's Day!" I could hardly keep from laughing.

During our time in the Twin Cities, we met quite a few other foster and group home parents. One of those I worked closely with was Jerry. Jerry was a huge man and had a mouth to match. We couldn't have been more different, and we definitely had polar opposite ways of dealing with kids. Jerry was always yelling at his kids. Mine, on the other hand, knew that, if I was yelling at them, they'd better start planning their own funeral. Yelling was for special occasions only.

The Trip to Hell

The summer of 1988 was hotter than a French cathouse on opening night. Everybody seemed to be hot and ornery all summer long, and our kids were no different. Every year, Jerry took his kids on a ten day long fishing trip to the Rainy River, up around the Canadian border. He asked me to go with him. He was going to take five kids, and I would do likewise.

I didn't particularly like the idea of putting myself and my kids in Jerry's hands, but I wanted to get a few of mine out of the house, for a while, and take the pressure off Donna. So I agreed to go, with reservations.

We were to take this rather long trip in a rather large, old van. We managed to get everything packed, but by the time we took off, it was mid-evening.

The first thing I concluded was that my kids were going to have a very difficult time putting up with Jerry's constant yelling. Secondly, I should have run personality tests on the kids in order to figure out if they were going to be able to live with each other for ten days.

We managed to make it to the Rainey River, International Falls, Minnesota, and Jerry's hometown, at approximately 4:00 am. The kids were all hot, tired, sweaty, and that was without their girlfriends and before they were all told to set up their tents.

There were several signs that indicated this was going to be a very long vacation. First of all, when we arrived, I turned on my radio. The all weather channel announced that International Falls was the hottest place in the nation. Anyone who watches a weather channel knows that International Falls, Minnesota usually qualifies as the coldest place in the nation, not the hottest. I also checked out the other local radio channels. What I was able to pick up was an all-French speaking channel and an all-talk station. There was also an all religion station. These were not good signs.

Our campsite stood on a flat spot probably twenty feet above the river. The shoreline was rocky, and right below us was a spot, carved out of the shoreline that had a huge rock protruding from the center.

As we explained to all of the kids practically before we got out of the van, the American-Canadian border ran through the center of the river. Anyone crossing from the American side to the Canadian side would therefore be entering Canada illegally. That meant possible trouble with the Royal Canadian Mounted Police, and we sure didn't want any of that kind of trouble. Naturally, before we got camp set up, some of the kids were yelling and waving at us from the Canadian side of the border. Geez, it was going to be a long, long ten days.

The Hero

As I mentioned, Jerry and his family were natives of International Falls, and Jerry's father still lived there. Jerry had invited him to our campsite for a day of shooting the bull, and of course, fishing.

After having a meal with all of us, Jerry, Sr. decided he wanted to do some fishing. He opened the trunk of his car and grabbed a folding chair. He grabbed his fishing rod and some bait and began walking down the path toward the river.

Some of the kids and I were right above Jerry, Sr. as he pushed the metal folding chair into the rocks. He sat down, baited his hook, and cast his line into the water. After a few minutes, he stood up, picked up the chair, and again, pushed it into the rocks to steady it. After resuming his fishing, I watched him lean forward to grab his hook. As he did so, the chair went forward and deposited Jerry, face down, in the water.

Kenny was standing beside me and saw the old man fall into the water. He took off like a shot and ran down the path to the river. I knew Jerry, Sr. was conscious because I watched him pushing on the slippery rocks of the river, trying to get his face out of the water. Ken quickly rolled Jerry over onto his back, holding his head up with his right arm. When Ken was satisfied that the old man wasn't seriously injured, he pulled him out of the water and onto the stony shore. By this time, other kids had gotten to the river to help. With

255

some help, Jerry, Sr. was able to negotiate the path to the campsite.

For the rest of the day, Kenny became the apple of Jerry, Sr's eye. He was thanked repeatedly, hugged, and in any way possible made to feel like nothing short of a hero. And he deserved it. I was very, very proud of him.

The heat was relentless but, somehow, we all managed to make it through the ten day ordeal. Some of us had been in the Rainy River for bathing purposes, but some of us had not. About halfway through the ten days, we decided to rent a motel room exclusively for the purpose of taking showers. When we did get home, some of the kids didn't seem to know whether or not to let me in the house because I had not shaved since I left. Even though I was certain I wouldn't be going on anymore fishing trips with Jerry and his family, this trip was probably worth the trouble just to watch one kid grow up and calm down, if only for a little while. I don't know where Ken is today, but I hope he hasn't forgotten that day at the Rainy River.

The Story of Robert

If I fail to remember the day I met any of my approximately 125 foster kids, I will always remember Robert's. This kid looked like he was about eight years old, although he was the ripe old age of twelve. He looked like he weighed about forty pounds with his pockets full of rocks. He had big blue eyes and curly hair, and a personality that could sell snowballs to Eskimos.

This little kid sat in a chair and kicked his legs back and forth constantly while his social worker gave me some of his personal background. Robert had been born in the projects of St. Paul and into a very unstable family. As I recall, both parents were drinkers and at least one parent, mother, was and is a drug user.

I remember being told about father's using a pellet gun on this boy when he was angry or drunk. Many years later, Robert told me his father used to play Russian roulette with a loaded pistol when he was very young. As this story was being told, I must have given Robert the impression that I didn't believe the social worker. Maybe he saw me shaking my head and thought I was calling him a liar or something, because suddenly he stood up, dropped his pants, and pulled up his shirt. It quickly became obvious that his father wasn't a very good shot, or he didn't believe in discrimination, because there were pellet gun wounds all over this boy's body.

I also remember a story about someone, I believe it was the father, who, when he wanted to scare Robert, would break a glass or bottle, put the pieces of glass in his mouth and chew on them until blood would drip out of his mouth and scare the kid. I'd heard a lot of stories in my career, but this one took the prize.

If you haven't guessed it already, I agreed to take this kid. I was told that I would need to take him to psychologist appointments at the Wilder Foundation. I had no problem with that. God knows he needed some help and support.

The first thing I learned about Robert was that he loved to be touched, e.g., a hug, which I strongly believe in under most circumstances, a pat on the back or head or an arm draped over the shoulders. He seemed to take every opportunity to sit next to me and loved to have me drape my arm over his shoulders.

As I recall, Robert used to have weekly appointments with his Wilder psychologist, Karen Brandt. Karen was an older lady who tended to play the role of grandmother in Robert's case. The problem was that Robert knew it and took full advantage. I think Karen knew Robert was manipulating her, but I don't think it mattered to her.

Way back in this book, I spoke about the things that people say to us that are immensely complimentary, things that make you want to go on when things get tough. In Robert's case, Karen used to tell me that "You are the only man in this boy's life that actually likes him." I'm not sure I ever understood what that meant, because I was never aware of anything about this kid that I disliked. There were things about his history that made me concerned and fearful, but he was optimistic and very socially adept.

The Search for Home

Remember the kids that Donna and I brought back to our house home after Russ's death? Those kids were John, Billy, David and Scott. When I think back to these days, I don't remember any agency people ever giving us any trouble because of the extra kids we had in the house. I'd like to believe that the reason was because they knew it wouldn't do any good for them to complain.

Donna and I did have some rules for these "extras" we had in the house. First, they stayed out of our way where the other kids were concerned, and they did not get involved with the other kids. Second, they had to find a job or get into a school or some sort of training program. Third, everyone had to be working toward becoming independent, and that included living on their own.

Back To Billy

During the course of the time that Bill was with me in Duluth, which was between a year and two years, I came to feel like he was leading a secret life. I began to feel strongly that he was gay. In time, that feeling was confirmed, but no one in my house ever even suggested that they thought, or knew, Bill was gay.

Shortly after we moved to the Twin Cities, Bill became one of four Duluth kids who also moved to the Cities and in with us. Our moving didn't lessen their need for homes and support, and we did have nine bedrooms and four and a half bathrooms in the first home we bought.

That first home was purchased eight months after our move. It was located a block from the State Fairgrounds and right across the street from the Hubert H. Humphrey Job Corp. Center.

Bill qualified for schooling at Job Corp. As I recall, he expressed an interest in the Culinary Arts Program. A physical was a part of the admission process. One morning, while he was in class, he was asked, over the classroom's PA system, to come to the nurse's office immediately. When he got there, he was told that he had HIV. They discharged him immediately. I'm not sure it was even legal to do so.

He walked out of school and across the street to our house. In one day, he managed to get kicked out of school, find out he had HIV, and find himself with no permanent home. And to add insult to injury, he didn't want to go home to his mother and stepdad. Actually, he desperately wanted to go home, but he still wasn't getting along with mother.

During the next day or two, while Bill, Donna, and I were all

258

getting over the shock of Bill's diagnosis, I was trying to figure out how to broker a peace between Bill and his mother so that he could be home with his family, where he belonged. Bill gave me permission to talk to his mother, tell her about the diagnosis, and try and convince her that home is where he belonged. Much to my surprise, she was very willing to have Bill come home. I told her that we would get his belongings packed up, and I would bring him home.

The night before we left for Duluth, Bill and I found ourselves sitting in my darkened kitchen drinking coffee together. I asked him why he'd been unable to tell me he was gay. He said that he was afraid I'd never let him in the house again.

I was shocked by the statement. I'd always told the kids never to be afraid of telling me anything. It saddened me to think that any of the kids would listen to me say that and feel the exact opposite.

The next morning, Bill and I packed his belongings in the car and took off for Duluth. I dropped him off at his mother and stepfather's home, gave him a hug, and asked both him and his mother to keep me posted.

Over the next several months, Bill's relationship with his mother and stepfather deteriorated. I don't remember if things ever got to the point where he left the house, but it appeared like things were going in that direction.

At the same time, Bill's health was getting worse. His situation had advanced from HIV to AIDS and eventually, he entered the St. Mary's Medical Center's Hospice Unit.

Around the first of December, 1991, Bill's mother called to tell me that his doctor had advised her to "call the troops home," that Bill's condition was, in fact, critical. I told her that I would be there the following day.

It was a long trip home. I was wondering what I was going to see when I walked in his room.

I went directly to the hospital. I asked for Bill's room number and then headed down the hall. His room was facing me at the end of the hallway. The door was open. As I got close to the door, the doorway was filled by none other than Bill. I was shocked, based on yesterday's phone conversation with his mom. I expected to find him in bed and close to death. Instead, he was walking and talking and looking quite strong.

Larry Bauer-Scandin

We greeted each other with a hug and retired to his bedroom. He sat on the bed, and I took a chair several feet in front of him. The first thing I saw when I looked at Bill, was a young man who knew he was dying. He also looked as if he was at peace with it, and with himself.

It didn't take long for me to start witnessing AIDS in action. As we talked, Bill began to cough and choke. I thought he was throwing up, so I grabbed something to hold under his mouth. Instead of throwing up the contents of his stomach, he started to throw up blood clots. As this was taking place, I was trying to locate the emergency light to summon a nurse. A nurse came in and took over.

As a result of this episode, I learned that Bill was also wearing diapers, as he apparently had lost bladder and/or bowel control. After the blood clot incident, the look on Bill's face indicated that he was having pain in his throat. The nurse gave him a cup of something, which, I was to learn, he gargled in order to numb his throat so he could eat.

As it was approaching the supper hour, we ended our visit for the day. I promised Bill that I would return the following day. As I walked down the hall and away from his room, I was wondering how much worse things would get before the end would come.

The next day, Bill was still in bed when I got to the hospital. I left the room, went into the sun room, and poured myself a cup of coffee.

As I sat there, thinking and staring out the window, a lady approached me and introduced herself as the hospice Chaplain. She asked me which of the hospice patients I was there to visit. When I told her, she asked what my relationship with Bill was. I told her that he had been a foster son of mine.

We got involved in a conversation about foster parenting, teen suicides, the rash of teen suicides in Duluth in 1986, and young people dying in general. I told her that I wasn't unfamiliar with youngsters dying for many reasons. She was curious about that experience, so we talked about it. As we did, I looked up and saw tears in her eyes. I smiled at her and asked if it wasn't she who was supposed to be consoling me. We both smiled, and as we parted, she said she'd learned a few things from our conversation and she promised to keep an eye on Bill for me. I never saw her again.

Over the next eight days, Bill and I spent most of the time talking about his plans for his own funeral, developing a list of people he wanted to have present, as well as a list of music he wanted played during the funeral service. After ten days with him, I decided that I had to go home and relieve Donna of the responsibility of taking care of all of the kids alone. Saying goodbye was hard because I didn't think I'd ever see him alive again. It's very hard to walk away from a person under those circumstances.

Bill's mother and I communicated several times over the next few weeks. She called me on December 23, his birthday, to tell me he'd passed away peacefully in his sleep. I told her that I was surprised that he had survived so long after the doctor's suggestion that she call the troops home.

I've mentioned that Bill had been raised by his mother and stepfather, but his biological father lived in Duluth. They just never had anything to do with each other. When dad found out about Bill's diagnosis and his being in a local hospice unit, he showed up at the hospital showing all sorts of emotion. According to what mom told me, Bill wasn't very happy to see him.

At some point, Bill had a conversation with his stepfather, Bob, and told him that he wanted to change his name from that of his biological father to his. Bob went to the courthouse, spoke to a judge about Bill's request, and the judge put the matter on a fast track, wanting to get the task accomplished before Bill passed away. Bill called his biological father and asked him to come to the hospital. When he did so, Bill told him about the plan to change his name. His father was furious and stormed out of Bill's room. The name change became legal in a very short period of time, and Bill passed away the same night. I think we all knew the reason why Bill seemed to be refusing to die up until this time.

Losing Another Good Friend

Before this autobiography comes to an end, I feel the necessity to say more about friendship, and what I think it is. A friend of mine once told me that he thought I was a little odd because I always seemed to be there for him, even in tough times. I don't think that's so odd or unusual. I think that sticking by a person in bad times is the very

261

definition of the word, "friend." I'm thinking of my best friend Marty, who, when we were ten years old, was spending his time sitting with and entertaining a sick friend instead of playing with healthy friends across the street.

And I think of Merle J. Micheau (Mich), who probably taught me more about life, kids, and the power of humor than anyone I've ever known. I think I owe it to you to tell you a little more about him.

While we were still in foster care, in Duluth Mich and his wife, Diane, took a little vacation in Florida. Actually, they were taking a little break from one of Duluth's winters. During the flight back to Minnesota, the pilot announced that there was a snow storm going on, in Minneapolis. Mich looked at Diane and said, "It's taken me sixty years to miss a Minnesota snow storm. Why the hell are we going north?"

When they got home to Duluth, Mich called me and asked if I knew anyone who might want to buy a big old house. I said, "No. Do you know someone who has one to sell?" He told me about hearing about the snowstorm while they were on the plane, and before they landed, they'd decided to move to Florida.

Within a matter of a few months, one of my very best friends moved to the other side of the United States. I was sad beyond description, but the telephone was put to good use.

Some months after their move, I was talking to Mich, and he told me that he was beginning to notice some numbing in his body. That numbness spread over the next several months, and finally, I suggested that he might want to check into the possibility of getting to the Mayo Clinic. He had recently been hired as a social worker at the prison/jail in Valuscia County, Florida, and he didn't have enough sick days accumulated to allow for such a trip.

Over time, the numbness became more complete and was spreading. Still, he had the problem of not having enough accumulated sick days to be able to be evaluated at the Mayo Clinic.

One night, he called and told me that he was coming to Minnesota to go through the Mayo Clinic. I asked him how he managed to pull that off. The jail's staff members donated a day or two of their sick leave to him so he could be checked out. It almost made me cry.

I asked him how long he thought it might take to go through the

Clinic. He told me that they had told him to count on seven days. I asked him who was going to go with him. Diane had to stay home and work, and none of his five kids could go with him. I told him that I would go with him. The numbness had affected his ability to move, so he needed to be in a wheelchair at times. I also wanted to be there as I was sure that the evenings were going to be very long.

I met him at the home of his parents in Elk River, Minnesota. We drove to Rochester, Minnesota, and checked into a motel near the Clinic.

For the next six days and nights, we walked from one test to another and little else. The evenings were spent drinking coffee in the motel restaurant and talking about "the good ol' days" when the two of us were chasing kids all over the State of Minnesota. We had a great time, except for the fact that we both knew there was something terribly wrong, and we needed to find out what is was.

As a part of that search, Mich was scheduled for a spinal tap. These aren't real pleasant tests, and I wanted to be in the room with him while it was being done. When we got in the test room, he introduced me to the young lady who would do the test and told her, "This is my friend, Larry, the best friend a man could ever have." I wish every person had one occasion during their lifetime to be honored by such a statement.

At the last meeting with the doctor, he labeled the problem but blamed it on a Duluth doctor who had placed Mich on what he called a toxic dose of a vitamin. There was nothing that could be done.

In the months that followed, Mich continued to get worse. His body eventually forced him to quit his job. He had seen a local doctor who performed a CAT scan on his pelvis. That doctor told Mich that he found a tumor that covered the entire front of his pelvic bone, wrapped around one side, and encircled the spine. He had bone cancer.

For several reasons, including availability of the needed medical services and closeness to family, Mich and Diane decided to move back to Minnesota, and specifically to the Twin Cities area. Eventually, an appropriate condo was found in Plymouth, Minnesota, a western suburb of Minneapolis and maybe thirty minutes from my home.

Diane was able to find a position as a legal assistant at a St. Cloud, Minnesota, legal firm. Unfortunately though, she had to drive about an hour each way per day. That made for very long, tiring days.

Periodically, I would babysit with Mich on weekends, so she could take a break and drive to Duluth to see the kids. By this time, he was confined to a power chair, and his toileting, showering, and getting onto, and out of, his chair had to be monitored. We always enjoyed being together and talking about kids.

After a year of so, Mich and Diane decided to move back to Florida, primarily to take advantage of the weather. By this time, it was apparent that his time was coming. Even though everyone knew that his condition was terminal, we never talked about it until one day, Diane called to tell me that Mich was in the hospital on morphine and in a lot of pain. The doctors were telling her he didn't have much time. She said that, if I'd like to see him, I should get on a plane as soon as possible.

I managed to catch a flight the following day, and Diane picked me up at the Orlando Airport. It was early evening. She drove me directly to the hospital.

When we walked in the room, his head was rolling from side to side, and he looked like he was in a considerable amount of pain. I walked around to one side of the bed and took his hand. He looked at me and smiled. He tried to say something, but he couldn't quite fight his way through the morphine. I told him to take it easy and not worry about talking. I told him that this was going to be the first time I ever got the last word in! He smiled, so I knew he realized it was me, and he understood what I was saying. I didn't want him to continue to try and fight off the medication, so I told him to get a good night's sleep, and I would see him in the morning.

The next morning, Diane found out that the hospital was going to discharge Mich and send him home. It was a surprise to everyone. Diane was concerned because he would be coming home on oxygen, and she had no idea how to use or maintain the equipment. We did know that we wouldn't have any trouble maneuvering him or the hospital bed coming with him, because all five of his kids were there.

Early in the afternoon, the ambulance showed up with Mich. They brought him in on a gurney, wheeled him to their bedroom, and gently placed him in a hospital bed he'd been using prior to his recent hospitalization. The ambulance staff then gave Diane a quick lesson in the use and maintenance of the oxygen equipment.

When things quieted down, I asked Diane where the other

bedrooms in the house were located. She pointed them out to me. I said, "Good. You get yourself set up in that bedroom," pointing to one at the very opposite side of the house from their bedroom, "and I'll move into your room and take care of Mich. You need some sleep." She didn't argue.

Diane and Mae, Mich's mother, set about the task of making supper for the whole crew, at least nine people, and Mich went to sleep. During the early part of the evening, the Micheau kids, Mae, Diane, and I just sat around relaxing and talking. But it didn't take long for fatigue to set in, so it was an early bedtime.

By this time, Mich was awake and looking like the pain was under control. We talked and laughed and remembered the many fun times we had together in Duluth, chasing runaways, raiding pool halls, and visiting kids and staff at Minnesota's correctional facilities. I can't describe how much fun we had that night, laughing and talking about how much fun we'd had over the past twenty-five years, realizing all the time that it would shortly come to an end.

Neither one of us slept that night. We talked, watched TV, I rubbed his back for him and got the urinal for him when he needed it. Sooner than we were aware of, the night had come to an end, and we both fell asleep. It felt strange to be lying in Mich and Diane's bed, but I wanted to be near in case he needed anything.

After another day or two, I had to return to Minnesota. I knew when I left that I'd never see my friend again, even though we said our goodbyes as if we would be seeing each other very soon.

During the first or second week of December, 1993, Mich called and apologized for not being able to spend enough time with me because his kids were all there during my visit. I told him that his kids were where they should have been at that time.

Then, he made another one of those statements that, for me, was saying something special. He said that, "When my kids go home, I'd like you to come back down so just the two of us can visit. And you can sleep in the bed right beside me again."

My friend passed away on New Years Eve, 1993. I suppose you think this was the end of it? Not quite!

Diane had Mich's body cremated. She called me and asked what I thought she should do with his ashes. She mentioned that he loved walking on the beach. I told her that that sounded like a great idea, but whatever she decided, she shouldn't consider throwing the ashes in the ocean because he couldn't swim. We laughed about it, and she determined that she would sprinkle the ashes on the beach.

On a Saturday morning, she drove the seventy miles to Orlando and picked up the urn containing Mich's ashes. She drove seventy miles back to the beach by their home, got out of the car and opened the trunk. It was a beautiful, sunny day with not a whisper of wind. When she opened the box and removed the urn, she discovered that the urn contained someone else's cremains.

She got back in her car and returned to Orlando. She got the right ashes and drove back to the beach. She opened the trunk, picked up the box containing the urn, opened it, and then opened the urn.

Just as she opened the urn, a wind came up off the ocean. As Diane was telling me this on the phone, I started to laugh. My friend, Merle J. Micheau, was still trying to run things, even from heaven!

Ending One Career and Beginning Another

Once in a very long while, Donna and I were lucky enough to find someone who was willing to stay with our brood while we took a weekend off. As a matter of fact, that happened exactly four times in fourteen years.

One of those times was in 1992. A friend of mine and his wife were going out of town, and they offered us their home for the weekend. We were all of thirty minutes from our house.

On Saturday morning, we received a call from the St. Paul Police Department notifying us that they had just arrested Lloyd and were about to start investigating his possible involvement in some delinquent activity. We, of course, went home.

We anguished through the weekend. On Monday, we received a visit from Mike Stephens and others representing law enforcement and Ramsey County. Mike's boss had made the determination that our group home could not remain open if Lloyd remained in the house. Therefore, we had two possible choices. We could stay together and close our doors to foster care, or we could think of a way to get Lloyd out of the house while the Police Department conducted its investigation, and hope and keep our fingers crossed.

After talking about it, Donna and I decided that we would find an apartment for her and Lloyd for whatever time was necessary. We found an apartment a very short distance from the house.

The investigation by the Police Department took about nine weeks. The official finding was that evidence would not support a successful prosecution, so the entire matter was dropped, except that Ramsey County would not allow Lloyd to move back into the house. Being that he was fifteen years old, we were not going to allow him to live on his own.

I protested the Department's decision, believing that since the investigation precluded prosecution, it was the Department that should eat crow, but they didn't see it that way.

I figured that we had nothing to lose by applying a little pressure on the Director. I contacted an attorney. I told him the story, and he felt that a warning letter to the Director was warranted. At least, that's what he said.

I knew that when the Director received the letter from the attorney, our career in foster care would more than likely be over. Shortly after the letter was received, I began getting visits from her subordinates warning me that if I ever wanted employment in the correctional field in the State of Minnesota, I'd better stop the pressuring. It was suggested by one of the Director's subordinates that the Department might force me out of foster care in one of two ways. It could either starve me for placements, thereby cutting off my income. The other way it could be done would be by flooding me with so many inappropriate placements that the program would fall apart, and placement sources would dry up.

One day, I was called and asked to accept, as I recall, six kids, about four of them right out of the courtroom. I determined that the plan was to flood me with inappropriate placements. When one of those placements showed up at the house one night with a loaded revolver, I made the decision to begin looking for other employment. It was, in fact, all over.

I began looking for another job. I called a friend of mine who was the director of a four-county community corrections setup in Western Minnesota. He had an opening and said he'd be more than happy to have me, but the salary was meager and his counties were poor.

Then one night I received a call from my barber. He'd been

looking for another job due to some medical problems. I asked him how the search was going. He said, "I haven't found anything for me, but I just may have found something for you."

Summary

I hope that you've enjoyed reading this autobiography. I hope that you've learned something, laughed at something or thought about something, or were reminded of somebody. But most of all, I hope it's given you some ideas about making some changes in your life that will make you happier, healthier, more productive, optimistic, aware, and more concerned about your family, friends, neighbors, and community.

To quote a line from a movie: "We either get busy living or get busy dying." Our individual clocks are ticking from the moment of conception. We can either use the time, whatever its length, to do some good, to be productive, and to live as if every man was our neighbor, or we can choose to be selfish, counter-productive, and in conflict with our neighbors. I see our world as needing more of the former and less of the latter.

I see parenting as the most satisfying and important thing that any of us will ever do in our lifetime. How we prepare ourselves and our children for this role will, in large part, determine the fate of this country, and perhaps the world.

We'd better start giving more than a little thought to why one in 30 adults in this country is in prison, jail, or on some form of supervised release. Why is it that when ninety-five percent of Minnesota inmates eventually are freed, the system doesn't pay more attention to helping new releases find adequate housing, employment, medical/psychological help, etc? If Minnesotans pay about $100/day to incarcerate an individual, what is it willing to invest per day when the individual is free, and again presenting a possible danger to the public? How does a parolee explain to a potential employer that the crime listed on the job application might not be what it reads like, because most defendants accept plea bargains?

I'm not what they used to call a bleeding heart liberal when it comes to crime and criminals. What I am saying is that I believe there are some who are doing too much time, and others who are doing far too little time, where the safety of the public is concerned. When I think about it, I wonder if we would be any worse off if we reduced all sentences by thirty days. Would the public be in any more danger if we saved three thousand dollars per month per inmate? A very recent (December, 2009) check of Minnesota Department of Corrections statistics indicated there were some 7800 adults incarcerated in the state's prisons. Give it some thought.

When are we going to figure out that the best way to assure America of responsible, happy, well-adjusted, productive adults is to work at raising responsible, well-disciplined, well-adjusted and happy kids? We have to show them that we care. We have to talk to them. We have to hug them. We have to discipline them.

I'll bet you're thinking, "I wonder if he believes in, heaven forbid, spanking? You bet I do. I believe in spankings, but I do not believe in beatings. You wouldn't believe the number of adult offenders I've worked with who have told me, in front of other offenders that they would feel a lot better about the hurt they caused if somebody would take a strap to them.

I'm particularly concerned about our schools. Long ago, we became very interested in the rights of the individual. I have no problem with that, unless those rights come at the expense of the rights of the majority. They say that our children have a right to a good education. I completely agree with that, unless a student is behaving in such a way that makes others feel unsafe, threatened, or are not getting the attention they deserve from their teachers because they have to deal with constant behavioral problems. These kids should be educated separately and away from other kids who know how to behave and take advantage of an education.

One thing I've learned about kids over the past forty-two years is this: You cannot gain control of an unwilling, uncooperative child unless he can be shown that his body can, and will, be controlled, and even confined, if necessary. Kids respect power. We adults seem to have given up on using it, and the result has been tragic. I believe that in a strange way, gangs attract kids because of the discipline and rules they offer.

And what are we teaching our kids, in school? Are we teaching civics anymore? Do kids know anything about our government or their part in it? Why do I know so many fourteen, fifteen, and sixteen year olds who can't write legibly? Are we still teaching the basics, you remember, reading, writing and arithmetic? If not, what the hell are we teaching them, and why are we graduating them?

And most important of all, we need to get a God back into our lives and those of our kids. We can't pass on what we know nothing about. Without a God, kids grow up without a well-developed conscience and may tend to believe that there is nothing out there that's more powerful than they are.

And finally, to everyone but to young people in particular, I would quote an unknown author. "Always shoot for the moon, because even if you miss, you'll still land among the stars!"

The End